From the Gulf States
and Beyond

From the Gulf States and Beyond

The Legacy of Lee Pederson and LAGS

Edited by

Michael B. Montgomery

Thomas E. Nunnally

The University of Alabama Press
Tuscaloosa and London

Copyright © 1998
The University of Alabama Press
Tuscaloosa, Alabama 35487-0380
All rights reserved
Manufactured in the United States of America

∞

The paper on which this book is printed meets the minimum requirements of
American National Standard for Information Science-Permanence of Paper
for Printed Library Materials, ANSI Z39.48-1984

Library of Congress Cataloging-in-Publication Data

From the Gulf states and beyond : the legacy of Lee Pederson and LAGS
    / edited by Michael B. Montgomery, Thomas E. Nunnally.
        p.   cm.
    Includes bibliographical references and index.
    ISBN 0-8173-0948-9 (alk. paper)
    1. English language—Dialects—Gulf States—Cartography.
2. Americanism—Gulf States—Cartography. 3. Linguistic atlas of the
Gulf States. 4. Pederson, Lee, 1930–   —Influence.
I. Pederson, Lee, 1930–   . II. Montgomery, Michael, 1950–   .
III. Nunnally, Thomas.
PE2970.G85F76   1998
427'.976—dc21   98-35175

British Library Cataloguing-in-Publication Data available

*To the informants, fieldworkers, and scribes
of the Linguistic Atlas of the Gulf States,
to whom the profession will long be grateful*

Contents

Acknowledgments

In few academic efforts is teamwork more crucial than the editing of a book-length collection of essays by many authors. The editors are acutely aware of this and wish to thank the following, whose assistance made this volume possible:

Susan Leas McDaniel, for help in organizing a list of contributors in the early stages of the project.

Our academic institutions, the University of South Carolina at Columbia and Auburn University, and our departments of English for research funding and equipment.

The staff at The University of Alabama Press, for their generous and timely assistance and expertise.

Lee Pederson, for providing a list of publications, the basis for the appendix to this book.

The Belknap Press of Harvard University Press, Southern Illinois University Press, UMI, The University of Alabama Press, University of Georgia Press, and University of Michigan Press for permission to reprint materials.

Two anonymous reviewers for The University of Alabama Press, for many useful comments.

The contributors to this volume, whose willingness to follow suggestions has been unfailing.

Michael B. Montgomery
Thomas E. Nunnally

From the Gulf States and Beyond

INTRODUCTION

Lee Pederson and LAGS
Michael B. Montgomery

The essays in this volume honor Professor Lee Pederson of Emory University and offer some measure of the value and inspiration of his career work, the Linguistic Atlas of the Gulf States (LAGS), a project in linguistic geography that was conceived in 1966 and became the centerpiece of Pederson's scholarship for the next quarter-century. LAGS is both an abiding contribution to current and future generations of scholars and the key to an informed understanding of the language and cultural history of the Interior South. Rarely has a scholar worked so tirelessly, as has Pederson with LAGS, to make so much available to colleagues in linguistics and other fields. And as the contributors to this volume endeavor to show, rarely has one scholar done so much to make possible the work of others by providing them with both data and invaluable research tools.

LAGS is the most signal of Lee Pederson's works and, as the list of his publications indicates (see the appendix), the principal focus of his writing. But the project hardly forms the full compass of Pederson's scholarly record. His first publication was on Thoreau, one of his several important essays on American literature. Nor are Pederson's scholarly achievements the measure of his distinguished career, which has featured considerable contributions and service to others, as in training students and atlas staff, donating material to projects such as the *Dictionary of American Regional English* (see Joan Hall's essay, this volume), and teaching courses in American literature, Shakespeare, and American English. Always approachable by other scholars and by the media, he has contributed much to public education about variation in American English.

Trained at the University of Chicago by Raven I. McDavid, Jr. (to whom LAGS is dedicated), Lee Pederson came south to Emory University in 1966. Motivated by a pre-publication version of McDavid's 'Needed Research in Southern Dialect' (1967), he had already begun to formulate the idea of an atlas of Southern speech. To ensure continuity with previous atlas work and to draw on existing knowledge of linguistic variation in the South, he organized a planning conference of dialectologists familiar with the goals of the Linguistic Atlas of the United States and Canada project, along with teachers and curriculum planners. Drawing from their advice, he and three associates produced A *Manual for Dialect Research in the Southern States* (later published as Pederson, McDavid, Foster and Billiard 1972), which included the LAGS questionnaire and other material. Then he organized two pilot projects to test the questionnaire, field procedures, and the grid framework for the subsequent region-wide survey, and before long LAGS was up and running.

With the groundwork laid and the scope of the work envisioned, Pederson began recruiting others to help. Over the next two-and-a-half decades, hundreds of students, colleagues, and volunteers lent a hand with interviewing and many other tasks, all supervised by Pederson. Most important of all to LAGS were the informants, 1,121 of them, whose interviews were taped in their entirety for the first time for an atlas project. As a result, 5,300 hours of recorded speech were produced, a staggering assemblage but still only a portion of the unprecedented amount of LAGS material (the components of LAGS are discussed in detail in the next chapter).

Of the many ways to estimate the value of LAGS, here is one: the *Annotated Bibliography of Southern American English* (McMillan and Montgomery 1989) reveals that more than two and one-half thousand publications—from notes to dissertations—had been written about Southern American English by the late 1980s. In LAGS, Pederson has made available as much data as is contained in all those studies combined—at least for the states covered by the project.

For a linguistic atlas project its size, LAGS was finished in record time, attributable to the fact that Pederson stayed at home and worked, doing his share of the interviews, transcriptions, and other tasks. Few in the profession could have managed such a long-term project, maintaining allegiance to a traditional atlas framework while exploiting the possibilities of developing technology to meet the demands of future researchers. Lee Pederson is such a person. Along with Hans Kurath, he is one of the two great innovators in 20th century American linguistic geography. Many others (especially Raven I. McDavid, Jr.) have contributed greatly to atlas work, but it is Kurath and Pederson who combined the talents and abilities of conceiving, planning, and executing a project and editing its material to completion, while incorporating innovations in design along the way. For both men, their commitment to atlas work grew from a fundamental interest in exploring American cultural history. Both changed our understanding of what a linguistic atlas could be.

Early in the 20th century linguistic geography and dialectology were considered integral to historical linguistics and a subject of general importance to linguists: Saussure 1959[1916] and Bloomfield 1933 each had two chapters on these subjects. However, this situation changed radically, and over the past half-century, linguistic atlases have fallen out of awareness for most contemporary researchers on American English, especially following the paradigm shifts of the 1960s. Nowhere is this more obvious than in contemporary textbooks on sociolinguistics, whose lack of coverage is almost total. Wardhaugh's *Sociolinguistics* (1992), among others, devotes more attention to 19th-century German dialectology than to 20th-century American work, despite a tradition of innovation by Kurath and, more recently, Pederson, and despite the fact that since the days of Kurath, American linguistic geography has had a strong interest in social variation in language. Though not mappable like regional variation, differences between social classes has much to suggest about language change—and LAGS is one project that inter-viewed a wide range of both sexes, all ages, and several ethnic groups. Yet almost without exception, American sociolinguists have ignored atlas data. Indeed, outside one or two scholarly journals, linguistic atlas research is rarely published nowadays, and mainstream research on language variation in the United States seldom draws on atlas data. The general estimation seems to be that atlas work is peripheral to issues of current interest and is largely anachronistic, bound by a design and methodology perhaps appropriate for investigating rural speech a generation or more ago. However, any serious consideration of LAGS and the kinds of data Pederson has designed the project to make available shows how uninformed such a view is.

In part as a result of Pederson's single-minded production of LAGS and the work of personnel he trained, recent years have witnessed a resurgence of interest in linguistic atlas material. The present volume seeks to continue that movement by offering ways in which data from LAGS, the most contemporary of American atlas projects, can be used in informed, robust ways. LAGS can be used for innumerable projects to test questions large and small and address issues in new and exciting ways, only a few of which are suggested here.

Seven currents of recent research utilizing atlases can be cited.

Linguistic atlas work not only collects material from large numbers of speakers, but it provides detailed social profiles of those speakers that can be used to explore social correlates of language usage. The Susan McDaniel and Virginia McDavid essays herein do this for gender variation in vocabulary and verb principal parts, respectively. Michael Montgomery's essay on multiple modals does so for less conventional factors such as the sex of the interviewer. (Innumerable studies are made possible by the variety of information on speakers and interviews gathered by LAGS fieldworkers.)

One can also cite the usefulness of LAGS data in assessing the location and integrity of linguistic boundaries, which two of the essays in this volume undertake. Anne Malone Fitts examines the evidence for a Midland/Southern boundary in Alabama, while Edgar Schneider examines the LAGS evidence for a regional boundary (the Chatta-hoochee River) proposed by another researcher, Gordon Wood.

The field has witnessed interest in using lexical (Johnson 1996) and other data from linguistic atlases to provide cross-generational comparisons. Guy Bailey (e.g. Bailey et al.1991) and his students (Tillery 1989, Brown 1991 in particular) have shown how LAGS phonological data can be used to explore language change in progress. Montgomery's essay on multiple modals in this volume also shows how LAGS can help researchers make tentative statements about language change in grammatical features.

Until fairly recently it was unclear how and whether linguistic atlas data were amenable to quantitative analysis, but over the past decade a number of quantitative tools and indices have been developed, espe-cially by Pederson (see the following essay and seven volumes of Pederson et al.'s book text), and also by several contributors to this volume: William Kretzschmar, Jr., Michael Miller, Susan McDaniel, and Edgar Schneider. One must cite in particular the work of

Kretzschmar and Schneider over the past decade, especially for data from the Linguistic Atlas of the Middle and South Atlantic States (Kretzschmar 1992, Kretzschmar and Schneider 1996, Schneider 1988, Schneider and Kretzschmar 1989). Not only has the quantitative movement arrived in atlas work, but because atlas data has inspired researchers to develop new and creative approaches, the range of analytical tools now at hand for students of language variation has broadened significantly.

The advent of LAGS has also inspired renewed interest in grammatical variation. Pederson's instructions to fieldworkers to note any form potentially of interest and the compilation of these in the project's *Concordance* and other formats have made possible the study of such features as habitual *be* (Bailey and Bassett 1986), auxiliary deletion (Bailey and Schnebly 1988), finite *bes* (Bernstein 1988), and multiple modals (Montgomery, this volume).

Further, one can cite how LAGS, a project formulated to answer questions of cultural interest, has inspired similar studies, such as the ones herein by John Algeo on *bubba* and Stanley Rich on church names in west Alabama. Finally, researchers have demonstrated how atlas work is fundamental to larger issues, such as the nature and definition of 'dialect' and how such a construct is operationalized (Kretzschmar, this volume), and has been used to test fundamental linguistic constructs such as 'apparent time' (Bailey et al. 1991).

Despite recent advances, the LAGS project and its publications are generally not well known—certainly far less well known to the profession than they deserve to be, either to the range of linguists who work on social and regional varieties of American English or to the cultural geographers, folklorists, and other social scientists who wish to understand how language reflects larger patterns of American cultural history and diversity. Recent work has only begun to tap the incomparable resource that is LAGS. This volume collects essays that continue the work and show what Lee Pederson made possible for others to study and explore.

The Treasury of LAGS:
Its History, Organization,
and Accomplishments

Michael B. Montgomery

The Linguistic Atlas of the Gulf States (LAGS) is the most contemporary of American linguistic atlas projects, completing in 1992 a quarter-century course from planning to fieldwork to publication of its seventh and final hard-back volume.[1] As a comprehensive survey of the speech of eight states in the American South, LAGS is one of a series of autonomous regional atlases that have developed under the auspices of the Linguistic Atlas of the United States and Canada (LAUSC), the project in linguistic geography founded by Hans Kurath in the 1920s and envisioned to survey the English-speaking parts of North America. Throughout its history, LAGS was directed by Lee Pederson of Emory University.[2] The material generated by LAGS merits extended discussion for a variety of reasons, not only because of its immense size and many forms, but also because of professional currents (discussed in the introduction to this volume) which have underestimated and often ignored the value of LAGS.

This essay provides a comprehensive view of the aims, methods, applications, and accomplishments of the project by surveying principal LAGS publications from 1981 to 1992.[3] These publications fall into two main divisions: 1) two microform collections, the *Basic Materials* (1981) and the *Concordance* (1986), published by University Microfilms International; and 2) the seven-volume series of books published from 1986–92 by the University of Georgia Press.

In its broadest sense LAGS has four interdependent components: in Pederson's terminology, these are the tape text (the recorded interviews, which in LAGS are called 'field records', a term that in previous atlas work referred to the notebooks in which informant responses were transcribed phonetically during interviews; cf. Pederson 1974b), and three 'analogues' of the tape text: 1) the fiche text (*Basic Materials*, consisting largely of the 'protocols', which is what LAGS calls the notebooks with the transcribed data from each speaker (arranged by questionnaire or work sheet item) and the *Concordance*); 2) the disk text (microcomputer files); and 3) the book text (the *Handbook*, two indexes, and four volumes called the Descriptive Materials). Cumulatively, this material may be schematized as in figure 1.

Figure 1. Components of LAGS

$$
\begin{array}{c}
\text{Disk Text} \leftrightarrow \text{Book Text} \leftrightarrow \left\{
\begin{array}{l}
\textit{Technical Index}\ (\text{v.3}) \\
\textit{Regional Matrix}\ (\text{v.4}) \\
\textit{Regional Pattern}\ (\text{v.5}) \\
\textit{Social Matrix}\ (\text{v.6}) \\
\textit{Social Pattern}\ (\text{v.7})
\end{array}\right.
\end{array}
$$

Tape Text ⇔ Fiche Text (*Basic Materials*)

Concordance ⇔ *General Index* (v.2)

From left to right in this figure we follow the outline of the LAGS editorial process, i.e., how components were derived from one another, with the book text being the most refined and farthest removed from the field recordings/tape text (N.B.: the *Handbook*, properly speaking the first volume of the book text, is not shown because, as a bridge between the *Basic Materials* and the *Concordance/General Index* and between the *Basic Materials* and the rest of the book text, it cannot be situated on this figure). From right to left the figure indicates how users can move from the most-edited to the least-edited parts of LAGS, depending on the information sought. As shown in this essay, the different 'text types' can be employed together in many types of research.

AN OVERVIEW OF LAGS

LAGS is one of the most important scholarly achievements in American English linguistics in the 20th century. As an extensive survey of seven Southern states (Alabama, Arkansas, Florida, Georgia,

Louisiana, Mississippi, and Tennessee) and part of an eighth (East Texas), a region of nearly a half-million square miles, LAGS surpasses all other studies of Southern American English in size and breath, furnishing invaluable tools for the study of Southern speech in its socio-historical contexts.[4] The complex picture of speech subregions it outlines argues strongly for revision of the simple Upper South vs. Lower South dichotomy traditionally presented in the linguistic literature. LAGS provides abundant, fascinating evidence for such subregions as the Piney Woods of the Lower South and the Mississippi Delta as being distinct speech areas, hitherto unidentified and unde-scribed.[5]

LAGS assembles more data from a wider range of speakers than do all other studies of Southern speech combined. Generational differ-ences, particularly in lexis, are more easily charted in LAGS than in any other major database on American English. For innumerable issues involving change and variation in Southern speech, LAGS offers a broad overview and points of departure for further investigations. Whatever limitations there are, LAGS data can be used to explore virtually every major regional and social issue in Southern American English, or its varieties, that researchers have identified.

THE BACKGROUND OF LAGS

The Linguistic Atlas of the United States and Canada, from which LAGS ultimately derives, took original inspiration from European forerunners (especially Jaberg and Jud's *Sprach- und Sachatlas Italiens und der Südschweiz*, 1928–40) and was organized by Kurath, with the help of Fries, Sturtevant, Bloomfield, and other members of the Linguistic Society of America, in the late 1920s. Sponsored in succeed-ing years mainly by the American Council of Learned Societies,[6] it was designed to collect basic information about native speech habits in a consistent way, with the aims of detailing linguistic patterns and ultimately correlating these with such cultural and historical phenomena as settlement and migration (McDavid 1958, Viereck 1973). Early on, Kurath and his associates expanded the European model (which surveyed older, rural, 'folk' speakers), determining to explore both regional and social distribution of forms by interviewing younger and old-fashioned speakers, as well as cultured and rustic ones. (In response, European linguistic geographers criticized Kurath for seeking any items other than traditional, rural ones directly related to folk culture. In their view it made no sense to collect verb principal parts and other grammatical forms; one of them, the Swiss Eugen Dieth (1948:76) called the questionnaire designed for the American atlas 'alarmingly modern'). Kurath initiated the study of social dialects in atlas work, but as Miller observes (1990–95:84), 'If LANE originated the study of social dialects, then LAGS has carried this idea to its logical conclusion'.

In the 1930s the LAUSC divided eastern North America into subsidiary regional projects. Of first interest was the Atlantic seaboard, the areas in which primary settlement (i.e. directly from Europe) took place prior to the American Revolution. This territory was surveyed by the Linguistic Atlas of New England (LANE) in the early 1930s and the Linguistic Atlas of the Middle and South Atlantic States (LAMSAS) in the late 1930s and 1940s. Only after fieldwork for these two projects was completed or well under way did attention turn to territories whose settlement derived from the Atlantic coast. These regions of secondary settlement included the Middle West (six states encompassed by LANCS, the Linguistic Atlas of the North Central States, and four by LAUM, the Linguistic Atlas of the Upper Midwest) and the Interior South, eventually to be covered by LAGS. Raven I. McDavid, Jr.,'s 1949 paper, 'Application of the Linguistic Atlas Method to Dialect Study in the South-Central Area', which called for a linguistic atlas of the Gulf states and lower Mississippi Valley and outlined what such a project could learn from atlas work elsewhere, was the first published discussion of the project that two decades later became LAGS.

HALLMARKS OF LAGS

From the beginning LAGS has had four hallmarks. First, it emphasized consistency with previous linguistic atlas projects. In its orientation to collecting data through one-on-one interviews using essentially the same detailed questionnaire (usually called 'work sheets'), LAGS parallels the efforts of other American atlases to document the speech closest to the settlement period by questioning many older, rural speakers about traditional folk culture, including domestic and farm life. This was to ensure the comparability of LAGS data with those gathered by other atlas projects. LAGS is based on an extensive survey of 1,121 speakers from 699 localities in 452 counties and parishes. Of these speakers, 914 were classified as primary informants (considered such by providing more or less full interviews, fulfilling the survey's requirements of local nativity, and representing a particular LAGS grid unit) and 207 as secondary informants (if they did not meet these exact qualifications—e.g., LAGS sometimes interviewed speakers who represented redundant coverage within a grid unit).[7] Using standard work sheets, LAGS sought from each speaker (normally a native of the immediate vicinity) the contrastive reflexes of lexical, phonological, and grammatical items for which, on the basis of previous observation or citation in the linguistic literature, there was reason to expect an areal or social pattern of variation.

Judged in its own terms, linguistic atlas work complements rather than competes with or substitutes for sociolinguistic work. The two differ in design, goals, and in other regards. One surveys an extensive territory, investigates hundreds of forms, and is qualitative and inventorial in design; the other most often involves the intensive study of a given community, focuses on a small handful of structures, and is quantitative in design. Atlas work does not seek to answer the same questions as sociolinguistic research, but does identify many contexts in which the latter may be fruitful. Linguistic geography seeks an extremely broad, taxonomic assemblage of data useful not only for addressing larger historical and cultural issues, but also to provide the widest baseline and most points of departure for future work. For both of these ends, it is important for linguistic geography to concentrate on surveying, like many other types of cultural study, older informants both native to the community and having parents who were native. It is, of course, equally crucial that regional patterns then discovered not be ascribed to the general population, but that discussions about dialect regions be stated as based on the native and older segments of society.

LAGS combines the traditional atlas framework and approach with much that is new, offering a comprehensive database on folk culture and language in the Interior South along with many new interpretive possibilities for understanding the linguistic complexion and dynamics of the region. Consistency with a design dating from the 1920s hardly precluded the incorporation of many new features, as will shortly be seen.

A second hallmark of LAGS is its innovations. Pederson addressed many of the limitations of earlier atlas work by broadening and recasting LAGS methodology. Chiefly because of his long-standing interest in investigating language change, he extended the sampling practices inherited from the atlas tradition by surveying an even wider range of speakers than previous projects, As a result, the range of informants in some respects approximated the demography of the region to a degree unprecedented in linguistic atlas work.

More than a fifth of primary informants were blacks: 197/914 (21.6%). Approximately 15 interviews were conducted by black fieldworkers; the rest were done by whites, who, given the insularity of many rural Southern communities in the 1960s and 1970s, may have been the only ones who could have interviewed black speakers successfully. The NORM ('non-mobile, older, rural male'; cf. Chambers and Trudgill 1980:33), the archetypal informant for much earlier, especially European, linguistic geography, became no longer the dominant type. Nearly half of LAGS primary speakers were women (423/914, 46.3%, compared to 30.7% for LAMSAS and less for other atlases), and the imbalance toward older individuals was not nearly so great as in previous atlases. Of the primary informants, 63.7% (582/914) were over sixty years old, 24.5% were between 31 and 60, and 11.8% were 30 years old or younger. The mean age of LAGS speakers was 62 (but for speakers in urban areas it was only 40). More than half of primary informants were classified as middle class (514/914, slightly a third (295/914, 32.3%) as lower class, and a ninth (105/914, 11.5%) as upper class. Forty bilinguals whose first language was not English were interviewed by LAGS: ten Spanish/English speakers in Texas and Florida, 24 French/English in Louisiana, five German/English in Texas and Arkansas, and one Choctaw/English in Mississippi.

In addition, LAGS fieldworkers elicited differing, but often considerable, amounts of conversation from speakers. Freed from direct, short-answer questioning by the recording in full of all interviews, they could focus the interview on broad semantic fields, and other new possibilities were opened such as the regular transcription of stress patterns, while LAGS maintained its traditional design and aims.[8] Also LAGS focused on urban speech far more than earlier atlases. When early fieldwork in East Tennessee showed that Knoxville and Chattanooga informants were often unfamiliar with rural and old-fashioned vocabulary known in smaller communities, Pederson decided that urban localities needed special study and developed an 'Urban Complement' (later called 'Urban Supplement') of 201 additional questions (about types of streets, automobiles, home appliances, etc.) posed to 164 speakers. Most of these informants were urban, but a few younger, rural ones were included in order to produce lexical evidence for the transition from rural to urban culture and the influence of the latter upon the former, and also to assess the significance of urbanization in the region; cf. Pederson and Billiard 1979).[9] LAGS also features many innovations in data format and presentation, as detailed below, that make it more user friendly than other atlases.

Third, LAGS exploited developments in modern technology—the tape recorder, the microfilm camera, the microcomputer, and so on. Because all interviews were recorded in their entirety, the quantity of transcribable and publishable data grew exponentially, with the result that Pederson's views of what LAGS could and should be evolved and the concept of a linguistic atlas and the corpus of data it organizes were redefined.[10] In particular, the advent of the microcomputer played a key role in altering the publication plans of LAGS in the mid-1980s.

A fourth hallmark of LAGS is its concern for documentation and accountability. A manual was produced early on (Pederson, McDavid, Foster, and Billiard 1972, updated in 1974). As work progressed, Pederson issued periodic updates in the form of four interim reports (Pederson 1969, 1974a, 1976, 1981b), three series of Working Papers on microfiche appended to the *Basic Materials* and the *Concordance*, and the introductions to volumes of the Descriptive Materials. The *Handbook* (and the Working Papers in greater detail) reports and explains how fieldworkers were trained, interviews conducted, and editorial and scribal decisions made, all to minimize the effect of individual tendencies of LAGS fieldworkers and scribes (only eight of the latter were employed). Since the approximately 5,300 hours of LAGS interviews were recorded, all LAGS data are ultimately accessible in their original tape-recorded form.[11] From early on, Pederson's goal was the 'exhaustive description of [these] tape/text field records' (1981b:258), leading to an array of interdependent publications that make LAGS data available for interpretation in raw and edited forms. All told, the bibliography of LAGS publications generated by the project staff numbers more than sixty items, a roster longer than for any other American linguistic atlas.

In four volumes of the Descriptive Materials (volumes 4–7 of the book text), Pederson and his team have produced an atlas of the Gulf states speech, and in the fiche text, the first three volumes of the book text, and the disk text, they have crafted a massive set of research tools. The Descriptive Materials exemplify, but hardly begin to exhaust, the ways in which LAGS data may be displayed and mapped. Thus, LAGS provides a vast corpus of Southern speech and shows how it can be analyzed in many ways; it is not an analysis itself. Those who yearn for a synoptic, quick-reference analysis of Southern American English with isoglosses and data summaries (as in Kurath's *Word Geography of the Eastern United States* and Kurath and McDavid's *Pronunciation of English in the Atlantic States*) will not find in LAGS a single volume that simply and neatly demarcates speech areas or formulates isoglosses in the fashion of Kurath. Rather, Pederson has used a deductive approach that involves liberally mapped linguistic features in the Descriptive Materials that are found to be concentrated in one or more sociocultural regions of the LAGS territory. Few 'larger' questions may be immediately answerable by consulting LAGS, compared to the many requiring the investment of scrutiny and exploration, but the Descriptive Materials have much to reveal, and Pederson has designed them (along with the disk text) to enable users to seek answers to their own diverse questions. He viewed his mission to be to 'lay out information for analysis by the reader, without the prescriptive limitations of interpretative conclusions prior to a full disclosure of the facts' (1986a:2). With data so rich and plentiful, he has chosen to present a large selection of mappings of individual forms rather than a comprehensive interpretation of social and regional patterns, lest in doing so he encourage other scholars to rely on his views without working with the data themselves.

Each regional component of the LAUSC to have reached publication (LANE, LAMSAS, LANCS, and LAUM) has presented its material differently. Some publications have taken the form of discursive summaries (LANE, LAUM); others have offered lists of data (LAMSAS), maps (LANE, LAUM), raw phonetic transcriptions on microfilm (LAMSAS, LANCS), or a combination of two of these alternatives.[12] Pederson's ideas of how and what of LAGS to publish evolved considerably over the years, as the amount of editorial time required to produce certain components became clear and as the advent of computers afforded new possibilities.

In none of his four interim reports, nor in the LAGS *Handbook*, did Pederson envision the capability of computers, but once they arrived, he reconceived LAGS.[13] He designed a 'graphic plotter grid', a computer-drawn approximation of the eight-state region (Pederson 1986b) and developed a series of 'electronic matrix maps' (Pederson 1988) to categorize and display LAGS data. Given the advantages and attractiveness of easy, instantaneous computer generation of maps over the more costly, time-consuming cartographic methods employed by earlier linguistic atlases, Pederson devoted the Descriptive Materials largely to a compilation of computer-produced displays of five kinds: SecTotals, SocTotals, LagsMaps, CodeMaps, and Area Totals (all discussed below).

Thus, LAGS was transformed in form and function in the 1980s to become what Pederson termed an 'electronic atlas in microform' (Pederson 1986a), later called the 'Automatic Atlas in Microform' (AAM), which he characterized as 'that ultimate format, a linguistic atlas on a small number of 5.25 diskettes ("floppy disks"), [that] will offer the best we can provide. That text will file materials and programs for sorting and mapping and will give readers the resources to map all indexed LAGS data in whatever ways the programs allow or they see fit' (Pederson, McDaniel, and Adams 1988:xvi). He later released into the public domain the disk text—all the computer data files and programs from which the Descriptive Materials were generated.[14] The availability of this disk version, enabling the production of thousands of maps for on-screen reading or for printing (in other words, an infinitude of possibilities for plotting linguistic features) solidified LAGS as the most modern of American linguistic atlases. Nonetheless, however complete these modifications to LAGS were, they concern the presentation of data rather than the itemized approach to collecting it.

In terms of the latter, LAGS remains squarely within the tradition of conventional linguistic geography, becoming a thoroughly modern atlas while maintaining a legacy as a thoroughly traditional one.

This essay now turns to discuss specific components of LAGS—first the fiche text (the *Basic Materials* and *Concordance*) and then the seven hard-bound volumes of LAGS, beginning with the *Handbook*.

THE LAGS BASIC MATERIALS

When published in microform in 1981, the LAGS *Basic Materials* (Pederson, Billiard, Leas, Bailey, and Bassett 1981) represented the fulfillment of a long-stated commitment of Pederson to make public all data from the project. Yet the event went almost unnoted by the profession and on the conference circuit, and the *Basic Materials* were never reviewed in a scholarly journal. Whatever the reason for this neglect, few have invested the effort to use LAGS as a research tool—admittedly, researchers trained outside the LAGS project had to learn how to evaluate and employ such a massive collection of phonetically transcribed data. Though its microphotographic format has probably put off some potential users, this was the only form in which LAGS could have feasibly been published at the time; today a compact disc or on-line computer version would probably be utilized (the latter is, in the form of the Linguistic Atlas website at the University of Georgia—see endnote 14). The expense of the *Basic Materials*, while not great considering the amount of material, has limited the availability of LAGS principally to the libraries of research universities.[15]

LAGS was not the first American atlas to be microphotographed (that distinction goes to LANCS; cf. Payne 1976 and McDavid and Payne 1976–78), but the LAGS *Basic Materials* are unprecedented in size: approximately 130,000 pages of text (96% of which are in phonetic notation), appearing in two formats—a microfiche version on 1,199 cards arranges data by individual informant, and a microfilm one on 54 reels arranges data by Protocol page. Guides to the *Basic Materials* can be found in microfiche 1 and in chapter four of the LAGS *Handbook* (Pederson, McDaniel, Bailey, and Bassett 1986). In addition to the transcriptions of LAGS data (the Protocols on fiche 17–1134 and the urban supplements on fiche 1135–75), which form the heart of the materials, the collection includes other items that introduce, condense, and supplement these data, including a revised *Manual for Dialect Research in the Southern States* (fiche 2–4), the Idiolect Synopses (fiche 6–16), and the first series of LAGS Working Papers (16 papers, fiche 1177–97).

Each of the 1,118 Protocol fiche (three LAGS interviews conducted in New Orleans in 1983 were not published) begins with a personal data sheet on the speaker and a sketch that characterizes the informant, the community, and the course of the interview. Following are 108 pages with responses to more than 800 work sheet items (some of which contained more than one feature of interest, meaning that the data were eventually categorized into 1,297 separate files). Each page of a Protocol (see figure 2) identifies the LAGS sector (UM = Upper Mississippi), community (Drew), grid (DM 348.01), and at least five social characteristics of the informant (F = female; L = lower class; Y = white; 69 = age; 1A = atlas social type). These pages have three types of notation derived from the field records: phonetic transcriptions (very narrow, in conformity with atlas practice), scribal comments and additions (on the right-hand side of the page), and LAGS abbreviations for stylistic features and other matters. All these notations are keyed to and interpreted by items on the work sheets/questionnaire, which is reproduced in the manual (fiche 3) and in the *Handbook* (pp. 282–84), and were produced by scribes in the LAGS editorial office rather than, as for other atlases, by interviewers transcribing informant responses on the spot in the field.

While Protocol pages are often crowded with transcriptions and the comments of informants and scribes, it must be remembered that they present only a partial distillation of LAGS taped recordings. The latter remain the full phonic record of all interviews, the primary authority for all LAGS data, and the ultimate record from which data can be retrieved for verification or alternative interpretation. Protocol transcriptions are often indexed to the field recording by the reel, side, and tape counter number, to enable this retrieval, and are often cross-referenced to other locations in the Protocols.

Moreover, transcription involved less guesswork than for earlier atlas work, since indistinct forms could be reaudited before transcription was

Michael B. Montgomery

Figure 2. Sample Protocol page
(From LAGS *Handbook*, p. 296)

Page 57 of Protocol DM 348.01 (Informant 548)
Transcribed by Lee Pederson

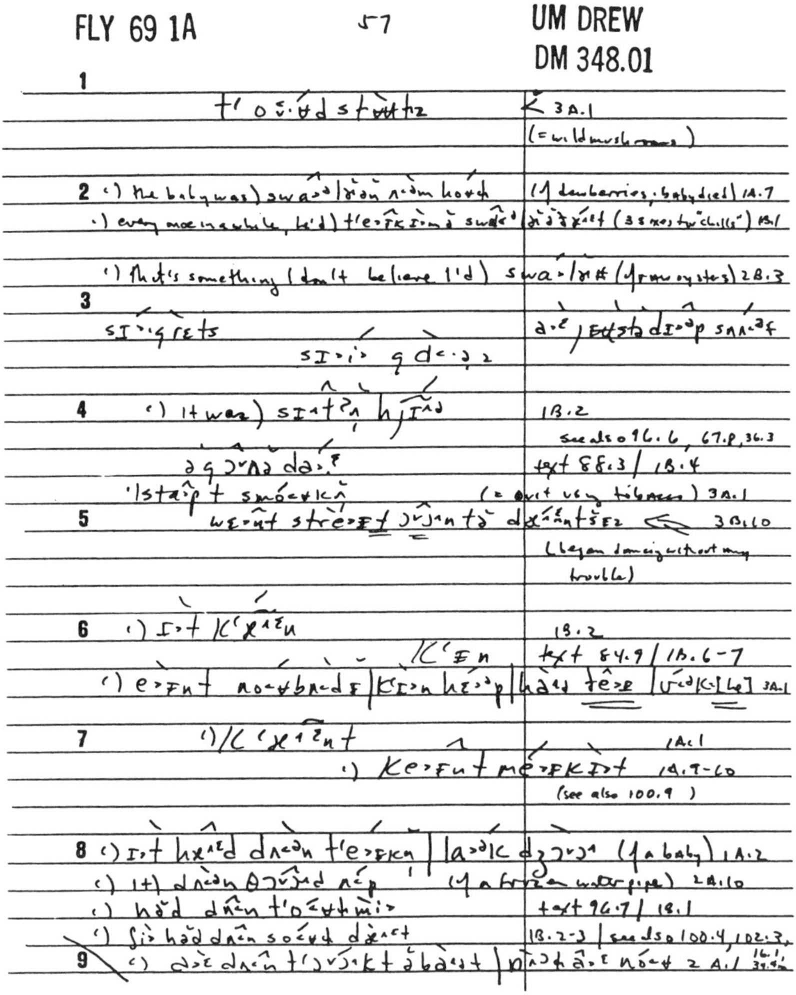

FLY 69 1A   ꜱ7   **UM DREW**
                                                      DM 348.01

From *Linguistic Atlas of the Gulf States*, Volume I, by Lee Pederson. Copyright © 1986 by the University of Georgia Press. Reprinted by permission.

attempted. Scribes could systematically include many types of information that conventional fieldwork without recorders could only sporadically manage: intonation (mainly stress patterns), comments about the status of forms (their naturalness, etc.), multiple responses (occasionally citing as many as half a dozen responses for the same work sheet item), syntactic contexts, and so on. Scribes could far more regularly note informant comments and judgments on the social status of forms and could indicate when responses were suggested by the fieldworker. As a result, LAGS grammatical data in particular are more detailed and interesting than those gathered by other atlases. Nearly all LAGS citations of multiple modals, for example, come from free conversation, rather than in response to a short-answer question, as we can tell by the phrases and clauses in which they are embedded in Protocol entries. The decision to tape record all LAGS interviews led, in short, to a substantially modified and enlarged database.

The LAGS Idiolect Synopsis, designed by Pederson as 'an extension of the vowel synopses in *PEAS* [Kurath and McDavid 1961]' (Pederson 1981b:247), is a one-page abstract of each informant's speech, a summary set of phonological, grammatical, and lexical forms in transcription from each Protocol.[16] Listed in narrow phonetic notation in each synopsis (see figure 3) are forms illustrating the incidence of 1) 15 vowel phonemes in five environments (preceding a voiceless obstruent, a voiced obstruent or pause, a nasal, a lateral, and a retroflex); 2) 24 consonants; 3) five plural forms (*pounds, shrimp*, etc.); 4) five function words (*toward(s), minutes till/to/of*, etc.); 5) principal parts of eight verbs (*rise, dive, eat, help*, etc.); and 6) 28 lexical forms (reflexes for *andiron, paper bag, dragonfly*, etc.) In including all phonetic segments of each citation word and in providing lexical and grammatical forms, these synopses contain much more information about an individual's speech than their counterparts in *PEAS*.

Because they are so compact and are grouped together in the *Basic Materials*, these synopses can be consulted for many speakers quickly and are appropriate for student projects, not only for quick inter-speaker comparisons but also for tracking pronunciation changes, especially vowel shifts and mergers across environments, as well as other types of sound change in progress (e.g. Tillery 1989, Kerr 1989). Indeed, the Idiolect Synopses and the *Concordance* are the two components of

Figure 3. Sample Idiolect Synopsis
(From LAGS *Handbook*, p. 290)

Idiolect Synopsis of Protocol DM 348.01 (Informant 548)

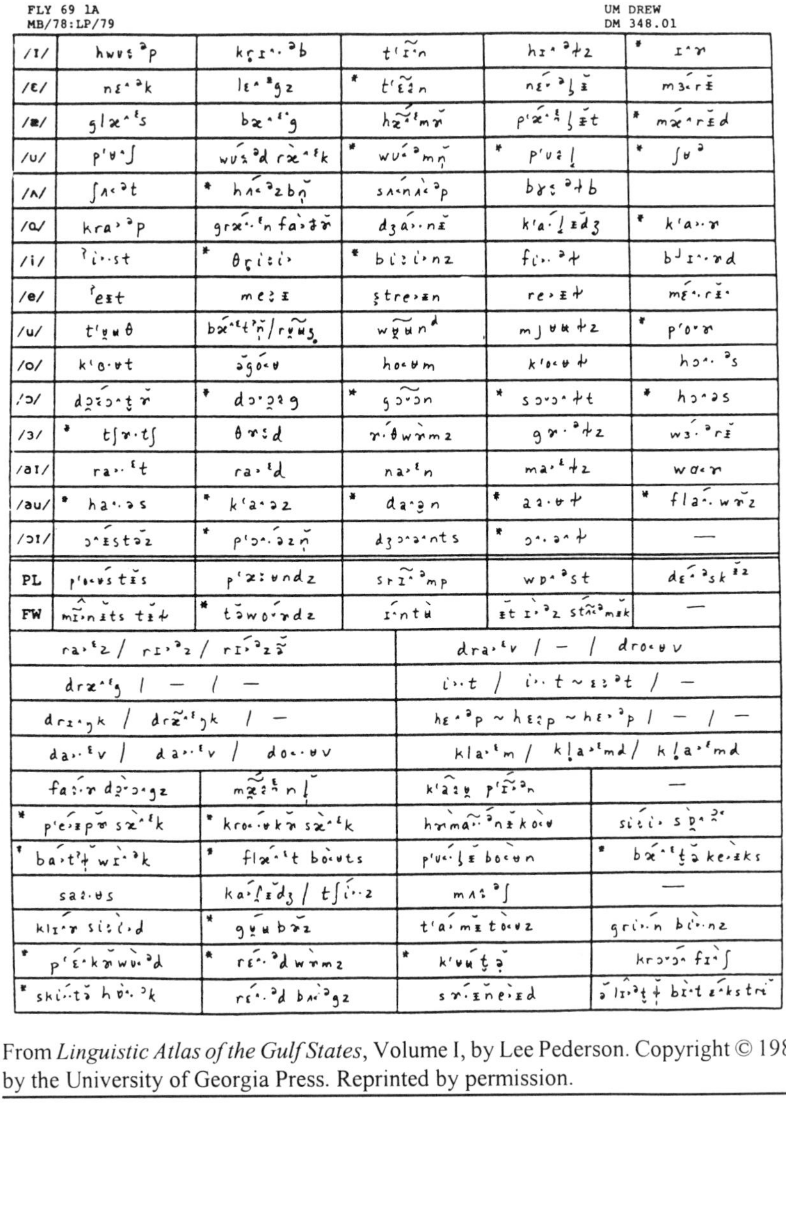

From *Linguistic Atlas of the Gulf States*, Volume I, by Lee Pederson. Copyright © 1986 by the University of Georgia Press. Reprinted by permission.

LAGS that require the least time to learn to use. The words chosen to exhibit vowels normally match those in *PEAS* synopses; special notations indicate when this was not possible (and a substitution was provided) and when only one of two or more appropriate responses to an item was included on the page (space permitted only one).[17] Nearly all the items in the Idiolect Synopses are presented for the cumulative LAGS corpus in the Descriptive Materials, displayed either on maps or charts outlining their areal and social distribution.

Finally, the 16 Working Papers appendixed to the Protocols not only discuss the editorial practices of LAGS in their greatest detail, but also document the internal history of the first 12 years of the project. A brief summary of each number in the first and second series of Working Papers (the latter published with the *Concordance*) appears in the LAGS *Handbook* (pp. 311–13).

THE LAGS CONCORDANCE

If potential users of LAGS are daunted by the imposing size of the *Basic Materials*, the component of LAGS published next provides far more convenient access to much of the data collected by the project. This is the *Concordance* (Pederson, McDaniel, and Bassett 1986) of all Protocol forms (from both primary and secondary informants) converted to standard orthography, indexed alphabetically, and coded to simplify and enhance their retrieval from the Protocols. Pederson characterizes the *Concordance* as 'a finder's list of all words and phrases in the LAGS protocols' (1981b:245).

The LAGS *Concordance*, prefaced by the second and third series of LAGS Working Papers,[18] comprises 154 microfiche and is the only item of its kind among American linguistic atlases. LAGS editors required from five to 20 hours to convert each Protocol's phonetic entries into *Concordance* orthographic forms. Since it also parses all phrasal and clausal entries from the Protocols and indexes each word from these, the computer-generated *Concordance* totals roughly three million entries on 40,934 pages. As a complete catalogue of forms in the Protocols and an indicator of the types and range of information to be found there, it organizes LAGS data by individual form.

Each line in the *Concordance* has five columns preceding the indexed linguistic form (see figure 4). Three of these columns specify the informant, page, and line number where the form can be found in transcription in the relevant Protocol. A *Concordance* entry sometimes includes a 'Scribal Gloss' (encompassing scribal judgments, such as 'false start or hesitation') that enables users to ascertain the linguistic status of Protocol entries, and a 'Grammatical Gloss', which indicates the formal or functional category of an item if such information is found in the Protocols. The *Concordance* then lists the indexed linguistic form (ranging from a word to a clause) and, finally, any scribal commentary and clarifications in the Protocol such as informant statements noting the perceived social status of the form or a comment disambiguating the form from synonyms.

Most entries are of single words with no scribal commentary (e.g. seven pages of *just*), which gives a bare appearance to many pages; this resulted because the *Concordance* was designed to be the complete inventory of forms from the Protocols. The *Concordance* groups in one place forms which are entered on more than one page in the Protocols (e.g., if they appear as a different part of speech or if they are an element in a compound). Consulting the *Concordance* ensures that all instances of a form are found in the Protocols. Multiple modals will normally be found on page 58, line 7, of Protocols (e.g., figure 4), but occasionally elsewhere. The *Concordance* indicates those locations.

Pederson, McDaniel, and Bassett (1984:332) state that 'within the atlas design, the *Concordance* serves as the central reference', since it stands between the Protocols and the Descriptive Materials and can be used with either one or both of these or as an independent research tool. Because of its orthographic format and alphabetic organization, it is the component of LAGS having a wide potential usership; nonlinguists, indeed 'any person interested in the heritage of the South' (Pederson, McDaniel, and Bassett 1986:1) will find its data fairly simple to use. A twelve-page introduction by the editors discusses on microfiche 1 the relation of the *Concordance* to other components of LAGS and spells out the conventions it employs.

The *Concordance* has no phonological information (other than indication of the stress patterns of some compounds), only showing where certain forms of phonological interest can be found in the

Figure 4. Sample Concordance page
(From LAGS *Concordance*, p. 21952)

```
BOOK  PAGE LINE SG    GG   ENTRY                                              21952

0784  058   7              might could
0784  058   7              might could
0806  058   7              might could <wouldn't ordinarily say/might say>
0824  058   7    f         might could <uses habitually>
0826  058   7              might could <he wouldn't say/has heard it>
0827  058   7              might could <"doesn't sound right">
0831  058   7              might could
0835  058   7              might could
0836  058   7              might could
0857  058   7              might could
0870  058   7              might could <rejects/sounds "uneducated">
0873  058   7              might could <she might use>
0888  058   7              might could
0900  058   2              might could <sounds funny/might say occasionally>
0908  058   7              might could <future reference>
0850  058   7              might could answer
0105  058   7              might could be
0678  058   7              might could be a call
0153  058   7              might could be a dreary day <it>
0815  058   7              might could be called <valleys>
0435  058   7              might could call it a shock, you
0595  058   7              might could call them, you
0111A 058   7    d         might could car(ry) you to the doctor, he <*take>
0149  058   7              might could catch some
0792  058   7              might could do for me, he <he thought of something>
0093A 058   7              might could do it
0095  058   7              might could do it <I>
0173  058   7              might could do it
0327  058   7              might could do it
0428  058   7              might could do it
0583  058   6    b         might could do it
0584  058   7              might could do it
0791  058   7              might could do it
0796  058   7              migh. could do it,<"I guess I might say it">
0823  058   7              might could do it
0864  058   7              might could do it
0876  058   7              might could do it <might say>
0868  058   7              might could do it by next week
0024  058   7              might could do it, I <heard/probably wouldn't say>
0043  058   7              might could do it, I
0064  058   7              might could do it, I
0072  058   7              might could do it, I
0074A 058   7              might could do it, I
0157  058   7              might could do it, I
0160  058   7              might could do it, I
0235  058   6              might could do it, I
0242  058   8              might could do it, I
0278  058   7              might could do it, I <quite natural>
0427  058   7              might could do it, I
0469  058   7              might could do it, I
0492  058   7              might could do it, I
0656  058   7              might could do it, I <sounds awkward>
0662  058   6    b         might could do it, I <seemed pretty natural to him>
0707  058   8              might could do it, I
```

From *Concordance to the Linguistic Atlas of the Gulf States*, edited by Lee Pederson.
Copyright © 1986 by UMI. Used by permission.

Protocols (hence the lengthy tally of *just*). More importantly, it is an indispensable research tool for lexical and grammatical variation. Indeed, since grammatical forms like multiple modals are very often cited in syntactic context, the *Concordance* can easily be employed to study the range of environments for such forms and to suggest what linguistic factors constrain their occurrence. Pederson, McDaniel, and Bassett (1984:334) state that 'without recourse to the field record, one can organize a useful grammatical statement' from the *Concordance* alone—although only, as we shall see, for individual forms rather than for a competing set of forms. Among grammatical data of potential interest are zero forms, 11 kinds of which were noted by LAGS scribes (zero copula verbs, conjunctions, prepositions, relative pronouns, auxiliary verbs, plural and agreement inflections, etc.) The *Concordance* offers a mine of raw material for exploring phonological and syntactic constraints on these zero forms, all of which are indexed in its appendix.

Perhaps most immediately obvious from the *Concordance* is the tremendous variety of lexical forms collected by LAGS, resulting from the scribes' patient culling of field records and the editorial decision to include in Protocols so much material, both outcomes made possible by the taping of interviews. Because fieldworkers were freed from on-the-spot transcription, they could elicit many synonyms, giving scribes more forms of possible interest to cite than has traditionally been the case in linguistic atlas projects.[19]

One can easily discover the number of speakers who used specific lexical forms (e.g. *poor white trash*) and grammatical forms (e.g. *y'all*) and study the scribal comments and contextual information pertaining to them. And since the *Concordance* cross-references informant numbers to the *Handbook*, it can be used in tandem with the latter, with its social and geographical profile of each informant, to compose broad, tentative statements about areal and social prevalence of forms (the Descriptive Materials do this cartographically for hundreds of items, but far from exhaust the possibilities). Or one can use the *Concordance* as a phonological finding aid to pinpoint forms of interest in the Protocols.

But comparative work (e.g. to examine the distribution of alternative terms for rural poor whites) is impossible with the *Concordance* alone. To discover which form is used by given types of speakers (e.g. who uses *poor white trash* vs. who uses *redneck*), readers must first consult either the Protocols or, more efficiently, the *Technical Index* (discussed below, which approximates a thesaurus), to identify which responses were made for a given work sheet item. Only a Protocol indicates which forms a given speaker uses for a specific item. Only the *Technical Index* identifies the inventory of different terms (i.e. the set of potentially competing forms) noted by LAGS scribes as appropriate responses[20] for each work sheet item (13 for item 043.5 *you-all*, a staggering 212 for 069.7 *poor whites* [*white usage*]) and cites the number of speakers offering each response. With information from the *Technical Index*, users can return to the *Concordance* and compare responses; the issue of whether or not these responses can be viewed as 'variants' or competing forms is discussed below.

While the *Concordance* offers countless opportunities for studying lexical variation (especially in conjunction with the *Technical Index*), we must consider more closely the statement cited earlier that 'without recourse to the field record, one can organize a useful grammatical statement' from the *Concordance* alone. The key word here is *useful*. The researcher can often draw from the *Concordance* information about grammatical constraints and, with the help of the *Technical Index* and the *Handbook*, information about grammatical variation across groups of speakers. Determining a speaker's range of responses to a work sheet item and the incidence of variants is often of substantial importance, but the *Concordance* cannot be used to explore variation within an informant's speech or to compare individual speakers except in the roughest way. The Protocols (and sometimes the field records) are required for this. Because of the inventorial organization of LAGS, the *Concordance* and the two index volumes reveal the number of speakers in the LAGS territory who used given forms, not the actual frequency of the forms themselves. We cannot tell whether an informant used a form once or a dozen times. The *Concordance*/Indexes provide a fairly good sense of how common many grammatical forms are in Southern American speech—but suggest only roughly the comparative frequency of variants.

This fact is usually inconsequential for lexical forms, but crucial for grammatical variants (e.g. finite *be*). LAGS treats grammatical forms, in effect, as lexical items. The *Concordance* lists, for instance, multiple modal combinations, including negative forms of them (*might not could*, etc.), but tells us nothing about other matters of interest: how often given speakers use multiple modals, how often they use them in comparison to single modals, nor whether multiple modals are used in the same semantic and pragmatic environments as single modals, and so on (some of these matters could be determined if the interviews had been transcribed completely; others are basic analytical challenges in variationist studies). These limitations flow from the design of the project and must be understood by users, who may be tempted to interpret LAGS data in unintended ways and to consider them not as tentative, as they are meant to be, but as definitive. In the final analysis, a researcher can always return to the field record and audit the interview to recover intraspeaker frequency of occurrence of forms or to undertake quantitative analysis of linguistic variables. Finally, it must be remembered that the *Concordance* is referenced to the Protocols, which should be consulted if questions about any details of *Concordance* forms arise.

THE LAGS HANDBOOK

The *Handbook* (Pederson, McDaniel, Bailey, and Bassett 1986), the first of the seven hard-bound volumes of the book text, is the principal reference guide to LAGS. It is the key to the *Basic Materials* and, to a lesser extent (because their exact format was unanticipated when the *Handbook* was composed), the Descriptive Materials (book text volumes 3–7). Patterned largely on the *Handbook* to the Linguistic Atlas of New England (Kurath et al. 1939), it consists of four chapters, which provide the background, plan, and rationale for LAGS, a survey of the geography and history of the Gulf states, detailed sketches of communities and informants, and an introduction to the *Basic Materials*. Appended is a bibliography of 1730 items on linguistics, cultural geography, and regional and local history to which the text is cross-referenced and which were used by LAGS editors in formulating the project, designing the LAGS grid, deciding in which communities to conduct fieldwork, or in some other way.

Among other matters, the first chapter of the *Handbook* ('Methods', pp. 1–40) explains the goals and history of the project and the basics of fieldwork (the grid design, the criteria for informant selection, the form of the work sheets, the editorial work, and the classification of informants). It summarizes LAGS fieldwork and scribal work and provides an account of compositional and transcriptional practices, conventions, and notations used in the *Basic Materials* sufficient to interpret the Protocol data fully. An important section of the chapter discusses the importance of classifying LAGS speakers by their social status and elucidates how this was done. LAGS tackled the three goals of being consistent with the Kurathian subjective system of social types (based on reading habits, social contact, amount of education, etc.), of being sensitive to a traditional social framework of two racial castes, and of taking more modern sociological constructs into account in its categorization of speakers. Classification was achieved through a series of overlapping formal and functional categories, a multiple set of indexes employed in the later descriptive volumes to compare social groupings of speakers. To simplify the process that was followed, one might say that fieldworkers first ranked informants using subjective criteria, including social experience and breadth of world view; then 'after ordering the informants within each community through the social indexes, editors assigned formal classifications' (Pederson, McDaniel, Bailey, and Bassett 1986:37) that were derived from LANE and other sources. Finally, LAGS editors included in the informant sketches in chapter three of the *Handbook* a multitude of characteristics on which the various indexes were based, providing readers with the raw material used in assigning social categorizations. The considerable detail found in informant sketches brings LAGS closer to an important goal of survey methodology—replicability—in the sense that an investigator could return to the same communities and identify similar informants of a later generation (using LAMSAS informant profiles, Johnson 1996 has recently done this for South Carolina and Georgia).

Chapter Two, 'The Geography of the Gulf States' (pp. 41–79), is the section of the *Handbook* of interest to the widest readership because of its 32 maps and its splendid synopsis of the extensive literature on the land regions, settlement history, land use, and cultural areas of the Gulf states.[21] The chapter is a compact atlas of Southern cultural history, providing the necessary background for interpreting larger patterns of geographical and social variation in the region's speech, and is especially adept in tracing the interplay of white and black settlement. Instead of a chapter corresponding to Kurath et al.'s 'The Dialect Areas of New England' or to McDavid 1994's 'Dialect Areas of the LAMSAS Region', the LAGS *Handbook* has only a section of ten pages, six of them taken by maps, called 'Dialect Areas'. This offers, based on selected evidence from the Idiolect Synopses, a preliminary sketch of the speech areas of the Gulf states. The maps (e.g. for the distribution of *pullybone* vs. *wishbone* and *red bug* vs. *chigger*, and the subregional variants of *burlap bag* and *dragonfly*) suggest that the traditional twofold division of the upper and lower South is oversimplified and that river valleys and cities often affect the distribution of vocabulary, but leaves much detail to be inferred from later volumes.

The third chapter of the *Handbook*, 'The Communities and Informants' (pp. 81–280), describes each community surveyed and every informant interviewed. It collates and combines the Protocol personal data sheets (the social and biographical vignette of each speaker, written by the fieldworker, citing each informant's ancestry, educational and occupational history, church membership, travel, etc.) and the interview sketches (a detailed characterization of the interview, written by the scribe, noting whether the informant was cooperative, self-conscious, etc., and other points of interest, such as the amount of free conversation); see figure 5.

Since every interview was a unique social encounter between individuals, the *Handbook* explicitly indicates the general success of each interview and the idiosyncrasies and sensibilities of each informant. These accounts remind us of the very personal side to linguistic fieldwork. Since the sketches identify the fieldworker and the scribe for each interview, researchers can evaluate and compare the tendencies of LAGS workers for themselves. Unlike in the LANE *Handbook*, each sketch here is prefaced by codes and indices (explained in chapter 4) for the gender, social class, racial caste, age, and atlas type of the speaker. The biographical details used to classify speakers socially are full and explicit, so that users can contest how any LAGS informant is categorized, if they choose. The length of each interview is also cited.

Figure 5. Sample informant Sketch
(From LAGS *Handbook*, p. 238)

705 LITTLE ROCK FG 458.09 MMY 85 1B: b.
Little Rock. Department store clerk, printer's
devil, also worked for lumber company,
florist, stores; Baptist; 5th gr. Mason,
American Legion. Travel to Ariz.,
Washington, St. Louis, and other parts of U.S.
Mother: b. Tenn.; little education; hw. MGP:
Tenn.; ca. 4th gr.; farmers. Father: b. Tenn.;
little education; peace officer. PGP: Tenn.;
ca. 4th gr. PGF: judge, farmer. Wife: 75;
schoolteacher; college; father from Lonoke
Co. Pleasant, talkative, intelligent informant.
Considerable conversation; explanations
sometimes unclear. Urban Supplement
included. MM-1/78:SL/79 12 hr. 10 min.

As mentioned earlier, the fourth chapter, 'The Basic Materials' (pp.
281–331), introduces the Protocol and Idiolect Synopsis microform
collection published in 1981. It includes a condensed version of the
work sheets (with the Urban Supplement), the indexes employed to
classify speakers, a detailed classification of work sheet items by
linguistic type or level, 14 sample Protocol pages, and other materials.
   The LAGS *Handbook* provides the most accessible overview of the
project through the early 1980s and answers most questions about what
was done, by whom, how, where, when, and why. It is from spending
time with this component of LAGS that users best come to understand
the uniqueness of the project and become acquainted with its special
terminology. The *Handbook* also functions as the technical key to the

Protocols and *Concordance*; only the very experienced researcher can dispense with it as a companion in working with LAGS data.

THE LAGS GENERAL INDEX

The LAGS *General Index* (volume two of the book text) is essentially a stripped-down, reorganized version of the *Concordance*. It indexes the complete data base from the Protocols orthographically, listing every form that occurs in the Protocols/*Concordance* and citing its part of speech, relevant Protocol page and line number, and number of entries. It lacks the ancillary information found in the *Concordance* such as scribal glosses and the phrasal context of forms. Since some *Concordance* entries are reports or comments on usage rather than actual citations of usage, the number of entries of a form in the *General Index* may surpass the number of speakers using it, but whether a form occurs in the *Basic Materials* and its rough frequency of occurrence there can most quickly be discovered by consulting the *General Index*. In this index the user can also see at a glance the range of derivatives and compounds based on a given form because these are subsumed under a head word; there are four columns of forms under the headword *corn*, for instance. Many hundreds of names for local communities, bodies of water, and so on, are also indexed here. The *General Index* and the *Concordance* from which it derives hardly form a dictionary, but are the closest thing that LAGS has to one and would likely be the starting point, had a LAGS dictionary been contemplated. As it is, *DARE* is making thorough use of these resources (see Hall, this volume).

THE LAGS TECHNICAL INDEX

Between the completion of the *Handbook* and the conception of the *Technical Index* (the third volume of the book text) two things happened to LAGS. First, it became clear that synoptic volumes describing the phonology and grammar of Gulf states speech, planned earlier, would be very time consuming to prepare. Second, the advent of microcomputer programs to sort and map data persuaded Pederson to mold the remaining LAGS publications not into traditional reference works, but into a disk version of LAGS that 'has the capacity to produce hundreds of thousands of different maps in a simple and inexpensive program' (Pederson, McDaniel, and Adams 1988:xviii). This format comprises ASCII files for the work sheet items plus the sorting and versatile mapping programs, all of which are conveniently summarized and illustrated in McDaniel 1989, collectively called the AAM (Automatic Atlas in Microform).

The *Technical Index* shows the consequences of converting LAGS to a disk text that 'reorganizes the LAGS data base as entries in a set of microcomputer files' (Pederson, McDaniel, Adams, and Liao 1989:ix). It indicates everything that can be mapped using the programs of the Automatic Atlas in Microform. Whereas the *General Index* arranges material alphabetically, the *Technical Index* organizes it by work sheet item. Unlike the *General Index*, the latter counts only actual forms (those used or acknowledged by speakers) from the Protocols, not ones reported or attributed to others. The *Technical Index* might appear to be a reshuffling of material in the previous volume, but this is only partially the case. The *General Index*, since it is derived from the *Concordance*, indexes only orthographic forms, while the *Technical Index* encodes forms in various ways, detailed below. The *General Index* enters place names, the latter does not. The *General Index* includes data from secondary informants and counts these as well as multiple citations of forms from a speaker (to the extent that these occur in the Protocols, they are usually phonological variants), while the *Technical Index* does not. This means that the two indexes rarely, if ever, show the same counts of forms. The *Technical Index* cites 376 instances of (i.e. speakers using) *y'all* and 118 instances of *y'all's*, far fewer than the figures in the *General Index*, which has 616 for *y'all* and 144 for *y'all's*. These two indexes show the diversity of Southern American speech in the numerous responses to many LAGS work sheet items, even though the majority of responses occur only once (e.g. 173 of the 287 responses for *rustic*, work sheet item 069.9, are nonce). While linguists searching for larger social or areal patterns may find nonce forms of little concern, the proliferation of terms may hold considerable interest to those exploring the creativity of language, types of folk metaphor, and many other aspects of language.

The *Technical Index* lists all appropriate response types[22] of the 914 LAGS primary informants for each work sheet item, beginning numerically with 001.1 A P *one* (the numeral).[23] Data from the Protocols are arranged in 1,297 microcomputer 'list files' of five kinds. Phonological files (the 423 LAGS pronunciation items) and 51 grammatical files for verb principal parts appear in 'Automatic Book Code' or 'ABC', a graphophonemic system, intermediate between phonetic and orthographic notation, created by Pederson to capture the phonemic dimensions of phonetic strings and the phonological modifications to such strings (Pederson 1987). An additional 158 grammatical files (e.g. 058.7 *might could*) and the 591 lexical files (including 201 from the Urban Supplement) are presented as alphabetically ordered orthographic forms, keyed by an alphabetic code used in the sorting/mapping programs (figure 6). Finally, 74 Systematic Phonetic files encode forms of 15 stressed vowels and diphthongs in five environments from the LAGS Idiolect Synopses (a 16th, /ɔɪr/, was rarely found), using the specially devised, abstract Systematic Phonetic Code (SPC) notational system (Pederson 1985)[24] for three kinds of phonetic features: Primary or Positional (Front, Back, High, etc.), Secondary or Conditional (Tense, Nasal, etc.), and Tertiary or Modificational (Raised, Retracted, etc.) details of each phone. While translating transcriptions to SPC entailed some simplification of LAGS phonetics, the original, more detailed transcriptions can of course be consulted in the Protocols. Two appendices list the names of the files, one by number, the other alphabetically. While the *Technical Index* resembles a thesaurus, users must remember that the categories represented by work sheet items are sometimes more inclusive than thesaurus entries. That is, responses to a LAGS question, some of which were quite broad, may not be close synonyms and there is sometimes no way to know this. This is not a problem for a work sheet item like 064.1, *grandfather*, the responses to which are denotationally equivalent and can be viewed as linguistic variants, but it is a serious one for 044.5, *corn breads*, or 069.7, *poor whites* [*white usage*], the responses to which cannot be assumed to be the same referentially.

Fortunately, comments in the Protocols/*Concordance* occasionally help to discriminate terms, but one would have considerable difficulty constructing a glossary or anything approaching a dictionary entry for many items using LAGS materials. This is in the nature of the project: when speakers provided several responses to a question, fieldworkers often could not ask them to differentiate between them. Sometimes speakers provided three, four, or more terms judged by the scribe to be appropriate responses, but the extent to which they were interchangeable denotatively or would be consistent in sense across speakers may not be apparent. There is the possibility that speakers with more than one response (e.g. the well-known item, 060A.4 *dragonfly*) may not use them synonymously, but this must be examined in follow-up study. LAGS suggests the general picture.

Figure 6. Sample entries
(From LAGS *Technical Index*, p. 150)

043.5 G you-all
  No Response (253)
  A   all [P-0] y'all (1)
  B   all of you (12)
  C   all of y(ou) ones (1)
  D   guys (1)
  E   y'all (376)
  F   y'all guys (1)
  G   you (92)
  H   you-all (380)
  I   you folks (4)
  J   you guys (1)
  K   you ones (8)
  L   you oneses (1)
  M   you people (3)

043.6 G you-all's
  No Response (507)
  A   all of your (1)
  B   all y'all's (1)
  C   y'all[M-k] (9)
  D   y'all's (118)
  E   y'all'ses (2)
  F   you-all[M-k] (3)
  G   you-all's (60)
  H   you folks's (1)
  I   your (298)
  J   your-all's (10)
  K   yournses (1)
  L   yours (1)

Those who read the introduction to the *Technical Index* are impressed with the straightforward organization of the Automatic Atlas in Microform and should have little difficulty visualizing how it generated the Descriptive Materials. Now that the AAM files are in the public domain, investigators will have little difficulty undertaking their own explorations of social or areal dimensions of LAGS items. A form of interest in either index can be checked against the *Concordance* to see which speaker(s) used it, and relevant social information about the speaker(s) can be quickly obtained from the *Handbook*. It is thus seen how integrated Pederson's atlas is: all later materials derive in a straightforward manner from the *Basic Materials* (which in turn are based on the tape-recorded field records), and the researcher can work his or her way from any of the Descriptive Materials backward, depending on how much detail is desired. This view of the relationships between components of LAGS shows how little information has been obscured between the first publications of LAGS in 1981 and the last ones in 1992. Even though much editing took place in the interim, users have no difficulty going to any map in the *Regional Matrix* or *Social Matrix* volumes (see below) and identifying the location of the user(s) of a given form because the Graphic Plotter Grid used in LagsMaps and CodeMaps (see below) displays data on a coded alphabetic/numeric layout that is keyed to informant biographies in the *Handbook*.

THE LAGS REGIONAL AND SOCIAL MATRIX AND PATTERN

Using the disk version of the atlas, LAGS rapidly published from 1990 to 1992 volumes 4–7 of the book text, which sort and display a large selection of the data collected by the project. Called cumulatively the Descriptive Materials and respectively the *Regional Matrix* (Pederson, McDaniel, Adams, and Montgomery 1990), *Regional Pattern* (Pederson, McDaniel, and Adams 1991), *Social Matrix* (Pederson, McDaniel, Adams, and Montgomery 1991), and *Social Pattern* (Pederson and McDaniel 1992), these volumes take the responses of the 914 primary informants as arranged in *Technical Index* files and organize them in data matrices and maps in the most refined distillation of LAGS material. They illustrate what is possible for an investigator to outline, given the AAM disk text, and what LAGS has chosen to present as a sample from near limitless possibilities.

Embodying Pederson's 'deductive' methodological approach (Pederson, McDaniel, and Adams 1991:xi), these volumes map features in two general ways. First, they take individual inventorial items (lexical or grammatical forms or phonetic strings) and explore their broad areal and social distribution. Second, they take the main and subsidiary land and vegetation zones of the Gulf states (based on the second chapter of the *Handbook*) and five broad social categories as the basis for classifying linguistic data and for discovering which and how many forms correlate with different areal and social divisions.

For the second approach the original 16 LAGS sectors are reconstituted into 33 physiographic subregions of six major land regions (Highlands, Piedmont, Coast, Plains, Piney Woods, and Delta). The boundaries of the subregions 'fundamentally reflect their physical properties, [but] . . . were also adjusted to accommodate significant economic and historic settlement histories' (Pederson, McDaniel and Adams 1991:xiv). As a result, geographers can examine the correlation of settlement, migration, topographical influences, and various social and cultural patterns with the distribution of individual linguistic forms in the eight-state region. These volumes are, in short, the centerpiece of LAGS.

Using the SecTotal and SocTotal computer programs, the *Regional Matrix* and *Social Matrix* volumes (4 and 6) present four-by-four numerical matrices, 24 per page, that are compact data summaries for 6,578 forms (i.e. an average of five for each LAGS item). SecTotals arrange figures from left to right and up to down to correspond to the sixteen-sector LAGS grid from west to east and north to south, displaying succinctly the regional distribution of lexical, phonological, and grammatical forms from LAGS interviews. SocTotals tabulate the number of speakers who use each form by two genders, two racial castes, four age groups, four educational levels, and four social status levels. In addition, the Matrix volumes each feature approximately 400 electronic matrix maps, generated by the LagsMap (for the *Regional Matrix*) and CodeMap (for the *Social Matrix*) programs. These maps display data using alphabetic and numeric symbols on the point-by-point Graphic Plotter Grid. The *Regional Pattern* and *Social Pattern* volumes (5 and 7) present data summaries (in the form of Area Total and Social Total tables) and Pattern Maps of 211 and 150 forms, respectively, nearly all of which forms are also mapped in the *Regional Matrix* and *Social Matrix* volumes.

Cumulatively, the four volumes detail the broad spatial and social dimensions of many forms collected by LAGS; to enhance the perception of these, each volume includes (inside back cover) a set of one or more overlay transparencies that, superimposed on the computer-generated maps, enable the user to visualize how the distribution of forms matches state boundaries and physiographical regions in the Gulf states.

SecTotal and SocTotal displays begin with a two-line header identifying the relevant linguistic form, the type of item (lexical, systematic phonetic, etc.), and the item number (see figure 7). They are arranged by work sheet page and line number and within an item are listed alphabetically (e.g., SecTotals/SocTotals are given for 15 terms under 069.7 *poor whites* [*white usage*], beginning with *bums, crackers*, and so on). Lexical and grammatical items were chosen for display if they occurred a minimum of 20 times in the Gulf states region, but were mapped at lower frequencies if they had a striking nature or distribution—e.g. were foreign loanwords having potential significance subregionally or were responses to the Urban Supplement work sheets. Phonological items were chosen if they occurred 50 times in the LAGS territory. The SecTotal for *y'all* shows 28 occurrences in Arkansas, 11 in West Tennessee, 13 in Middle Tennessee, but only eight in East Tennessee; on the other hand, *you-all* occurred for 21 Arkansans, nine West Tennesseans, 22 Middle Tennesseans, and 33 East Tennesseans. While these figures cannot be compared directly with one another (because different numbers of speakers were interviewed in each sector—sixty in East Tennessee, 33 in West Tennessee, etc.), LAGS suggests here that *you-all* is dominant over *y'all* for the East Tennessee sector and that the two forms have rough parity in the other three sectors. SocTotals show that *y'all* was used by 186 women and 190 men, 93 blacks and 283 whites, and so on.

However, a caveat: Percentages of occurrence based on SecTotals and SocTotals are not provided in the Matrix volumes. Such figures would have permitted direct comparison across LAGS sectors and

Figure 7. SocTotal for item 069.7, *poor whites* [*white usage*]
(From LAGS *Social Matrix*, p. 182)

069.7La (24)
bums

12	12	1	23
8	7	3	6
4	5	9	6
4	11	9	0

069.7Lb (39) crackers +

20	19	9	30
5	13	11	10
11	10	11	7
8	17	10	4

069.7Lc (16) Georgia Crackers

7	9	1	15
2	4	5	5
6	4	6	0
3	7	5	1

069.7Ld (46) lazy

22	24	2	44
7	11	20	8
16	11	11	8
7	30	8	1

069.7Le (26) no-(ac)count +

9	17	2	24
2	4	6	14
4	9	8	5
3	12	9	2

069.7Lf (25) no-good

4	21	0	25
4	8	6	7
7	4	11	3
4	13	5	3

069.7Lg (19) peckerwoods

6	13	6	13
4	4	1	10
5	4	5	5
3	8	7	1

069.7Lh (22) poor people

11	11	2	20
3	3	6	10
6	8	5	3
6	12	3	1

069.7Li (120) poor white trash

66	54	5	115
27	39	27	27
14	18	39	49
6	41	59	14

069.7Lj (30) poor whites

18	12	2	28
9	8	8	5
1	2	9	18
1	6	17	6

069.7Lk (36) red-necks

18	18	6	30
16	7	5	8
5	6	5	20
5	8	18	5

069.7Ll (22) sorry

9	13	0	22
5	5	5	7
3	5	11	3
5	11	6	0

069.7Lm (88) trash

40	48	3	85
15	14	31	28
21	23	22	22
16	40	25	7

069.7Ln (19) trifling +

7	12	0	19
2	4	6	7
4	7	6	2
3	12	4	0

social groups, but they would have been misleading because of the reality of missing data. SecTotals and SocTotals give us numerators; we cannot know the denominators. The latter might appear to be, for SecTotals, the number of speakers interviewed in a given sector, but this makes the doubtful assumption that every single speaker was asked a given item. This reality of *non-response* means that we must either assume that it occurred to the same extent across sectors and speaker groups, in order to compare percentages of use, or acknowledge that the percentages calculated are at best rough. The user of the Pattern volumes must remember this. The LAGS *Technical Index* does indicate the overall number of primary informants having 'No Response' to each work sheet item (e.g. 253 for 043.5G *you-all*, 210 for 060A.9 *chigger*, 40 for 044.5 *corn breads*), but this information is not available for individual sectors or social groupings. Non-response can be calculated from the computer data files or from the Protocols, but ultimately we cannot be sure, without consulting the field records, whether the gaps in data indicate that speakers were not asked a given question or that they did not have a response to it.

The *Regional Matrix* and *Regional Pattern* volumes group data so that we can surmise rough correlations between many linguistic forms and geographical areas. Pederson's goal here and in the *Social Matrix/Pattern* volumes is to present individual word geography and not to postulate what dialectology has conventionally called an isogloss. The semblance of such a demarcation might have emerged if LAGS had taken the approach of Kurath and McDavid in their *PEAS*, wherein two or more responses to an item are plotted on a single map, but the two *Regional* volumes do not approach mapping in this way. Each LagsMap in the *Regional Matrix* features two forms and each Pattern Map in the *Regional Pattern* four, the forms on each map being chosen because their incidence corresponds to a certain land region, subregion, or combination of these. The *Regional* volumes never map competing forms (and thus do not reveal what the *Handbook* maps of *chigger* vs. *red bug* and so on do). Users can map competing forms for themselves using the LagsMap program.

Unlike in subsequent volumes, the criterion for choosing items to map in the *Regional Matrix* is not clear; the introduction says only that mapped items 'are arranged according to the land regions in which the items show the most significant incidence, although many appear in several regions' (xxv). Beginning with the six major land regions and their 33 subregions and using the 844 mapped items, the *Regional Matrix* and *Regional Pattern* abstract 29 different geographical configurations having 'shared linguistic habits', six of which are inclusive (encompassing all or parts of more than one of the major land regions) and 16 are exclusive (consisting of one region or one or more subregions within a region). For example, in the *Regional Matrix* 24 forms (*pinders, cow pen, mantel board*, etc.) are judged to illustrate a Piney Woods distribution, ten an Eastern Piney Woods one (*fat lightard, spider*, etc.), and 16 a Western Piney Woods one (*corn dodger, jackleg*, etc.). Twenty forms are classified as Delta, 14 as Mississippi Delta, eight as Lower Mississippi Delta, and ten as Atchafalaya Delta. Where a glance at a map does not suggest these patterns for the LagsMaps in the *Regional Matrix*, overlay transparencies come to assistance; there are eight transparencies for the *Regional Matrix*, outlining the LAGS sectors and land regions.

The criteria for mapping items in the *Social Matrix* (vol. 5) and two *Pattern* volumes (6–7) are explicitly stated: for example, if their incidence in one or more of the 33 physiographic divisions of the Gulf states is equal to or higher than that in the LAGS territory as a whole, provided at least three speakers used the form in each division. This incidence is shown on a tabular data summary that accompanies each Pattern Map (for sample data summaries of *sauce* and *yeast bread* see McDaniel, this volume, figures 10 and 11; for a Pattern Map of *chigger*, see figure 8 below). For example, the following four items are mapped in the *Regional Pattern* (pp. 280–81) and called the 'Western Piney Woods Pattern 2': *jackleg* (untrained carpenter), *deaf* (pronounced with [i]), *beard* (also pronounced with [i]), and *free jack* (mulatto). All four occur at higher than the overall LAGS rate in the Piney Woods area from the Alabama/Mississippi state line westward across Mississippi to the Mississippi River in Louisiana. The first three occur at a higher rate than average in other divisions of the Piney Woods, especially in East Texas and Western Louisiana. A table summarizing the data for each form cites the region-wide rate of occurrence and then breaks this down for each of the 33 divisions, overshading those whose rate meets or exceeds that of the overall LAGS territory. On the accompanying Pattern Map each item is plotted in the areas with higher than average incidence with a different lining or shading. Again an overlay map is helpful in labeling the physiographic divisions and giving a quick overview.

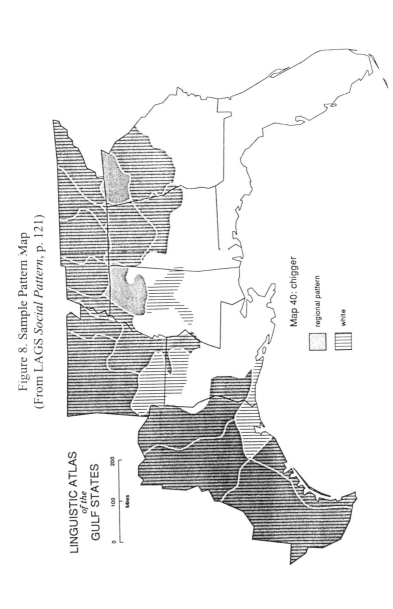

Figure 8. Sample Pattern Map
(From LAGS *Social Pattern*, p. 121)

LINGUISTIC ATLAS
of the
GULF STATES

0   100   200
Miles

Map 40: chigger

regional pattern

white

As the LagsMaps in the *Regional Matrix* are a precursor to the Pattern Maps of the *Regional Pattern*, the 397 CodeMaps of the *Social Matrix* are preliminary to the Pattern Maps of the *Social Pattern*. CodeMaps are grouped in the *Social Matrix* by the geographical or social patterns they show. Ninety-seven (in the *Social Matrix*) are cited for regional distribution (49 as 'Interior Southern', 48 as 'Coastal Southern'; the overlay accompanying the *Social Matrix* outlines how LAGS demarcates these two large regions). One-hundred fifty other items, called 'social markers', are mapped because their 'percentage of usage was at least double for one [social] factor in each set of two (e.g., the percentage of black usage was double that of white usage)' (Pederson and McDaniel 1992:x) and this differential measured at least ten percentage points. Fifteen CodeMaps identify 'Black' forms (e.g. *passed*, 'died'), two 'Black/Age 66+' forms (e.g. *battercakes*), 14 'Black/Education 10-' (e.g. *pecans* with initial stress), and so on. A one-page table in both the *Social Matrix* and *Social Pattern* gives a classification of all 150 markers.

Each CodeMap features one form and plots, by an alphabetic/numeric code, the distribution of the form across the LAGS grid by social categories of speakers (see McDaniel essay and Montgomery, 'Multiple Modals', this volume). Two maps present a three-way breakdown (by 'Race/Sex/Social Status' and 'Race/Age/Education') for each of the 150 forms in the *Social Matrix*. Within each CodeMap a tabular insert identifies the code for the categories mapped and indicates how many speakers in each category used the item. For example, *ashcake*, which occurred 72 times overall, is labeled as a 'Black' term; 22 of the 84 'B/F/L' (i.e. Black/Female/Lower-class speakers) used it (encoded by 'A' on the map), as did 24 of the 74 'B/M/L' ones (encoded by 'B'); by contrast, only five of the 174 lower-class white females used it. CodeMaps in the *Social Matrix* and Pattern Maps in the *Social Pattern* thus present concentrated information on each form they map, showing both the regional and social distribution of data collected by LAGS and suggesting in some cases an interaction of geographical and social factors. The combined regional and social displays suggest the social forces that contribute to the composition of the dialect areas in the Gulf states. While data shown in CodeMaps are drawn from the SocTotals that constitute the first half of the *Social Matrix* volume, CodeMaps sometimes combine SocTotals, as for compounds having a common denominating element (as with *cracker*, which incorporates *Georgia cracker*, etc.). Item numbers are not indicated on the published CodeMaps, so users must be alert to use the index of the *Social Matrix* to identify these.

The maps of the two Matrix volumes lead in to the more interpretive presentation in the Pattern volumes, where the more conventional Pattern Maps with areas of higher than average incidence of forms overshaded give the most insightful picture of geographic patterning. The *Social Pattern*, the final volume of LAGS, integrates information from the *Regional Pattern* and the *Social Matrix*, its Pattern Maps helping, in Pederson's terminology, to 'particularize the significance of the regional pattern as a sociogeographic entity' (Pederson and McDaniel 1992:xix) by examining the patterning of the 150 'social markers' in three ways: through a data summary (see McDaniel this volume), a pattern map (see above), and a dendrogram (see McDaniel this volume). The *Social Pattern* also provides a comprehensive index to all maps and data matrices in volumes four through seven and an appendix listing the 1,437 items considered for inclusion in the volume and indicating the degree of differentiation by major social factor for each one.

Data summaries in the *Social Pattern* identify the incidence and percentage of use for both the 33 subregions and four social categories (racial caste, sex, age, and educational level, but not social status). As with the *Regional Matrix*, these percentages determine the areas shaded in the data summary and shaded or lined in the associated Pattern Maps. Dendrograms break down the occurrences of each of the 150 forms in a binary fashion to five degrees: first by region (Interior vs. Coastal South), then by racial caste, gender, age (with 65 being the cutoff), and education level (10 or fewer years vs. 11 or more). Like the data summaries, dendrograms present percentages, but these are calculated differently from the summaries. In the dendrograms, the total number of speakers responding with a form across a binary social category is taken as the denominator, the number in one or the other social group as the numerator. In the data summaries, it is the number of speakers interviewed in one or another regional unit or social category that is the denominator, while the number of speakers using the form represents the numerator. For *passed* (078.5L, 'died'), for instance, 64 speakers in the Coastal South used the term; 51 (80%) of these were black, 13 (20%) white. In the Interior South the disjuncture is 67%/33%. The accompanying data summary for the form indicates that 44% (86/197) of all black speakers used *passed*, while only 4% (31/717) of the whites did. Two effects of this approach to analyzing the LAGS data are noteworthy. One is that framing social variation within the larger Coastal vs. Interior South division identifies the possible interaction of social and regional forces in the composition of Gulf states dialects. The data summaries and maps of the *Social Pattern* organize data in ways that likewise contribute to this. The other effect is that, since the dendrograms are based on the number of speakers responding with a form rather than the number of speakers interviewed, their percentages do not make assumptions about missing data, as the percentages in the data summaries do.

The introduction to each Matrix and Pattern volume is both programmatic and substantive, providing technical keys to using the volume, background on and discussion of its composition, and in most cases a brief, preliminary interpretation of findings. In the *Social Pattern* we find Pederson's most considered statements about the distinct dialect regions of the Gulf states:

> Reconsidering the distribution of all 844 regional markers (the data of Volume 5), one finds a basic regional pattern within these divisions, with the Eastern Highlands (A1–3) and the Central Gulf Coast/Lower Delta (C5/F4–5) as the respective core areas . . . a preliminary reorganization suggests the Eastern Highlands (A1–3), the Nashville Basin (A5, D3), and Western Highlands (A6, D7) as one major Interior subdivision, the Piedmont (B1–2, A4) and Central Plains (D4–5) another, and the Upper Delta (F1–2) as a third. The Coastal set includes perhaps five subdivisions, the Atlantic Coast (C1–2), the Gulf Coast (C3–4), the Coastal Black Belt (D2, D1), the Piney Woods (E1–5, D6, F3, F6), and the Lower Delta (F4–5, C5). (Pederson and McDaniel 1992:x)

To use the four Matrix and Pattern volumes, one must consult the introductions frequently to interpret Automatic Book Code notation and various other conventions. Whatever the merits of the ABC for encoding data for computer sorting, its use in labeling maps of phonological forms throughout the Matrix and Pattern volumes is debatable. Why should readers master a special code of LAGS when they are familiar already with standard phonetic transcription? The overlays reduce the need to consult the introductions, but additional transparencies would also have been helpful, such as for the SecTotal and SocTotal displays or for the dendrograms, on none of which the categories are labeled.

However, these requirements facing users of the LAGS Descriptive Materials are minor compared to the rewards of investing the time to familiarize themselves with the conventions and practices of LAGS and with understanding, through the wealth of data that LAGS organizes, the complexity of the Gulf South as a speech region of American English.

USES OF LAGS

It has been shown how that LAGS data can be appropriately and profitably analyzed in a number of ways. Much more than a reference work, LAGS publications, especially the *Basic Materials* and the *Concordance*, can be used in innumerable ways to explore Gulf states speech, particularly to undertake more intensive study of specific forms than provided in the Descriptive Materials. This section consolidates and exemplifies how LAGS publications can be used to pursue different types of research, outlining only some of the possibilities beyond what is offered directly in the Descriptive Materials.

Just as the field records are the final authority and source against which data in the Protocols can be checked, the Protocols serve the same function for the *Concordance* and the Descriptive Materials, since both of these are derived from the Protocols. It is the Protocols which contain the rawest and fullest data to which researchers can resort, and questions will sometimes arise in using derivative publications that can be answered only by reference to the Protocols. For example, any numerical figures in the Descriptive Materials may be double checked by consulting the Protocols.

Using the *Handbook* and the *Concordance* a researcher can creatively explore the patterning of any specific linguistic form collected by

LAGS. The *Concordance* identifies and the *Handbook* describes and classifies the speakers who use a form, so one may determine whether these constitute a group of any kind. That *peckerwood* is used primarily by blacks and *redneck* by whites can be discovered from the *Social Matrix*. But beyond major social categories used in the Descriptive Materials (gender, racial caste, age, educational level, and social status), speakers can be classified in any number of ways—by the size of community they grew up in, the age of speakers more finely (e.g. by decade of birth) than the *Social Matrix/Pattern* display, their occupation (do farmers form a recognizable group linguistically?), church denomination (do Episcopalians pattern differently from Baptists?), and so on. The possibilities are many, because individual informant biographies in the *Handbook* spell out more information about the speakers than in any other study of American English. As a result, the speakers hardly seem like anonymous individuals, and students of language variation may choose to classify them in many ways in their own examination of Gulf states speech. In studying multiple modals, Montgomery (this volume) classifies LAGS primary and secondary speakers on several bases that, it was hypothesized, might relate to the occurrence of multiple modals in a LAGS interview.

Using the Idiolect Synopses (in the *Basic Materials*) and the *Handbook*, those with little training can compare the pronunciation of speakers and explore phonological variables and sound change in progress, that is, across apparent time. Crisp transcription in the synopses may be quite useful in teaching some aspects of phonetics as well.

The *Concordance*, *Handbook*, and *Technical Index* can be used together to explore which types of speakers use which synonymous forms for a given work sheet item. Which terms are used for 'poor whites' by whites (item 069.7) and by blacks (item 069.8)? The *Technical Index* lists 212 and 105 different ones, respectively. Which groups of speakers use *War between the States* (295 responses) or *Confederate War* (66 responses) for the mid-19th-century conflict (085.8 *Civil War*)? Which use *Christmas Gift* (351 responses) or *Happy Christmas* (68 responses) for the holiday greeting (093.2 *Merry Christmas*)? Many such questions are answered in the *Regional Matrix* and *Social Matrix* volumes, but many others remain to be examined, requiring only careful use of the *Concordance*.

The Protocols and the *Handbook* may be used together to investigate any number of linguistic variables beyond those for which the data are presented in the Idiolect Synopses. For example, Montgomery 1995, drawing from Protocol transcriptions, examines to what extent speakers in the three traditional 'grand divisions' of Tennessee (East, Middle, and West) differ in pronouncing the major place names of the state (*Knoxville, Chattanooga, Memphis, Nashville,* and *Tennessee*), these forms being chosen because they involve a number of different phonological variables and occur at a high response rate for Tennessee informants (thus minimizing the problem of missing data). Some of the phonological features in those names are synopsized in the Descriptive Materials, but the Protocols contain much raw material not dealt with there, such as variation in vowel off-glides in the initial syllables of *Memphis* and *Tennessee*. It is often wise to consult the Protocols in doing one's own comparisons in any case, because a mistake does once in a while slip into the Descriptive Materials; practically speaking, the Protocols are the arbiter.

GENERAL DISCUSSION AND CONCLUSIONS

Research for the Linguistic Atlas of the United States and Canada, while laborious and often delayed, has successfully collected data from a remarkably large number of informants over an extended territory—indeed, most of the United States. Using a standard questionnaire, it has sought the responses of speakers, although overwhelmingly those who were older and taking nearly a half century to do so, that provide our best opportunity, along with the material gathered by *DARE*, for identifying the larger patterns of differentiation and dispersion and for investigating many questions of change and spread in American English. The LAUSC has sought nothing less than, at the broadest level, to reconstruct the sociocultural history of the English-speaking parts of the continent, while in a narrow sense it could only document the patterning of individual linguistic items.

How does LAGS fit into this grand design? Is it possible to say how many dialect areas there appear to be in the South? The *Handbook* offers some tantalizing, preliminary notions, and the *Regional Matrix* and *Regional Pattern* present evidence for at least distinct regional patterns involving at least four linguistic forms each, discriminated not in the sense of isogloss bundling, but on the basis of higher than region-wide incidence of those forms in certain areas. These regional patterns include a 'Piney Woods' type of speech extending discontinuously from Florida and Southern Georgia to East Texas (see Pederson 1996). The Matrix and Pattern volumes outline the dimensions of hundreds of items, and it now remains for the profession to take the information that LAGS has generated and determine everything that it reveals to us. Regardless of one's theoretical preferences, LAGS provides a tremendous wealth of data that are retrievable and amenable for interpretations.

In an era when so much research in language variation takes the form of case studies and intensive micro-studies of linguistic sub-systems, LAGS may seem to some to be an anachronism. Yet like its counterparts in other regions, LAGS was designed to provide not just an atlas—a product of research—but the stimulus to further research. LAGS has succeeded admirably in these regards by providing a magnificent set of research tools and an inexhaustible database. Countless questions about change in American English should utilize linguistic atlas data, and a few sociolinguistic studies have (e.g. Labov 1963). However, current and recent students of American English have by and large paid too little attention to the data made available by linguistic geography.

To summarize, the resulting new paradigm of linguistic atlas that is LAGS represents a significant rethinking of format and requires that existing discussions of linguistic geography take note and be revised. LAGS offers four degrees of abstraction from the field recordings:

1) the *Basic Materials*, a distillation of contrastive forms represented in phonetics for which variation was expected and whose regional and social distribution is or may be explored; presented in Protocols and Idiolect Synopses, these data tell us about individual speakers;

2) the *Concordance*, taking all Protocol data and assembling them orthographically and alphabetically, reveals the comparative

frequency of individual linguistic forms, their social evaluation, and in some cases the range of environments in which they occur;

3) the electronic atlas or disk text, which represents the ultimate in quick and multifold data manipulation, translates much of the data into Automatic Book Code and Systematic Phonetic Code; and

4) the book text, which uses the disk text to map the data and, through its presentation in thousands of data matrices and hundreds of maps, outlines many of the regional and social patterns of Gulf states speech.

The expectation of the public and probably of much of the profession is that a linguistic atlas will sift through its countless data and offer a view grand in scope and incontrovertible in detail about the identity and relations of dialect areas. Do these reflect settlement history? Do they reflect our modern perceptions of regions? Despite our natural wishes that LAGS had addressed these questions more directly, we must recall that the initial publications from atlas projects are designed to be descriptive. The three interpretive volumes (Kurath 1949, Atwood 1953, Kurath and McDavid 1961) were by-products of atlas investigations, and the appeal and accessibility of these interpretive publications is not a fair standard for LAGS.

Linguistic atlas work will always have its detractors who dispute the time (and ultimately the funds) devoted to large-scale projects focusing on traditional rural vocabulary. However, comparability of all atlas surveys conducted since LANE a half-century earlier was too precious a goal for LAGS to abandon in formulating its design. With the cumulative publication of LAGS, the ongoing publication of LAMSAS in electronic form[25], and the advent of three volumes of *DARE* (Cassidy 1985– , with three more to come) and its derivatives like Carver 1987, fulfillment of the long-held promise of linguistic geography to provide a fuller and broader understanding of American cultural patterns has begun to emerge. Those who utilize the riches of LAGS for research will play an important role in fulfilling this goal.

NOTES

1. This chapter is based on a cumulative review of LAGS material published in *American Speech* 68:263–318 (1993). I have updated it where appropriate and changed the focus to be more utilitarian. I am especially grateful to Tom Nunnally for his helpful advice in this effort.

2. This statement in no way detracts from the invaluable contributions that others have made to the LAGS project. These are detailed in the LAGS *Handbook* (Pederson, McDaniel, Bailey, and Bassett 1986) and in the first series of LAGS Working Papers (included in Pederson, Billiard, Leas, Bailey and Bassett 1981).

3. Pederson covers some of the same ground in his 1993 essay, 'An Approach to Linguistic Geography'. In Montgomery 1993 I have reviewed the criticisms of linguistic atlas methodology and discussed in detail the limitations of using atlas data, especially the inappropriateness of using them for establishing certain quantitative indexes of variation. In the present essay I focus on the legitimate uses of LAGS for researchers.

4. The territory surveyed by LAGS was determined by social history, topography, and boundaries of previous regional atlases. The last factor meant that Tennessee and Arkansas were rather anomalously included as 'Gulf' states because it was crucial to fill in gaps between the territory of other regional atlas projects that had been completed.

5. For a detailed view of Piney Woods speech, see Pederson 1996.

6. A detailed account of activities in the late 1920s leading to the establishment of the atlas, including the selection of Kurath as Editor, is provided by O'Cain (1979:244ff.), an insightful essay on the early history of the atlas that adds notes from Kurath's personal records to the account in Kurath et al. (1939:x–xiii). A partial transcript of the August 2, 1929, conference sponsored by the American Council of Learned Societies to plan the atlas appears as Report 1929.

7. In addition, interviews were occasionally abandoned because of illness or inconvenience; the recordings of such partial intervews were nonetheless transcribed and used by LAGS, although only for certain purposes, as indicated later in this essay. Unlike previous linguistic atlas projects in the U.S., LAGS did not combine responses from more than one individual of a given type (a primary informant with one or more secondary ones) in a community into single field records. Thus, LAGS Protocols represent a compilation of idiolects rather than linguistic profiles of speaker types.

8. The amount of free conversation, as might be expected, varied greatly according to fieldworker and informant. The recording of all interviews liberated fieldworkers from eliciting items, such as grammatical forms, that

proved difficult to target with a short-answer question. Many of these could be expected to arise during conversation. It also enabled fieldworkers to use a broad, 'shotgun' approach by posing questions like 'What did you call the different rooms in the house?' rather than laboriously asking for single items. LAGS was not the first atlas project to seek free conversation. Raven McDavid characteristically elicited large amounts of it in his LAMSAS interviews (which, with few exceptions, were not recorded), and this differed sharply from other earlier fieldworkers. Recording LAGS interviews produced for the first time in an atlas project a division of labor which allowed the most talented fieldworkers to do the interviewing, the most experienced scribes the transcription, and so on. The freedom given the fieldworker from immediate transcription created at least a somewhat less pressured and more conversation-like event. On the other hand, it must be said that producing a transcription from a recording alone is in some respects (for certain consonantal distinctions, especially voiceless ones) more difficult than from a face-to-face interview.

9. Deriving in part from Pederson's dissertation survey of Chicago (Pederson 1965, 1971), the Urban Supplement was tested in 1974 and early 1975, further revised, and employed first in the summer of 1975. Pederson's rationale for adding this component to LAGS interviews was two-fold. One was to provide an adequate database for distinguishing urban areas: 'it was impossible to represent these complicated urban communities without a significantly elaborated sampling. More important, much of the old-fashioned and essentially rural-oriented vocabulary items of the basic work sheets had no currency—or even vague familiarity—among the natives of these metropolitan communities' (Pederson and Billiard 1979:46). Also noted was the 'failure of contemporary sociolinguistic research to investigate the vocabularies of the cities [that] has resulted in a paucity of lexical information about the composition of the contemporary urban vocabulary' (ibid.)

10. Interestingly, plans were made at the very beginning (1929) to record all linguistic atlas interviews, but were abandoned for economic reasons (O'Cain 1979:249, 251). Perhaps the stock-market crash shortly after the August 1929 ACLS gathering (see note 6) had something to do with this.

11. Complete recordings of all LAGS interviews are on deposit for consultation at the University of Georgia in Athens and at the Special Collections Department of the Woodruff Library at Emory University in Atlanta. Pederson has made arrangements with the latter not only to provide facilities for researchers to audit field records but also to reproduce individual interviews on cassette tape for researchers upon request.

12. Of these projects, only LAMSAS is still actively being edited.

13. For a detailed account of how Pederson's conception of LAGS evolved through these four reports, see Montgomery (1993:274–75).

14. Pederson has made arrangements to donate the computer files and programs to the American Dialect Society and to authorize the ADS to distribute copies of them at cost. At present LAGS files are available on line through the Linguistic Atlas website at the University of Georgia. William Kretzschmar, current Editor-in-Chief of the atlas, reports the following:

LAGS computer files are available through the Linguistic Atlas internet site at hyde.park.uga.edu (soon to change to us.english.uga.edu). After the change those who try the old address will be prompted to go to the new address. At that address users need only click on the LAGS section of the US map, or on the separate LAGS label, to be offered an opportunity to download any files or programs from the complete LAGS site. This site does not yet offer help in using the programs, or to interpret the results of the operation of the programs. There are plans to improve access to LAGS data and programs on the site, when appropriate funding becomes available.

15. The *Basic Materials* collection of 1199 fiche costs $3,750; the combined fiche and film set costs $6,250 (the film not being available separately). The fiche for individual states can be purchased by contacting the publisher, University Microfilms, International. The cost of the 154-fiche *Concordance* is currently $395.

16. Each idiolect synopsis is what it says it is—a profile of an individual's speech. The synopses in *PEAS* were sometimes based on more than one speaker. The use of multiple informants from a community was not uncommon for *DARE* or in linguistic atlas projects other than LAGS.

17. The atlas approach to surveying pronunciation meant that it is primarily interested in phonetic form, rather than phonemic contrast. Minimal pairs were usually not sought from which a phonemic inventory in the classical sense could be constructed, but similar to *PEAS*, the phonetic transcriptions in LAGS Idiolect Synopses permit a structuralist interpretation and sufficient information can still be extracted from them for a phonemic description.

18. The two papers in the second series of Working Papers (Pederson 1986c and Bailey 1986) elaborate on the first two chapters of the *Handbook*. The seven papers in series three outline the progress of LAGS editorial work that produced the later volumes of the Descriptive Materials. They are collectively called 'A Matrix for Word Geography' and are abstracted in the introduction to the *General Index* (Pederson, McDaniel, and Adams 1988:xvii–xix).

19. Among the most exotic of these are 11 types of what LAGS terms, very broadly, 'grunts' (which is where they are referenced in the *General Index*). These include interjections (e.g. item 092.2 *land's sake* has 199 different

responses), miscellaneous forms (item 012.6 has 51 forms of the tag questions), and sounds of farm animals. For some of these (particles for hesitation, affirmation, and negation) the LAGS *Technical Index* cites the pronunciations in Automatic Book Code (Pederson 1987).

20. A response was judged as 'inappropriate' when the informant was judged not to have understood the interviewer's query or not to have responded appropriately for any other reason.

21. A longer version of this chapter, 'A Social History of the Gulf States', was published as LAGS Working Papers no. 1, 2nd series.

22. Some responses were deemed not pertinent, as misunderstandings of the interviewer's query, etc.

23. Actually the range of material is even broader than this. Scribes recorded many forms outside those originally designated because the forms were considered to have potential interest to researchers, even though they were not systematically sought by fieldworkers.

24. The display of phonetic data to maximum effect on a map without ignoring the detail of atlas transcriptions presents an enormous challenge. On the oversized LANE maps, which incorporated all transcriptions, the latter were clear but difficult to group and compare systematically. In the effort of LAGS to computerize its raw material for display on maps, the Systematic Phonetic Code was born.

25. Also at the Linguistic Atlas website at the University of Georgia (see note 14 above).

LAGS Insights into Female Speech
Susan Leas McDaniel

The Linguistic Atlas of the Gulf States (LAGS) project, directed by Lee Pederson, consists of tape-recorded interviews (called 'field records') with 1,121 natives of communities in an eight-state region (Tennessee, Georgia, Florida, Alabama, Mississippi, Arkansas, Louisiana, and East Texas) conducted from 1968 to 1983. Of these, 914 were designated as primary and are used in most analyses of data collected by the project. *LAGS Volume 1: Handbook* describes how informants were selected and primary informants were determined. Fieldworkers generally sought an even representation of men and women to interview, but priority was given to older, less educated, rural informants, in order to record the oldest possible varieties of native speech across the region (Pederson, McDaniel, Bailey, and Bassett 1986:16–23; see Montgomery, 'Treasury', this volume, for additional information on the design of LAGS).

LAGS Volume 7: Social Pattern uses a binary breakdown of the primary informants according to social factors (the 'dendrogram' of figure 1) to analyze and display lexical, phonological, and grammatical data according to 1) region (Interior Southern [I]/Coastal Southern [C]); 2) racial caste (black [B]/white [W]); 3) sex (female [F]/male [M]); 4) age (65 or under [Y]/66 or over [O]); and 5) education (ten years or fewer [L]/eleven years or more [H]). In that volume, responses to LAGS work-sheet items frequently correlate with race, age, education, and social status, but of the five social factors the informant's sex seems to correlate least frequently with language usage across the Gulf States. For the items analyzed there, usage by females meets the stated criteria for mapping for only three forms: *coverlet*, *deep-dish pie*, and *sauce*. (Responses were mapped if the percentage of usage for one social group was at least double that of the other in a binary set and if the difference between the two percentages was ten points or more. For example, *sauce*, with 42% female and 21% male, shows a differential of 21.)

Susan Leas McDaniel

Figure 1. Binary breakdown of social factors

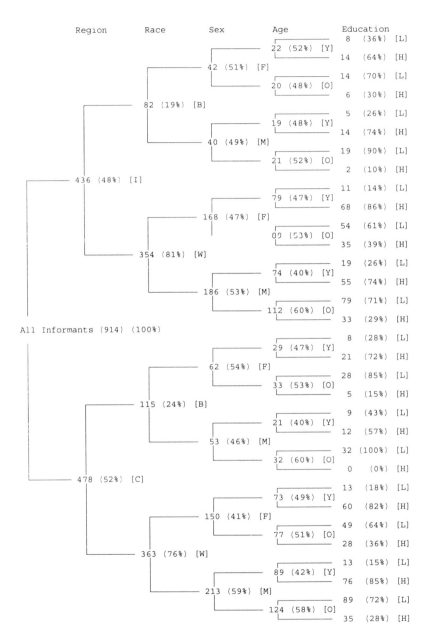

This paucity of evidence would suggest that the speech of women in the Gulf States is primarily determined, not by their gender, but rather by the subregion in which they live, their race, age, education, and social status, or the influence of the males with whom they associate. However, if we examine the data presented in *LAGS Volume 6: Social Matrix*, rather than in *LAGS Volume 7*, using a somewhat looser criterion, as is done in this paper, a number of female usages emerge that are distinct from those of their male counterparts. As a result, we can appreciate linguistic atlas data as a valuable source for exploring the relationship between gender and language variation. Whereas previous studies have used other atlases and dealt exclusively with grammatical items (Van Riper 1979, Maynor 1981, Allen 1986, McDavid, this volume), the present study draws on LAGS and examines lexical and phonological items as well as grammatical ones.

The first section of *LAGS Volume 6: Social Matrix* contains 6,578 Social Total matrices in 275 pages, arranged in order according to LAGS work-sheet page and line number (e.g. 048.3). Figure 2 contains a Social Total matrix showing totals in all categories, followed by a matrix for the term *deep-dish pie*, from worksheet item 048.3L. Each matrix begins with a two-line header, followed by four lines that show usage totals according to sex, racial caste, age, education, and social status.

Figure 2. Item 048.3L, synonyms for *cobbler*:

	Social Totals (914) All Informants				048.3Lc (63) deep-dish (pie)			
Sex/Race	422	492	197	717	56	7	9	54
Age	196	210	266	242	16	22	16	9
Education	234	216	224	240	3	10	21	29
Social Status	194	369	279	72	7	19	23	14

The first header-line for a specific item like *deep-dish pie* gives the page and line of the item from the LAGS worksheets, followed by an uppercase letter designating the category that contains the item

(Grammatical [G], Lexical [L], Phonological [P], Systematic Phonetics [S], Urban [U]), a lowercase letter to indicate the position of the response within the ordered set of matrices for an item, and a number in parentheses indicating the frequency of occurrence of the form. The second header-line gives the item name; names followed by a plus (+) sign represent a combination of two or more similar response forms to an item, as listed in *LAGS Volume 3: Technical Index*. Lexical and most grammatical forms are in conventional orthography; phonological items and verb forms are in the Automatic Book Code (ABC), for which see figure 3 below and Pederson 1987; and systematic phonetic items are entered in their own code, followed by the narrow phonetic equivalent.

For the Social Totals matrix (figure 2), the first two numbers on the first matrix-line give the totals according to sex (female 422, male 492); the next two, according to race (black 197, white 717). The second matrix-line contains the number of responses for four age groups (13–45, 46–65, 66–76, 77–99), the third line for the four education levels, in years (0–7, 8–10, 11–12, 13–16+), and the fourth line for four social class divisions (lower, lower middle, upper middle, upper). Thus, for age, education level, and social class, the *Social Matrix* volume presents a more refined breakdown of data than does the *Social Pattern* volume with its binary divisions (figure 1).

The first matrix-line of the Social Total for *deep-dish pie* (figure 2) clearly indicates that the gender factor is significant for this response (female 56, male 7) and racial caste almost equally so (black 9, white 54).[1] The second matrix-line, age groups, shows that the term occurs chiefly in the speech of informants under the age of 77 (16, 22, 16 versus 9). The third line indicates that the majority of occurrences are in the speech of those with more than ten years of schooling (21 and 29 versus 3 and 10). The fourth line shows that lower-class informants used the term the least (7 and 19 versus 23 and 14).

FEMALE SPEECH

As mentioned above, the present study uses a criterion different from those employed in the *LAGS Social Pattern*. An item is considered 'significant female usage' if the number of females using it (as shown

Figure 3. The Automatic Book Code

Stressed Vowels

\<a\>	pat	\<u\>	putt	\<ew\>	butte	\<ow\>	bout
\<e\>	pet	\<ai\>	bait	\<ie\>	bite	\<oy\>	boy
\<i\>	pit	\<aw\>	bought	\<oe\>	boat	\<ue\>	boot
\<o\>	pot	\<ee\>	beet	\<oo\>	put	\<ui\>	buoy

Consonants

\<p\>	pill	\<f\>	fill	\<m\>	mill
\<b\>	bill	\<v\>	villa	\<n\>	sin
\<t\>	till	\<th\>	ether	\<ng\>	sing
\<d\>	dill	\<dh\>	either	\<l\>	lieu
\<k\>	kill	\<s\>	sue	\<r\>	rill
\<g\>	gill	\<z\>	zoo	\<w\>	will
\<ch\>	chill	\<sh\>	shoe	\<y\>	you
\<j\>	pledger	\<zh\>	pleasure	\<h\>	hill

Weakly Stressed Vowels

\<A\>	coda	\<koedA=14\>		\<I\>	Cody	\<koedI=14\>

Syllabic Consonants

\<M\>	bottom	\<botM=14\>	\<L\>	bottle	\<botL=14\>
\<N\>	bacon	\<baikN=14\>	\<R\>	butter	\<butR=14\>
\<NG\>	baking	\<baikNG=14\>			

Degrees of Stress

\<=1\>	primary	\<=3\>	tertiary
\<=2\>	secondary	\<=4\>	weak

(additional ABC qualifiers used in figures below are listed in volume 6:xxvi)

in the Social Totals matrices) exceeds the number of males using it by at least 20; Systematic Phonetic and Urban Supplement items are excluded from consideration. Since only 46% of the primary informants are female, this criterion indicates responses for which more than 52% of the total usage is female. Although only three 'female' responses were mapped in the *Social Pattern* under the stricter criteria of at least a double percentage of usage and a difference in percentage of at least ten, the Social Totals in the *Social Matrix* nevertheless provide a striking male/female contrast in many instances if we use the somewhat looser criterion stated earlier in this paragraph.

Significant female usages occur, not surprisingly, most often in household terms, whereas men seem to have more knowledge of outdoor terms—animals, birds, fish, terrain, farm buildings, and farm implements. A second and perhaps less obvious category of female dominance is standard grammatical usage—pronouns, verb forms, and agreement. Female speech in the Gulf States also has a higher rate of usage of standard pronunciations and national, as opposed to regional, lexical forms. Indeed, the majority of regional markers appear in the speech of male informants.

Figure 4 lists the responses, selected from the Social Totals in the *Social Matrix*, that meet our criterion for significant female usage. These include national terms as well as regional variants and are presented in alphabetical order by category (Lexical, Grammatical, Verbs, Phonological). As stated earlier, a term followed by a plus sign (+) is a combination of two or more closely related forms for a given item (e.g. *curdled* + *curdled milk*). In meeting the criterion of being used by at least 20 more females than males, the items in figure 4 show a 52% or greater percentage of female usage, based on the total number of responses of that form to the worksheet item. Twenty-four terms with a 67% or greater female usage are listed in figure 5, arranged in descending order by percentage.

The 'domestic' lexical responses in figure 5 include foods (*deep-dish pie*, *giblets*, *yeast bread*, *spoon bread*, *salad tomato*), household items (*coverlet*, *buggy*, *comforter*), and a process (*perk coffee*). A comparison of the totals for other responses to the item reinforces the female usage trends. For example, in item 028.7L (synonyms for *bedspread*), the female-majority terms are *coverlet* (60/18) and *spread* (159/139). The terms with slight male majorities are the seemingly more commonplace ones, *bedspread* (232/247) and *cover* (11/15), but these cannot be called 'significant male usages', because *bedspread* has a higher percentage of female than male usage for the LAGS sample as a whole (55% vs. 50%). For the related item 029.1L (synonyms for *quilt*), the strongest female term is *comforter* (49/24).

A similar pattern appears for item 048.3L (*cobbler*). Of the synonyms that occur 20 or more times, female usage is dominant for *cobbler* (281/254 = 66%/52%) and *deep-dish pie* (56/7 = 13%/1%), whereas the sole male dominant term is *pie* (100/155 = 24%/32%).

The third female response mapped in the *Social Pattern, sauce* (item 048.5L, sweet sauce), occurs in the speech of 178 women (42%) and 105 men (21%). *Sauce* is the dominant response for this item, an item for which fieldworkers often had difficulty in eliciting an appropriate form, possibly because of the wording of the sample questions in the work sheets (the first question suggested for eliciting this item is, 'What do you call the sweet liquid that you pour over the pudding?' Gulf States informants, often not understanding *pudding* as a synonym for *cake*, consequently had no response). The forms for this item having slightly higher male usage are *syrup* (34/42 = 8%/9%) and *topping* (10/20 = 2%/4%).

Since many of the women interviewed in the Gulf States were housewives or farm wives who generally remained at home while their husbands worked, they were naturally more likely to be familiar with a variety of names for items concerned with home life, which their spouses would not necessarily adopt. To the farmer who has been working in the fields all day, the fruit-and-pastry dessert may be simply a pie, regardless of its form; no name may be necessary for a sweet liquid poured over cake; and the covering on the bed may, indeed, be merely a cover.

Figure 4. Female dominant terms
(Terms for which females responses outnumbered
male responses by 20 or more)

Term	Totals (F/M)		
a. LEXICAL RESPONSES		bath towel	100/79
afraid	264/229	bought bread	72/43
angry	143/88	buggy [=baby carriage]	82/37
appendicitis	194/145	bulge	256/214
barbed-wire fence	87/65	can't remember	113/93

carriage [=baby carriage]	162/122	jilted him	93/68
change purse	72/46	kissing	205/174
cherry tomato	112/80	load (of wood, etc.) +	84/52
chest of drawers	239/211	maid of honor +	139/72
chimney +	277/254	matron of honor +	76/27
clean (the house)	133/102	merry-go-round	216/184
cloth + [=washcloth]	200/174	moth	196/167
cobbler	281/254	mountain laurel	92/52
coin purse	93/62	pale	114/90
comforter	49/24	pancakes	332/310
corn on the cob	124/81	parlor	164/134
cottage cheese	264/204	path [=lane]	98/76
coverlet	60/18	perk (coffee)	60/27
crouch +	60/33	perspired	94/60
curdle(d) +	39/19	poach(ed) +	341/315
cut (flowers)	92/67	pupil	109/85
davenport	76/51	queer [=odd] +	185/160
dawn	73/52	reins	180/152
deep-dish pie	56/7	relatives	251/217
dish towel	158/92	rhododendron	108/63
dishcloth	127/81	rising [of wind]	68/47
dumplings +	77/48	rolls	143/88
expecting	118/83	salad tomato +	61/30
family [=relatives]	73/53	sauce [sweet]	178/105
froze {007.6}	156/127	scuttle +	156/135
giblets	49/15	sensitive	50/30
going steady	88/65	sheaf	55/32
Grandmamma	38/11	silks	147/109
green beans	187/141	spanking [n.]	220/188
green onions	168/130	spoon bread +	61/21
home {098.4}	57/34	spread [=bedspread]	159/139
horse [A/X frame] +	173/128	sprinkle [v.]	82/49
hydrant +	134/108	stack {041.7}	76/50
illegitimate +	190/131	stoop [=crouch]	69/48
jaundice	126/102	sunrise	183/160

sunset	142/111	there are/were	95/65
take/took you home	181/160	this way	244/212
took [=stole]	88/63	those were	69/40
touchy	171/150	we were(n't) /are(n't)	124/95
towel +	236/163	who	145/120
trench	68/38	whose	103/89
wardrobe	244/203	yes	243/203
washcloth	152/123	you and I	164/137
without cream/milk	120/94	yours	250/230
yeast bread	56/19		

c. VERB FORMS

b. GRAMMATICAL RESPONSES

		ask [inf.]	245/219
an (apple)	241/198	ask [p.p.]	91/71
anyway	169/145	begun [p.p.]	106/82
didn't use to	118/97	bitten [p.p.]	208/161
died of	147/126	blown [p.p.]	173/145
doesn't	195/158	broken [p.p.]	216/185
fell off the bed	111/85	catch [inf.] <!kach>	100/49
fine + {079.4}	157/130	climbed [p.p.]	215/165
giddyup	95/70	climbed [pret.]	243/207
goodness [exclamation]	35/14	come [p.p.]	185/153
heard of <hurdov=13>	79/53	dived [p.p.]	165/116
here are	104/76	dived [pret.]	204/161
here's	74/52	dragged [p.p.]	85/53
hers	264/219	dragged [pret.]	106/75
how are you?	159/100	dreamed [p.p.]	147/125
how do you do?	69/43	drew [pret.]	210/167
long way	97/77	drowned [p.p.]	146/117
more loving	91/57	drunk [p.p.]	130/107
named for	91/48	fallen [p.p.]	98/65
no, thank you	58/37	frozen [p.p.]	212/177
she and I	44/17	gave [pret.]	275/241
smell (that)	189/168	given [p.p.]	211/177
so glad (to see you)	52/12	help [inf.]	179/156
theirs	250/204	helped [p.p.]	96/63

helped [pret.]	135/104	harness <hornIs=14>	136/108
lay [pret.]	132/107	hundred <hundrId=14>	186/106
lie [inf.]	207/166	June <jewn>	80/50
ridden [p.p.]	196/159	knob <nob>	147/127
risen [p.p.]	187/167	Martha <morthA=14>	133/93
rose [pret.]	251/216	morning <mawrnNG=14>	50/26
sat [p.p.]	106/80	mother <mudhR=14>	194/170
sat [pret.]	151/128	mountain <mowntN=14>	87/66
shrank [pret.]	63/42	Mrs. <misIz=14>	38/15
sit [inf.]	212/190	November <noevembR=314>	78/50
swam [pret.]	217/182	orphan <awrfN=14>	53/33
swollen [p.p.]	232/212	post office <poestofIs=134>	103/56
taught [pret.] <*tawt>	279/250	pretty <pritI=14>	139/90
waked [pret.]	48/25	queer <kwir>	144/114
written [p.p.]	202/169	real <ril>	162/117
		rinse <rints>	126/83
		roof <roof>	68/34

d. PHONOLOGICAL RESPONSES

actress <aktrIs=14>	231/210	Sarah <sairA=14>	160/135
apron <aiprN=14>	224/182	sausage <s{o}sIj=14>	49/29
Asheville <ashvL=14>	136/111	scarce <skars>	56/32
Atlanta <atlantA=314>	70/48	second <sekNt=14>	180/152
chair <char>	104/67	September <septembR=314>	61/37
Civil War <sivLwawr=143>	69/47	seventh <sevNth=14>	242/209
colonel <kurnL=14>	213/191	seventy <sevNtI=144>	215/160
cough <k{aw}f>	71/34	stomp <stomp>	65/40
cow <k{au}>	118/98	sure <shur>	44/21
dog <d{ou}g>	71/34	swamp <swomp>	110/75
eleven <IlevN=144>	113/79	tassel <tasL=14>	159/137
far <for>	129/101	thrash <th{t}ash> [flap]	31/19
father <fodhR=14>	157/136	tube <t{ue}b>	84/52
February <febyuewerI=1324>	42/17	twenty <twintI=14>	37/15
fog <f{o}g>	95/64	umbrella <umbrelA=314>	78/49
forehead <for(h)Id=14>	69/47	uncle <unk{L}=14>	97/75
grease <grees> [inf.]	38/15	wasps <wosp(s)>	67/35
greasy <greesI=14>	79/49	wheelbarrow <wheelbarA=134>	141/113

with <with>   203/146   year ago, a <AyɪrAgoe=4143>   101/80
without <withowt=31>   80/46   yesterday <yestRdai=143>   102/68
worry <wurrl=14>   68/37

Figure 5. Highest percent female usage

deep-dish pie	(89%)
so glad (to see you)	(81%)
Grandmamma	(78%)
coverlet	(77%)
giblets	(77%)
yeast bread	(75%)
matron of honor +	(74%)
spoon bread +	(74%)
grease <grees> [inf.]	(72%)
Mrs. <misIz=14>	(72%)
she and I	(72%)
February <febyuewerI=1324>	(71%)
goodness [exclamation]	(71%)
twenty <twintI=14>	(71%)
buggy [=baby carriage]	(69%)
perk (coffee)	(69%)
cough <k{aw}f> [unrounded onset]	(68%)
dog <d{ou}g> [unrounded onset]	(68%)
sure <shur>	(68%)
catch <kach> [inf.]	(67%)
comforter [=bed covering]	(67%)
curdle(d) +	(67%)
roof <roof>	(67%)
salad tomato +	(67%)

SIGNIFICANT MALE USAGES

For almost all of the lexical items that relate to things used outside the household, to flora and fauna or to any area more closely related to males, the female total is less than the male (often greatly so), except for national forms. For example, for items on LAGS work-sheet page 21, dealing with parts of wagons, plows, and harrows, responses used by 50 or more men than women and with a percentage difference of more than ten points in favor of the males include the following:

felly +	(22F vs. 122M = 5%/25%)
tire +	(70/187 = 17%/38%)
singletree	(213/336 = 50%/68%)
doubletree	(116/302 = 27%/61%)
turning plow	(89/175 = 21%/36%)
disc harrow	(58/162 = 14%/33%)
axle	(268/363 = 64%/74%)

No corresponding lexical terms high in female usage are listed in figure 4(a) for items on this work sheet page. In a similar way, the usage of males is considerably higher for *cat squirrel* (34/126 = 8%/26%) and *gray squirrel* (160/234 = 38%/48%) for item 059.6L, and for *fox squirrel* (129/287 = 31%/58%) for item 059.7L. Men more often referred to a chipmunk as a *ground squirrel* than women did (92/149 = 22%/30%) for item 059.8L and to a woodpecker as a *peckerwood* (159/218 = 38%/044%) or *sapsucker* (19/80 = 5%/16%) for 059.3L.

Many terms that have a distinct areal distribution in the Gulf States territory are also found more often in male speech. For item 020.5L, *harmonica*, the national form itself is evenly divided numerically (215/215), with a higher female percentage (51%/ 47%). The form *harp*, prevalent throughout the Gulf States, has a slightly higher male total (164/170) with a higher female percentage (39%/35%), but the other three forms all show a ten or more numerical difference and a percentage in favor of male usage:

French harp	(118/174 = 28%/35%)
mouth harp	(28/44 = 7%/9%), and
mouth organ	(35/52 = 8%/11%)

In another example, item 060A.4L, *dragonfly*, the two dominant regional forms, *mosquito hawk* and *snake doctor*, both have higher male totals and percentages: 109/182 (26%/37%) and 118/158 (28%/32%), respectively. However, the regional form *snake feeder*, occurring primarily in the Eastern Highlands, is almost evenly divided between females and males (26/29 = 6%/6%).

In the area of euphemistic names for male animals, again the males in the sample seem to be more familiar, or at least more forthcoming, with a variety of terms. An example is item 034.1L, *stallion*, for all responses except *stud* as a taboo term (21/19 = 5%/4%). Male usage is considerably higher for all combinations of *stud* (162/287 = 38%/58%) and *studhorse* (29/90 = 7%/18%), and somewhat higher for *male horse* (18/32 = 4%/7%) and *stallion* + (175/228 = 41%/46%). Men also have a greater apparent familiarity with names for male hogs, item 035.3L:

boar +	(289/389 = 68%/80%)
boar hog +	(35/72 = 8%/15%)
male +	(51/102 = 12%/21%)
male hog	(34/54 = 8%/11%)
stock hog	(7/13 = 2%/3%)

GRAMMATICAL ITEMS

In grammatical usage, almost every worksheet item shows a higher female total and percentage for standard forms. Figure 4(c) above indicates a number of verb forms that are much higher, including the preterit and past participle of *dive* (item 095.3G) and the infinitive of *lie* (item 096.6G). In the former, the distribution of *dived* by gender is 204/161 (48%/33%) and 165/116 (39%/24%) for preterit and past participle, respectively, while the corresponding figures for *dove* are almost equal in percentage between the sexes: 117/140 (28%/28%) and 46/57 (11%/12%). For the nonstandard *div*, the male usage is higher: 9/30 (2%/6%) and 5/19 (1%/4%). For the verb *lie*, women often used the standard infinitive (207/166 = 49%/34%), in contrast to the higher use of *lay* as an intransitive infinitive by men (151/209 = 36%/42%).

There is also a distinct contrast between the sexes for other grammatical items, according to figure 4(b). Women used the determiner *an* more often before a vowel (241/198 = 57%/40%), as opposed to male usage of *a* plus vowel (142/228 = 34%/46%) for item 051.8G. Men

more often said *thataway* (50/178 = 12%/36%) and *thisaway* (71/166 =
17%/34%), and women said *this way* (244/212 = 58%/43%) for item
052.3G. Female informants in the Gulf States, while not necessarily
having more formal education than their male counterparts, seemed to
have more awareness of standard usage, at least in responding to the
direct interrogation of the interview situation.

Conclusions regarding phonological items are difficult to draw, based
on the evidence of the Social Totals alone, since these include only
responses occurring 50 or more times and do not show any combinations. The phonological items listed in figure 4(d), however, are for the
most part standard pronunciations: for example, for *pretty* (item
026.3AP) is *<pritI=14>* (139/90 = 33% /18%) rather than *<purtI=14>*
(57/77 = 14%/16%); for item 001A.2P is *<sevNtI=144>* (215/160 =
51%/33%) instead of *<sebMtI=144>* (32/83 = 8%/17%); or for item
008.1P is *chimney* (277/254 = 66%/52%) and not *chimley* (155/261 =
37%/53%). Again, these differences may result from a greater self-
consciousness that women may have felt in the presence of a language-
conscious fieldworker. The limited evidence of the Social Totals also
suggests that women less often use <aw> (i.e. [ɔ]) in terms such as *fog*
(item 006.7AP), *swamp* (item 029.6P), and *tassel* (item 056.3P), or
delete initial syllables in words such as *eleven* (item 001.6AP) and
appendicitis (item 080.1P). These and other contrastive sets are
illustrated in figure 6, which shows the total usage for each gender for
a number of responses, followed by the percentage by gender for all
informants.

Figure 6. Female/male terms (contrastive sets)
(Female terms highlighted)

Term		Total (F/M)	Percent (F/M)				
LEXICAL							
003.2	sunrise	183/160	43/33	022.7	merry-go-round	216/184	51/37
003.2	sunup	162/244	38/50	022.7	flying jenny	125/175	30/36
018.4	dish towel	158/92	37/19	039.1	reins +	180/152	43/31
018.4	rag +	46/129	11/26	039.1	lines +	185/294	44/60
022.1	horse +	173/128	41/26	045.3	pancakes	332/310	79/63
022.1	sawhorse +	142/240	34/48	045.3	flapjacks	85/136	20/28

048.3	cobbler	281/254	66/52
048.3	deep-dish pie	56/7	13/1
048.3	pie	100/155	24/32
056.2	corn on the cob	124/81	29/16
056.2	roasting ears	218/314	52/64
064.5	buggy	82/37	19/8
064.5	carriage	162/122	38/25
064.5	baby carriage	82/145	19/29
065.7	illegitimate +	190/131	45/27
065.7	bastard +	191/309	45/63
066.5	family	73/53	17/11
066.5	relatives	251/217	59/44
066.5	kinfolks	147/225	35/46

GRAMMATICAL

013.1	doesn't	195/158	46/32
013.1	don't (3rd sing.)	184/293	44/60
042.2	you and I	164/137	39/28
042.2	me + [noun]	59/129	14/26
051.8	an (apple)	241/198	57/40
051.8	a (apple)	142/228	34/46
052.3	this way	244/212	58/43
052.3	thataway	50/178	12/36
052.3	thisaway	71/166	17/34
091.3	yes	243/203	58/41
091.3	yeah	267/354	63/72

VERBS

006.3	blown [p.p.]	173/145	41/29
006.3	blowed [pret.]	56/126	13/26
096.6	lie [inf.]	207/166	49/34
096.6	lay [inf.]	151/209	36/42

102.1	gave [pret.]	275/241	65/49
102.1	give [pret.]	81/166	19/34
102.4	come [p.p.]	185/153	44/31
102.4	come [pret.]	175/286	41/58
104.4	drew [pret.]	210/167	50/34
104.4	drawed [pret.]	75/134	18/27

PHONOLOGICAL

001.6	<IlevN=144>	113/79	27/16
001.6	<(i)lebM=14>	22/100	5/20
001A.2	<sevNtI=144>	215/160	51/33
001A.2	<sebMtI=144>	32/83	8/17
001A.3	<sekNt=14>	180/152	43/31
001A.3	<sekN(d)=14>	161/226	38/46
003.5	<yestRdai=143>	102/68	24/14
003.5	<yest[R]dI=144>	46/102	11/21
006.7	<f{o}g>	95/64	23/13
006.7	<fawg>	118/195	28/40
008.1	chimney +	277/254	66/52
008.1	chimley +	155/261	37/53
029.6	<swomp>	110/75	26/15
029.6	<swawmp>	110/184	26/37
032.4	<with>	203/146	48/30
032.4	<wid>	17/67	4/14
032.4	<widh>	151/211	36/43
033.1	<d{ou}g>	71/34	17/7
033.1	<d{aw}g>	238/322	56/65
056.3	<tasL=14>	159/137	38/28
056.3	<tawsL=14>	54/117	13/24
080.1	appendicitis	194/145	46/29
080.1	(ap)pendicitis	150/214	35/43

Since all of an informant's social characteristics have a bearing on his or her speech, combinations of those factors help to reveal a pattern of usage. The second section of the *Social Matrix* consists of 397 Code

Maps. Like the LAGS Maps of *LAGS Volume 4: Regional Matrix*, these maps identify the regional distribution of responses according to points on a grid that approximates the shape of the Gulf States territory.

In addition to the areal distribution, the maps of the *Social Matrix* identify the informants according to combinations of the five social factors for 247 terms. These include 97 Interior or Coastal markers and 150 social markers, selected to illustrate responses according to race, sex, age, and education level. Using the binary division described above, the Code Maps show racial caste (indicated on all maps) as an uppercase letter from A to D (black) or a number from 1 to 4 (white). With race included on all maps, the factors yield six possible combinations of three binary factors each, as represented in six codes. As seen in figure 7, Codes 1–3 include the gender factor.

Figure 7. Social Matrix map coding

Code 1: Race/Sex/Age

1 = W/F/13–65 ###/152	A = B/F/13–65 ##/51
2 = W/M/13–65 ###/163	B = B/M/13–65 ##/40
3 = W/F/66–99 ###/166	C = B/F/66–99 ##/53
4 = W/M/66–99 ###/236	D = B/M/66–99 ##/53

Code 2: Race/Sex/Education

1 = W/F/00–10 ###/127	A = B/F/00–10 ##/58
2 = W/M/00–10 ###/200	B = B/M/00–10 ##/65
3 = W/F/11–16+ ###/191	C = B/F/11–16+ ##/46
4 = W/M/11–16+ ###/199	D = B/M/11–16+ ##/28

Code 3: Race/Sex/Social Status

1 = W/F/L ###/174	A = B/F/L ##/84
2 = W/M/L ###/231	B = B/M/L ##/74
3 = W/F/U ###/144	C = B/F/U ##/20
4 = W/M/U ###/168	D = B/M/U ##/19

In Code 3, for example, the informants ranked on the left-hand side are white (W), and those on the right are black (B). Number 1 represents lower or lower-middle-class white female informants. The number following the virgule (/) indicates the total number of informants in each category, for example, 174 white female, lower or lower middle class. On an actual map, the octothorpes (###) would be replaced by the number of informants in that category who used the response. Figure 8 is a Code Map of *snake feeder* (*dragonfly*), a term with a distinct regional distribution and an almost even female/male numerical split in usage. This map readily identifies the form as one limited primarily to the Blue Ridge and Valley (East and Middle Tennessee) and the Upper Cumberland Plateau of Upper Georgia. A further examination shows that the form is used by white informants only, with the female usage divided fairly evenly between the younger and older age categories, but with the male usage primarily among those over age 66.

A map showing a more distinct social, as opposed to regional, distribution is figure 9, *coverlet* (item 029.7L), for which 77% of the total number of responses are from females. This map gives the location of the females whose responses dominate this item, most of whom are white and better-educated, showing that, although absent in most of mainland Florida, the term occurs in many parts of the Gulf States, without being concentrated in any one region.

The features included as Code Maps in the *Social Matrix* were restricted to those that most strikingly illustrate the factors and are limited to 247 terms, primarily those that are significant according to the factors of regional distribution, racial caste, age, and years of schooling. Because only a few terms were mapped as being more significant in usage according to gender, they are of limited usefulness in analyzing female, as opposed to male, usage in the territory. In a study of this type, the primary value of the Code Maps is to supplement the information provided by the Social Totals by giving a geographical context for social factors.

Usage charts, another feature of *LAGS Volume 7: Social Pattern*, represent an additional means of analyzing the social factors and areal distribution in determining the usage of Gulf States informants. These charts give the percentage of usage among the total number of informants in each major social category, excluding social class, and also

Figure 8. Snake feeder {060A.4L} (55)

```
Code 1: Race/Sex/Age

1 = W/F/13-65    10/152      A = B/F/13-65    0/51
2 = W/M/13-65     4/163      B = B/M/13-65    0/40
3 = W/F/66-99    16/166      C = B/F/66-99    0/53
4 = W/M/66-99    25/236      D = B/M/66-99    0/53
```

Figure 9. Coverlet {028.7L} (78)

```
Code 2: Race/Sex/Education

1 = W/F/00-10    14/127    A = B/F/00-10    0/58
2 = W/M/00-10    10/200    B = B/M/00-10    0/65
3 = W/F/11-16+   44/191    C = B/F/11-16+   2/46
4 = W/M/11-16+    8/199    D = B/M/11-16+   0/28
```

```
              1         2         3         4         5         6         7
     12345678901234567890123456789012345678901234567890123456789012345678901234567890

A                                              ...........3.2.2......1              A
B                        .42..2..2. ...................1.......4....                B
C                        ...1..... ...................2.......1..                  C
D                        .................1....1........32..2..                    D
E                        ....1................23........                           E
F                        .....................313..                                F
G                        ...................33.3....3......                        G
H                .      ..  ..3............3..1.3.........3..                       H
I           .            ...................3.........3.........                   I
J           .     3      .   ....3...........2....C...3...3......                   J
K      . .C3            .1  3.                                                      K
L      ...     .4      .. 4.................334......3...3...3....                  L
M      1       .       3..............................3.........                   M
N      .                ....3....1.........................4....4.                 N
O           .          .  .................................3......                 O
P           .        ...  ........3...3.3......................                    P
Q     ..      ..      ..  .................1. ..........3......                    Q
R     .       ..      ....................3.............     .  .                  R
S                     .3................4....3  .   ....    ..                     S
T        .         3.. .....3...... ............ ..3. .   .. . ...                 T
U     ..  .  ..      .  .3........                      .. . ..                    U
V     1.    ...      .   ..........                     ... . .                    V
W     ...  . ..                                          .. . .                    W
X     . ..3   ...                                       ... .  .                   X
Y        ....                                            .. .  .                    Y
Z     .    ..3                                           ..... . .                  Z
AA        ..                                             ... .   AA
AB  ..    ..                                             .. . .. . AB
AC  ..    .                                              . .. . AC
AD   .. .                                                . . . AD
AE   ..                                                  .... AE
AF   ...                                                 ... AF
AG                                                       .   AG
AH                                              3         .  AH
              1         2         3         4         5         6         7
     12345678901234567890123456789012345678901234567890123456789012345678901234567890
```

according to the 33 subregions. The chart for sauce, figure 10, illustrates a response for which female usage is dominant (highlighted in the chart are the instances of sauce in female speech in subregions where the percentage is equal to or higher than the territorial average of 42% and where three or more informants used the term). For the other three factors represented, the percentages are higher for white informants under age 66 with more than a tenth-grade education. The chart also indicates that the areal distribution is not a major consideration for this term, which occurs at least once in each of the 33 subregions, with usage among all female informants in each subregion equaling 60% or above in A4, B2, C5, D4, D5, E5, and F2.

In another example (generated from the disk text), figure 11 is the percentage chart for *yeast bread* (from item 044.3L, *loaf bread*). The chart shows that the highest differential in percentage points is between female and male usage (13%/4%) and that its occurrence is also somewhat higher in the speech of white and better-educated informants, with age a negligible consideration. No instances of *yeast bread* occur in C5, C6, D8, F1, F3, F5, and F6, all in the west central and western portions of the LAGS territory and all except F1 in the Coastal Southern area. The highest usage is in the Highlands, eastern Piedmont, and eastern Piney Woods. An examination of the data from the percentage charts in figure 5 (Highest Percent Female Usage) reveals that for 16 of the 24 terms, the percentage differential between the binary factors is higher for white females under age 65 and with more than ten years of formal education. Only four of the responses (*Grandmamma*, *twenty* *<twintI=14>*, *buggy*, and *roof<roof>*) occur more often in the speech of black women (all younger and better-educated). For the remaining four terms, racial caste is not a significant factor for *giblets* or *she and I*; age is negligible for *yeast bread*, and, a sole exception to the general pattern, *so glad* is found more frequently in the speech of older and less-educated white women. The pattern of white/female/younger/better-educated seems to apply to a majority of mapped responses in the territory, with the reverse pattern (black/male/older/less-educated) also holding true in many instances for other forms.

The Social Total matrixes, supported by the Code Maps and percentage charts, give a reasonably clear picture of the speech of the 914 primary informants in the LAGS sample, based on the factors

Figure 10. Percentage chart for *sauce* [= sweet topping] {048.5L}

	Black: 57/197 29%	White: 226/717 32%	Female: 178/422 42%	Male: 105/492 21%	65(-) years: 153/406 38%	66(+) years: 130/508 26%	10(-) grades: 99/450 22%	11(+) grades: 184/464 40%	283/914 31%
	Black	White	Female	Male	65(-) years	66(+) years	10(-) grades	11(+) grades	
A1	3/6 50%	20/46 43%	12/22 55%	11/30 37%	13/21 62%	10/31 32%	5/26 19%	18/26 69%	
A2	0/3 0%	2/17 12%	2/11 18%	0/9 0%	1/8 13%	1/12 8%	0/12 0%	2/8 25%	
A3	0/0 0%	4/18 22%	4/12 33%	0/6 0%	2/5 40%	2/13 15%	2/11 18%	2/7 29%	
A4	3/9 33%	13/28 46%	14/20 70%	2/17 12%	8/19 42%	8/18 44%	8/16 50%	8/21 38%	
A5	1/5 20%	17/34 50%	8/15 53%	10/24 42%	9/21 43%	9/18 50%	8/17 47%	10/22 45%	
A6	0/0 0%	8/41 20%	6/20 30%	2/21 10%	7/20 35%	1/21 5%	1/23 4%	7/18 39%	
B1	6/12 50%	20/47 43%	19/35 54%	7/24 29%	12/22 55%	14/37 38%	8/28 29%	18/31 58%	
B2	5/7 71%	4/18 22%	5/8 63%	4/17 24%	7/14 50%	2/11 18%	2/7 29%	7/18 39%	
C1	0/4 0%	1/8 13%	1/6 17%	0/6 0%	0/6 0%	1/6 17%	1/6 17%	0/6 0%	
C2	2/8 25%	2/15 13%	2/10 20%	2/13 15%	2/16 13%	2/7 29%	3/7 43%	1/16 6%	
C3	1/8 13%	9/19 47%	5/12 42%	5/15 33%	8/18 44%	2/9 22%	1/10 10%	9/17 53%	
C4	2/7 29%	4/14 29%	1/7 14%	5/14 36%	4/13 31%	2/8 25%	2/5 40%	4/16 25%	
C5	2/5 40%	3/10 30%	4/6 67%	1/9 11%	2/9 22%	3/6 50%	3/9 33%	2/6 33%	
C6	0/2 0%	4/9 44%	1/7 14%	3/4 75%	2/4 50%	2/7 29%	0/4 0%	4/7 57%	
D1	1/4 25%	3/15 20%	0/8 0%	4/11 36%	1/6 17%	3/13 23%	2/10 20%	2/9 22%	
D2	3/9 33%	9/21 43%	9/19 47%	3/11 27%	7/12 58%	5/18 28%	3/14 21%	9/16 56%	
D3	0/1 0%	4/16 25%	2/7 29%	2/10 20%	3/9 33%	1/8 13%	1/8 13%	3/9 33%	
D4	3/7 43%	6/15 40%	7/9 78%	2/13 15%	4/10 40%	5/12 42%	1/9 11%	8/13 62%	
D5	3/8 38%	6/11 55%	6/9 67%	3/10 30%	2/8 25%	7/11 64%	5/10 50%	4/9 44%	
D6	1/4 25%	2/13 15%	2/6 33%	1/11 9%	0/6 0%	3/11 27%	3/9 33%	0/8 0%	
D7	2/4 50%	4/19 21%	5/13 38%	1/10 10%	3/6 50%	3/17 18%	2/11 18%	4/12 33%	
D8	0/2 0%	8/27 30%	5/13 38%	3/16 19%	6/16 38%	2/13 15%	2/10 20%	6/19 32%	
E1	1/7 14%	7/48 15%	5/27 19%	3/28 11%	5/21 24%	3/34 9%	4/39 10%	4/16 25%	
E2	0/5 0%	8/24 33%	5/16 31%	3/13 23%	5/11 45%	3/18 17%	2/17 12%	6/12 50%	
E3	2/9 22%	11/24 46%	8/16 50%	5/17 29%	7/15 47%	6/18 33%	4/15 27%	9/18 50%	
E4	1/9 11%	10/28 36%	7/13 54%	4/24 17%	4/10 40%	7/27 26%	5/22 23%	6/15 40%	
E5	3/6 50%	12/21 57%	9/12 75%	6/15 40%	9/13 69%	6/14 43%	6/12 50%	9/15 60%	
F1	0/4 0%	2/11 18%	1/9 11%	1/6 17%	1/6 17%	1/9 11%	1/8 13%	1/7 14%	
F2	7/16 44%	11/33 33%	12/20 60%	6/29 21%	13/25 52%	5/24 21%	5/23 22%	13/26 50%	
F3	1/4 25%	2/11 18%	2/7 29%	1/8 13%	1/5 20%	2/10 20%	2/8 25%	1/7 14%	
F4	3/11 27%	6/20 30%	6/13 46%	3/18 17%	4/15 27%	5/16 31%	4/12 33%	5/19 26%	
F5	0/7 0%	1/17 6%	1/8 13%	0/16 0%	0/9 0%	1/15 7%	1/17 6%	0/7 0%	
F6	1/4 25%	3/19 16%	2/6 33%	2/17 12%	1/7 14%	3/16 19%	2/15 13%	2/8 25%	

From *Linguistic Atlas of the Gulf States*, Volume VII, by Lee Pederson. Copyright © 1992 by the University of Georgia Press. Reprinted by permission.

Figure 11. Percentage chart for *yeast bread* {)44.3L} 75/914 8%

	Black: 7/197 4%		White: 68/717 9%		Female: 56/422 13%		Male: 19/492 4%		65(-) years: 34/406 8%		66(+) years: 41/508 8%		10(-) grades: 32/450 7%		11(+) grades: 43/464 9%	
	Black		White		Female		Male		65(-) years		66(+) years		10(-) grades		11(+) grades	
A1	1/6	17%	6/46	13%	5/22	23%	2/30	7%	2/21	10%	5/31	16%	2/26	8%	5/26	19%
A2	1/3	33%	4/17	24%	3/11	27%	2/9	22%	1/8	13%	4/12	33%	3/12	25%	2/8	25%
A3	0/0	0%	1/18	6%	1/12	8%	0/6	0%	1/5	20%	0/13	0%	0/11	0%	1/7	14%
A4	0/9	0%	4/28	14%	4/20	20%	0/17	0%	2/19	11%	2/18	11%	2/16	13%	2/21	10%
A5	0/5	0%	2/34	6%	2/15	13%	0/24	0%	1/21	5%	1/18	6%	0/17	0%	2/22	9%
A6	0/0	0%	5/41	12%	5/20	25%	0/21	0%	2/20	10%	3/21	14%	3/23	13%	2/18	11%
B1	1/12	8%	7/47	15%	8/35	23%	0/24	0%	3/22	14%	5/37	14%	2/28	7%	6/31	19%
B2	0/7	0%	2/18	11%	1/8	13%	1/17	6%	1/14	7%	1/11	9%	0/7	0%	2/18	11%
C1	0/4	0%	1/8	13%	1/6	17%	0/6	0%	0/6	0%	1/6	17%	1/6	17%	0/6	0%
C2	0/8	0%	2/15	13%	0/10	0%	2/13	15%	1/16	6%	1/7	14%	2/7	29%	0/16	0%
C3	0/8	0%	2/19	11%	1/12	8%	1/15	7%	2/18	11%	0/9	0%	0/10	0%	2/17	12%
C4	0/7	0%	2/14	14%	2/7	29%	0/14	0%	2/13	15%	0/8	0%	0/5	0%	2/16	13%
C5	0/5	0%	0/10	0%	0/6	0%	0/9	0%	0/9	0%	0/6	0%	0/9	0%	0/6	0%
C6	0/2	0%	0/9	0%	0/7	0%	0/4	0%	0/4	0%	0/7	0%	0/4	0%	0/7	0%
D1	1/4	25%	4/15	27%	2/8	25%	3/11	27%	2/6	33%	3/13	23%	3/10	30%	2/9	22%
D2	1/9	11%	2/21	10%	3/19	16%	0/11	0%	2/12	17%	1/18	6%	2/14	14%	1/16	6%
D3	0/1	0%	1/16	6%	1/7	14%	0/10	0%	1/9	11%	0/8	0%	0/8	0%	1/9	11%
D4	0/7	0%	1/15	7%	0/9	0%	1/13	8%	0/10	0%	1/12	8%	1/9	11%	0/13	0%
D5	1/8	13%	0/11	0%	1/9	11%	0/10	0%	0/8	0%	1/11	9%	0/10	0%	1/9	11%
D6	0/4	0%	1/13	8%	1/6	17%	0/11	0%	0/6	0%	1/11	9%	1/9	11%	0/8	0%
D7	0/4	0%	1/19	5%	1/13	8%	0/10	0%	0/6	0%	1/17	6%	1/11	9%	0/12	0%
D8	0/2	0%	0/27	0%	0/13	0%	0/16	0%	0/16	0%	0/13	0%	0/10	0%	0/19	0%
E1	1/7	14%	3/48	6%	1/27	4%	3/28	11%	1/21	5%	3/34	9%	3/39	8%	1/16	6%
E2	0/5	0%	4/24	17%	4/16	25%	0/13	0%	2/11	18%	2/18	11%	3/17	18%	1/12	8%
E3	0/9	0%	8/24	33%	5/16	31%	3/17	18%	4/15	27%	4/18	22%	2/15	13%	6/18	33%
E4	0/9	0%	1/28	4%	1/13	8%	0/24	0%	0/10	0%	1/27	4%	1/22	5%	0/15	0%
E5	0/6	0%	1/21	5%	0/12	0%	1/15	7%	1/13	8%	0/14	0%	0/12	0%	1/15	7%
F1	0/4	0%	0/11	0%	0/9	0%	0/6	0%	0/6	0%	0/9	0%	0/8	0%	0/7	0%
F2	0/16	0%	2/33	6%	2/20	10%	0/29	0%	2/25	8%	0/24	0%	0/23	0%	2/26	8%
F3	0/4	0%	0/11	0%	0/7	0%	0/8	0%	0/5	0%	0/10	0%	0/8	0%	0/7	0%
F4	0/11	0%	1/20	5%	1/13	8%	0/18	0%	1/15	7%	0/16	0%	0/12	0%	1/19	5%
F5	0/7	0%	0/17	0%	0/8	0%	0/16	0%	0/9	0%	0/15	0%	0/17	0%	0/7	0%
F6	0/4	0%	0/19	0%	0/6	0%	0/17	0%	0/7	0%	0/16	0%	0/15	0%	0/8	0%

Created by the author from disk text of the Linguistic Atlas of the Gulf States.

analyzed. Although gender appears to be the least significant of these, it nevertheless often shows a pattern of usage. The data examined in this study suggest that men are more likely to use those terms usually considered as regional markers: lexical forms and non-standard grammar and phonology. However, this is not the whole story in characterizing the speech of a region. The lexicon of household items and the incidence of standard grammatical forms and pronunciation, in a majority of cases, are features of the speech of women. And, since the social factors in combination yield more information than any one factor considered alone, the informants' gender may be a valuable element in establishing a social pattern across the territory.

NOTE

1. In this paper 'significance' is not used in the statistical sense of the term, but rather as a provisional descriptive device.

Packaging LAGS for *DARE*

Joan Houston Hall

In his provocatively titled note 'Hey, Lucy', Lee Pederson illustrates the 'lexicographical problem of editorial economics' (1981a:63) with an amusing vignette from one of the interviews conducted for the Linguistic Atlas of the Gulf States (LAGS) project. While doing fieldwork in east Tennessee, Pederson had asked about 'unpackaged material', hoping to elicit such terms as *loose* and *bulk*. An elderly informant from Jacksboro not only responded with *loose*, but also recounted a tale of the word's use by the local town drunk. After relating the anecdote from the taped interview, Pederson concludes

> If only the final sentence [of the story] finds its way into the legendry [i.e. the then-contemplated dictionary component of LAGS[1]], the style of the passage, as well as the marvelous compression of extemporaneous folk speech, will be lost. If we try to include the whole passage and others like it, we may find ourselves without a vessel and our data poured out loose, without even a table to support them. (63)

Now that the dictionary component of LAGS has been given up, the task of fashioning vessels for the LAGS lexical data falls to the editors of the *Dictionary of American Regional English* (*DARE*).[2] Given the tremendous amount and variety of LAGS material, that is a daunting task. But the value of the information dictates that we utilize it as fully as possible. And the production of each successive publication of LAGS has provided a new tool to make the task a little easier.

With the publication of the *LAGS Basic Materials* in 1981 (129,000 pages from the 'protocols',[3] reproduced on microfilm and microfiche), it was obvious to the *DARE* staff that we needed to take account of these data that had been so systematically and carefully collected. They did seem to be 'poured out loose', however, with no easy means of accessing or organizing them. The microfiche version contained each protocol, informant by informant; the microfilm reels were arranged question by question. One could browse through the materials and find much of interest, but it was impossible to have a very complete knowledge of what was there or where it could be found. Pederson and his staff were cooperative and generous in checking individual queries for us, and Volume I of *DARE* (A–C) includes numerous LAGS citations based on these informal exchanges. But systematic use of the data was not possible.

With the publication (in fiche) of the *LAGS Concordance* in 1986, however, the situation changed dramatically: all at once the data in the *Basic Materials* were accessible. We not only knew what words had been collected, but could correlate them with any of the 1,121 individual speakers (see figure 1). *DARE*'s use of the material often required laboriously counting instances of words in the *Concordance* and matching informant numbers with geographic localities, but the information was there and it was exciting in its breadth and depth. In 1988 the publication of the *LAGS General Index* provided further assistance. Much of the data had now been synthesized for us, obviating some of the tedious counting of instances in the *Concordance*.[4] And the appearance of the *LAGS Technical Index* in 1989 meant that synonymies were available for selected questions, and much phonological information had been analyzed and categorized.[5] Volume II of *DARE* (D–H), as a result, uses Pederson's data much more systematically, featuring approximately 300 instances in which we report data from LAGS.[6]

Once it was obvious that we would be using LAGS materials regularly in *DARE*, it was necessary to standardize our citation procedures and determine ways to condense the material into entry-sized capsules. Neither with our own sources nor with LAGS material can we routinely quote long passages such as the one in 'Hey, Lucy' that capture a speaker's unique style. But the problem of taking vignettes from the LAGS tapes and paring them down to quotable nuggets in *DARE* is now moot, for the mammoth plan to transcribe the entire corpus of tapes has had to be relinquished.[7] That leaves us with the voluminous materials in the *Concordance* that need packaging for presentation as lexical evidence from the Gulf States. How best to synthesize the data is the continuing challenge for editors at *DARE*.

The first question to deal with was the lack of congruence in our regional labels. For *DARE*, 'Gulf States' means Florida, Alabama,

Mississippi, Louisiana, and east Texas, while for LAGS the label includes Arkansas, Georgia, and Tennessee as well. Although *DARE* could have adopted the LAGS designation at the time our regional labels were being developed, the inclusion of the interior states as 'Gulf' states seemed counterintuitive. We recognized the reason for their being in LAGS, but decided to adopt a geographically more limited label for our own use. Had we accepted the LAGS designation originally, we would have saved ourselves some trouble; for as we began to cite LAGS regularly in Volume II of *DARE*, the lack of fit in labels became annoyingly obvious. To apply our 'Gulf States' label to Pederson's material would be confusing to readers, since the label is defined in the front matter as excluding Arkansas, Georgia, and Tennessee. But to use the label 'Gulf States, AK, GA, TN' would not only have been awkward, but would also have required verifying for each quote that some of the informant numbers in the *Concordance* did indeed refer to people from those various states. In the interests of accuracy and simplicity, we decided to apply the label 'Gulf Region' to the LAGS materials, using more specific designations such as 'inland Gulf Region' or 'coastal Gulf Region' as appropriate.[8] We have reserved the label 'Gulf States' for quotes from *DARE* materials.

A much greater challenge in packaging the LAGS materials for *DARE* results from the somewhat different aims and methods of the two projects. In *DARE*, absolute consistency in the asking of the questions was essential. Without it, we would have no basis for assuming that (most) responses are indeed synonymous. Because fieldworkers did not, as a rule, record the entire interview on tape, the Questionnaire had to be the source of last resort.[9]

In LAGS, however, where all the interviews were recorded in their entirety, fieldworkers had much greater leeway in terms of posing their questions. Sample elicitation frames were offered in the worksheets, but any format that was successful for a particular fieldworker was acceptable. Because the tapes were there as a backup, detailed notes in the protocols were less essential than they would otherwise have been; the transcribed tapes would provide context, sense, and style.

In 'Lexical Data from the Gulf States', in which he quoted from a LAGS tape that included a good conversational explanation of the terms *hillbilly*, *hillbilly people*, and *river nigger*, Pederson wrote:

> In addition to the phonological evidence . . . and grammatical evidence
> . . . considerable lexical information is preserved by the tape. The highly
> specialized senses of the three terms mentioned above could never be
> ascertained by analysis of morphemes or lexemes without elaborate
> marginal glosses by the fieldworker. (1980b:202)

But without such elaborate glosses, and now without the hope of having complete transcriptions of the interviews,[10] we are left with only the record of the word in the *Concordance* and whatever marginal notations *were* made in the protocols.

While the line number in the protocol (recorded also in the *Concordance*) tells us what basic question was being addressed, it does not let us know how the question was asked. In many cases, that much information is sufficient for *DARE*'s purposes: we can cite the material in such a way as to indicate that the word was used by a specific number of informants in designated places at a given time. But in those cases where the sense of the word is unclear, or where specialized meanings are likely, the lack of any contextual evidence is frustrating. *DARE* editors are left with a hard decision: whether to use LAGS evidence, knowing that we cannot be sure what was intended by individual informants, to use only part of it, or to pass it by. Uncomfortable compromises are sometimes the best solution. We can include a LAGS citation but bracket the information to indicate that the *DARE* editor is making a generalization based on his or her best interpretation of the data; we can use only the incontrovertible evidence; or, we can add editorial notes of the type, 'It is possible that some informants may be referring instead to sense **2** below'.

The term *galvanize*, an assimilated form of *galvanized*, provides a case in point. The *Concordance* has 17 examples in which the word is clearly adjectival, occurring in compounds such as *galvanize bucket* (see figure 1). There are 13 instances of the word alone, two of which have been marked in the protocols as adjectives by the 'x' in the fifth column.

In several other cases, marginal notes make it clear that the term is being used as a noun: 'bucket made of galvanize'; 'pipe made of galvanize'. But in others, the situation is ambiguous. Does the marginal note 'boat for fishing' mean that *galvanize* is here used as a noun

Figure 1. Sample fiche from the *LAGS Concordance*

```
BOCK  PAGE LINE SG   GG    ENTRY                                              13098

0716  064   9                gals, teenage
0531  064   9                gals, young
0134E 017   2    !           galvanize
0148  017   3    !           galvanize
0157A 017   3    !      x    galvanize
0359  017   3    f      !    galvanize <most common bucket is>
0394  017   2    !           galvanize <water bucket made of>
0438  017   2    !           galvanize <=galvanized bucket>
0545  017   3    !      x    galvanize
0583  024   6    !           galvanize <boat for fishing>
0587  017   3    f      !    galvanize
0676  017   2    !           galvanize <bucket made of>
0764  017   3    !           galvanize <"bucket" is tin, plastic, or>
0857  017   3    !           galvanize <milk pails made of>
0860  023   2    !           galvanize <pipe made of>
0860  020   3    !           galvanize banding <on barrels>
0237  017   3    !           galvanize bucket
0586  017   2    !           galvanize bucket
0648  017   3    !           galvanize bucket
0676  017   3    !           galvanize bucket
0857  023   1    !           galvanize bucket
0122B 017   4    !           galvanize bucket, a <"great big container">
0685  017   2    !           galvanize bucket, a
0798  017   3    !           galvanize bucket, a
0304  017   4    !           galvanize buckets
0425  016   3    c      !    galvanize fence
0851  126   1    !           galvanize fencing
0751  017   4    b      !    galvanize pail
0471  017   2    b      !    galvanize tin <pail usually made of>
0471  026   6    !           galvanize tin
0900  026   6    !           galvanize tin
0857  018   9    !           galvanize tub
0048  017   3                galvanized <buckets>
0217  070   9                galvanized
0330  026   6    f           galvanized
0337  017   2    !           galvanized <water buckets made of> <or aluminum>
0402  026   6                galvanized
0407  070   8    f           galvanized
0512  017   3    f           galvanized
0519  017   3                galvanized <milk bucket made of> <metal>
0542  017   2                galvanized
0717A 017   3                galvanized
0723  017   3                galvanized <metal buckets were> <or enamel>
0747  011   4                galvanized
0825  017   3    b           galvanized <well buckets usually>
0842  017   2    !      n    galvanized <bucket made of> <or granite>
0910  017   2                galvanized <bucket made of> <iron>
0165A 017   3                galvanized aluminum <bucket made of>
0006  017   3                galvanized bucket
0070  017   3    f           galvanized bucket
0288A 017   2                galvanized bucket
0333  017   2                galvanized bucket
0508  017   2                galvanized bucket
0616  017   2                galvanized bucket
```

synonymous with *fishing boat*? And does '= *galvanized bucket*' mean that *galvanize* itself is the noun, or does *galvanize* substitute for *galvanized* in the noun phrase? At *DARE* we were particularly interested in the noun uses, since the adjectival form with reduced consonant cluster is unremarkable. But for the dictionary citation from LAGS we chose to be cautious, and we omitted the questionable interpretations (see figure 2, sense 2 for the entry for *galvanize*). We would have preferred to include them, but without more detailed marginal notes in the protocols, we could not be sure that our interpretation of the evidence was accurate.

Figure 2. *DARE* entry for *galvanize*

galvanize n

1 The zinc coating on iron; by ext. nickel plating.   Cf **fertilize**
1917 *DN* 4.412 **wNC**, *Galvanize*. . . Nickel plating. "The galvanize wore off my pistol." **1940** Stuart *Trees of Heaven* 315 KY, There was a washpan layin there. Boliver grabbed it and seized it with his teeth. The galvanize flew off in tiny white flakes.

2 also *galvanized:* Galvanized iron.
1966–70 *DARE* (Qu. F30, *What is a pail made of?*) Inf MO8. It's usually made out of granite or galvanized: MT5. Tin or galvanized: NY70. Galvanized, granite: OH96, Galvanized, wood: VA45, Made of galvanized or plastic; (Qu. D30, *The strip of . . . metal that covers the ridge of a roof*) Inf WA21, Galvanized, galvanized tin. **1986** Pederson *LAGS Concordance* **Gulf Region,** 2 infs. (Water) bucket made of galvanize: 1 inf, Most common bucket is galvanize: 1 inf. "Bucket" is tin. plastic, or galvanize: 1 inf, Milk pails made of galvanize: 1 inf, Pipe made of galvanize: 1 inf, Water buckets made of galvanized or aluminum; 1 inf, Bucket made of galvanized or granite: 1 inf, It's made out of galvanized: 1 inf, Galvanize banding on barrels.

Similarly, for the word *hominy*, the marginal notes in the *Concordance* were inadequate to determine whether informants meant whole kernels of corn or the coarsely ground grits. Although the worksheets instructed fieldworkers to distinguish between the two, the efforts were often unsuccessful. Since hominy and grits have almost become cultural icons south of the Mason-Dixon line, with people throughout the country holding strong opinions about their edibility as well as their best means of preparation, it is disappointing not to have the full story from this most logical source of data. *DARE* editors had to be content with lumping both forms of the substance in a single dictionary sense, and making a generalization for the LAGS citation, based on what comments were provided.

A different kind of problem surfaced with the entry for *gallery*, meaning 'porch, veranda, balcony'. The *DARE* map (figure 3), with 53 occurrences, showed a distribution which we described as 'chiefly Gulf States, AK, TX'.[11] This seemed a perfect opportunity to check for LAGS verification or refinement of the regional label. The *Concordance* includes several pages of informants who offered the term *gallery*. There are copious marginal notes, so determining the appropriate sense was no problem. And writing a statement summarizing the use of approximately three hundred LAGS informants would have been relatively straightforward, since we could make generalizations as to the numbers who specified 'porch' as opposed to 'balcony', etc. The problem of editorial economics was not one of space. Instead, it was one of determining how much time to devote to gleaning from the list of informant numbers the geographic corroboration we suspected was there. To have discovered the regional distribution of the LAGS informants would have meant tediously copying down the informant numbers and correlating them with the list of informant locations in the *Handbook*. Since we already had a good *DARE* map, that was not a productive use of time. We had resigned ourselves to using the LAGS data less fully than we would have liked.

But receipt from Pederson of a prepublication copy of the fourth volume of *LAGS*, the *Regional Matrix*, solved the problem. This volume includes more than 400 maps showing distributions of 844 lexical, grammatical, and phonological features, as well as more than 6500 'sector totals', or matrices showing the number of informants from each geographic sector of the LAGS region who used a particular linguistic form. The *LAGS* map of *gallery* shows that within the Gulf States, the term is found most frequently in Louisiana, Mississippi, southern Alabama, and east Texas (see figure 4). While the *DARE* and LAGS maps are roughly congruent, the greater density of LAGS informants within the region[12] provides a more accurate (as well as a slightly more contemporary) picture of the distribution.

Figure 3. *DARE* map for *gallery*

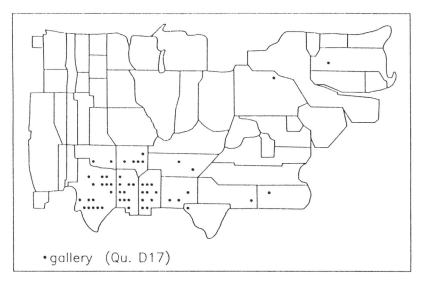

• gallery (Qu. D17)

From *Dictionary of American Regional English*, Volume II, edited by Frederic Cassidy and Joan Houston Hall. Copyright © 1991 by President and Fellows of Harvard College. Reprinted by permission of Harvard University Press.

Despite such relatively minor problems resulting from different methods, the LAGS data have been extremely useful to *DARE*. Often they corroborate already identified regional distributions, whether as broad as 'chiefly South, South Midland', or as narrow as 'especially east Tennessee'. In other cases, they suggest that a label applied on the basis of our other evidence is either too broad or too narrow. And in many other instances, they provide the justification for inclusion of otherwise inadequately documented entries.

It is no surprise to find strong LAGS support for such well established regionalisms as *dusk dark* ('chiefly South'), *funky* ('chiefly South, South Midland' for the sense 'musty, moldy, rancid'; 'esp among Black speakers' for the sense 'having noticeable body odor'), *grind rock* ('chiefly South, South Midland'), *guano sack* ('chiefly Central and South Atlantic'), or *hog's head cheese* ('chiefly South, South Midland, Northeast'). The Gulf States evidence is frosting on the cake of an

Figure 4. LAGS Regional Matrix map for *gallery*
(with LAGS sector outlines superimposed)

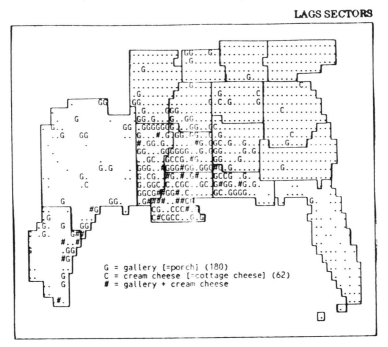

LAGS SECTORS

G = gallery [=porch] (180)
C = cream cheese [=cottage cheese] (62)
# = gallery + cream cheese

From *Linguistic Atlas of the Gulf States*, Volume IV, by Lee Pederson. Copyright ©
1990 by the University of Georgia Press. Reprinted by permission.

already substantial *DARE* entry. Occasionally, however, the LAGS
material is the determining factor in the way a *DARE* entry is constructed. In the case of the terms *goober* and *goober pea*, *DARE*
evidence showed wide use of *goober* throughout the South and South
Midland (figure 5), but somewhat more restricted use of *goober pea*,
chiefly in the South Midland. The *DARE* editor could have written a
single entry for *goober*, including *goober pea* as a variant there and
labeling the entry 'chiefly South, South Midland'. But when the LAGS
evidence became available, showing that 24 of the 34 *goober pea*
responses were from Tennessee, there was no question: that distribution
(figure 6) justified writing a separate *DARE* entry for *goober pea*, with
the narrower label 'chiefly South Midland'.

Figure 5. *DARE* map for *goober* n[1] 1

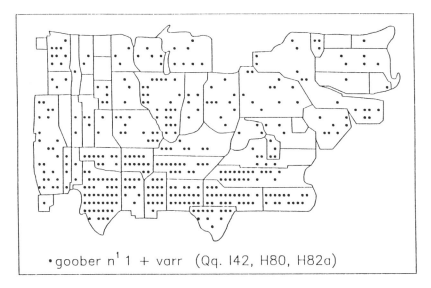

•goober n[1] 1 + varr   (Qq. 142, H80, H82a)

From *Dictionary of American Regional English*, Volume II, edited by Frederic Cassidy and Joan Houston Hall. Copyright © 1991 by President and Fellows of Harvard College. Reprinted by permission of Harvard University Press.

Because the LAGS mesh was much smaller than *DARE*'s (using 911 primary informants, plus 210 secondary ones in 699 localities in the Gulf States, as compared with *DARE*'s 2,777 informants in 1,002 communities throughout the country), LAGS data are particularly useful in describing smaller regions within the broad South, South Midland pattern. LAGS evidence for Louisiana French terms is especially valuable, since *DARE*'s grid could not provide detailed coverage there. But it has been useful in corroborating other narrowly defined regions as well.

Native Tennesseans, thoroughly conscious of at least a tripartite division of their state based on political, cultural, and linguistic grounds,[13] will not be surprised to hear that Pederson found the term *dairy*, referring to a room dug in a hillside for storage of dairy products in summer and vegetables in winter, to be restricted to east Tennessee (Pederson 1977b:88–89). Nor will it surprise them that all five LAGS

Figure 6. *DARE* map for *goober pea*

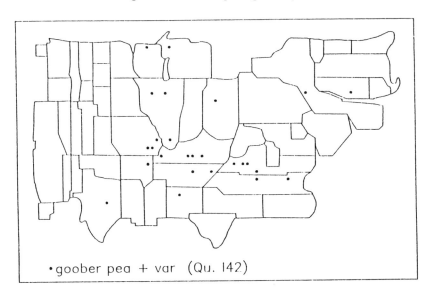

•goober pea + var (Qu. 142)

From *Dictionary of American Regional English*, Volume II, edited by Frederic Cassidy and Joan Houston Hall. Copyright © 1991 by President and Fellows of Harvard College. Reprinted by permission of Harvard University Press.

examples of *dryland fish*, a facetious term for a mushroom, were found in central Tennessee. (Most of *DARE*'s evidence for *dryland fish* was from Kentucky, so the Tennessee examples broadened our regional description.) Similarly, the LAGS evidence for *hog jaw* (as contrasted with *hog jowl*) comes primarily from central and western Tennessee. This kind of data is extremely useful for *DARE*, allowing editors to refine or confirm the labels suggested by our broader fieldwork mesh.

In addition to providing corroboration of regional labels, LAGS material often provides evidence that greatly strengthens an entry or even justifies including it at all. In the case of *dago*, for instance, used to refer to a low-lying meadow, *DARE* had only Raven McDavid's record of having collected it in northern Florida, and Gordon Wood's attestations from Oklahoma and Tennessee (one example from each state). Taken together, they formed a minimal but acceptable entry; but the discovery that a central Georgia LAGS informant had also used the word helped confirm not only the continued use of the word, but also its basic regionality.

LAGS information provides similar crucial support for the entries *daresome* 'afraid', *fodder shower* 'light rain', *future* 'resemble', *go-fetch-it* 'Adam's apple', *gritsmill* 'gristmill', *hen turd* or *hen dung tree* 'hackberry', and many others as well. In the case of the entry *hove* v², LAGS provides the sole quotation ('Couldn't hove it—couldn't wait, stay'), and proves that what both the *OED* and the *EDD* label 'Obsolete' was still in existence in central Mississippi when the LAGS intervi w was conducted there in the 1970s.

Not only do LAGS materials contribute substantially to the documentation of entries in *DARE*. Of equal importance, they validate the methods used in collecting data for *DARE*: the smaller-meshed survey corroborates the patterns suggested by the larger scale inventory. In each project, the fieldwork has yielded a tremendous amount of data, much of it valuable oral evidence that rarely finds its way into the print media.

In 'Calvary Camels and the Knockaway Tree', Pederson laments the fact that *knockaway tree*, a folk name for *anaqua* which a LAGS fieldworker had collected in Texas, was not 'flourishing in all our national dictionaries' (1980a:159). I am sure he was pleased five years later to find not only *knockaway*, but also *knackaway* and *nockaway* as variants in the *DARE* entry for *anaqua*. Had the LAGS evidence been available to us then, we would have been delighted to add its confirmation of this folk use. Now that most of the LAGS material *is* available, *DARE* can benefit tremendously from its carefully thought out fieldwork, extensive database of folk language, and innovative processes for manipulation of the data. *DARE*, in turn, can contribute to the fulfillment of Pederson's wish to see not just one, but all of our *'knockaway trees'* flourishing in at least one of our national dictionaries.

NOTES

1. In his preliminary *A Compositional Guide to the LAGS Project*, which was sent to the LAGS project consultants, Pederson explained that 'The legendary [later spelled *legendry*] will bear the essential characteristics of a historical

dictionary, specifically the current supplements to the *OED*. Three basic sets of entries will be ordered in an alphabetized word list: 1) PRIMARY ENTRIES, 2) SECONDARY ENTRIES, and 3) REFERENCE ENTRIES' (1977a:192). The 'primary entries' were to include phonological, grammatical, lexical, and semantic treatments, all of which would describe in detail the data collected through the fieldwork. In retrospect, it is obvious that the scope was much greater than could be accomplished in anything like a reasonable length of time.

2. The Dictionary of American Regional English (DARE) project is located at the University of Wisconsin-Madison. It is supported by grants from the National Endowment for the Humanities (an independent federal agency), the Andrew W. Mellon Foundation, the National Science Foundation, the University of Wisconsin-Madison Graduate School and College of Letters and Sciences, and other foundations and individuals. *DARE* Volume I, edited by Frederic G. Cassidy, containing extensive introductory matter and the letters A–C, was published by the Belknap Press of Harvard University Press in 1985. Volume II, edited by Frederic G. Cassidy and Joan Houston Hall, containing the letters D–H, appeared in 1991. Volume III, I–O, appeared in 1996.

3. The protocols are notebooks based on the tape-recorded interviews and arranged so that line numbers agree with question numbers in the worksheets. The protocols include narrow phonetic notation for the responses to the questions, as well as notes about context, stylistic features, grammatical designations, and other linguistic or paralinguistic features.

4. In cases where more than one part of speech is involved, it is essential that we use the *Concordance*, for the *General Index* lumps homophonous and homographic terms together. As Pederson says in the introduction to the *General Index*, it is a summary, but not a substitute for the *Concordance*.

5. Because the *Concordance* includes responses from all 1,121 of the informants and the *Technical Index* includes only those from the 914 primary informants, the two sources frequently differ in their lexical totals. In cases where *DARE* already has plenty of other information, we find it adequate to cite the less detailed *Technical Index*. In most cases, though, we find it preferable either to use the *General Index* or to go back to the raw data in the *Concordance*.

6. For sections of text which had already been edited when new volumes of *LAGS* became available, it was not always possible to check the LAGS materials.

7. Although we recognize that the cost of transcribing all of the tapes makes the original plan impossible, it is difficult not to lament the loss of all the syntactic information as well as the contextual evidence for the lexical items.

8. Pederson has identified 33 subregions within the Gulf States, which are illustrated by the maps in Volumes 4 (*Regional Matrix*) and 5 (*Regional*

Pattern). (See the essays by Montgomery and McDaniel in this volume for more discussion of the subregions.) For *DARE*, much broader designations must suffice.

9. This method was not without its problems. Even with a carefully framed question, it is possible for a response to fit either as a noun or as an adjective. (The term *high hat*, for instance, can be understood either way in some contexts.) The method required that fieldworkers take copious notes, ask questions, and write explanations of unfamiliar or unusual terms. The results, of course, varied from one fieldworker to the next. And at the present editorial stage, if the field notes were not taken adequately, there is no hope of retrieving the context.

10. Pederson has generously offered to check LAGS tapes for *DARE* in cases where context is essential to understanding; but no theory of editorial economics can justify the time that would take for any but the most crucial of entries.

11. The *DARE* maps are 'distorted' to reflect population density rather than geographical area, though the basic shapes of the states have been retained.

12. The maps in the *Regional Matrix* are based on the responses of the 911 primary informants from the LAGS region. The *DARE* map represents the responses of informants in 1,002 communities throughout the country, 159 of whom were in the region corresponding to that in LAGS.

13. See, for example, Michael Montgomery's 1995 article 'Does Tennessee Have Three "Grand" Dialects?: Evidence from the Linguistic Atlas of the Gulf States' or read the fiction of Peter Taylor for evidence of the belief in differences among the people of the various regions of Tennessee.

Multiple Modals in LAGS and LAMSAS

Michael B. Montgomery

One of the more unusual syntactic patterns in Southern American English (SAE), found apparently in all of its regional and social varieties, is the combination of modal auxiliaries in verb phrases like *might could have done better* and *might not can help*. To date, more than 40 different combinations of modals have been attested in SAE, although most of these are undoubtedly rare. While they have been cited anecdotally in the literature for nearly a century, such 'multiple modals' (MMs)[1] more recently have become profoundly intriguing to both descriptive and theoretical linguists, who have realized that little was known about their 1) syntactic nature, 2) historical source(s), or 3) regional and social variation. As a result, research on MMs has progressed, largely over the past 25 years along these three different dimensions.

No other syntactic patterns in SAE have inspired as much attention from syntacticians as have MMs. Much progress has been made in understanding both their syntax and history—though significant differences between speakers and varieties in the range of MMs permitted have left many questions open for further investigation. However, until quite recently, their regional distribution had been only partially sketched (Atwood 1953:35) and their social distribution no more than suggested.

The present paper shows how data collected by the Linguistic Atlas of the Middle and South Atlantic States (LAMSAS) and especially the Linguistic Atlas of the Gulf States (LAGS) can suggest a a great deal about their variation. The latter project, which interviewed over 1,100 individuals in eight Southern states from 1968 to 1983, affords the sharpest and broadest picture yet of the regional and social usage of MMs. Not only did LAMSAS and LAGS each collect nearly 500 instances of MMs (in LAGS mainly from free conversation), but sufficient personal information on atlas speakers is available to enable researchers to classify them in conventional and unconventional ways in order to explore correlations between the use of MMs (and indeed many other linguistic features) and a variety of social and situational variables.

THE SYNTACTIC DIMENSION

Beginning with Labov et al. 1968 (followed by Butters 1973, Pampell 1975, Coleman 1975, Boertien 1986, Di Paolo 1986, etc.; see Chapter 5, 'Morphology and Syntax', in McMillan and Montgomery 1989 for a complete listing of references through 1988), linguists sought the syntactic implications of the fact that MMs violated the assumed fundamental phrase-structure prohibition against combinations of true modal auxiliaries in English. It was apparent that MMs could not easily be accounted for by current syntactic models. While this implied either that MMs were not combinations of two fully tensed modal auxiliaries (but rather of an adverb and a modal auxiliary) or that syntactic models must be revised to accommodate them in some way, in actuality too little was known about MMs for many years for these concerns to be addressed adequately. Subsequent syntactic research undertook to establish the constituent structure of MMs, their relation to a more abstract level of structure, and the combinatory possibilities of individual modals with one another.

Because of the rarity of all but a few MMs, syntactic studies have normally relied entirely on data from directed elicitations from a small number of carefully selected informants, instead of from conversational interviews or natural observations. Elicitations typically allow an investigator to tap the judgments of native speakers about the relative acceptability of various combinations (as in such word-order permutations as interrogatives, negatives, and so on, in which MMs occur far less often than in affirmative declaratives) rather than to rely on the infrequent examples that occur naturally. Though they are invaluable for exploring infrequently occurring forms, the limitations of elicitations that use decontextualized sentences to seek judgments about grammaticality are problematic; a thorough exposition of all the advantages and disadvantages of syntactic elicitations has yet to be made, so far as this writer is aware.

The quest for the most appropriate theoretical accommodation of MMs is still at issue (Battistella 1990, 1991, 1995 are recent efforts within a Government and Binding framework). Today, as the result of elicitational research and three substantial observational studies in different parts of the South (Feagin 1979 in Alabama, Di Paolo 1986 in Texas, Mishoe and Montgomery 1994 in the Carolinas), there is consensus about much of the syntactic description, if not the analysis, of MMs in SAE:

1) The first modal is usually epistemic *might* or *may*, the second a deontic modal which most often is a historical preterit form (*could*, *would*, *should*, etc.), although *can* frequently occurs in second position as well.

2) Both elicitational and observational studies generally recognize, in descending order, *might could*, *used to could*, *might can*, and *might would* as the most common and most acceptable MMs. *Might could* appears to be common to and most frequent in all varieties of SAE; some speakers accept only this combination.

3) Studies generally agree in how MMs pattern in question formation and negation in SAE. The second modal is the usual candidate for yes-no question inversion (*She might could . . . => Could she might . . .*) and is the only pattern that has been observed by researchers, although Coleman 1975 reports that some speakers in North Carolina accept questions with both modals inverted (*Might could she . . .*), and Boertien 1986 reports the same for some Texas speakers. Questions formed by the traditional English practice of inverting the first auxiliary with the subject (*Might she could*) appear to be unattested and unacceptable.[2] These phenomena lend support to the analysis of the initial modal as being an adverb (Labov et al. 1968, Whitley 1975, Di Paolo 1986), though this view is disputable on other grounds, including negative formation. With regard to the latter, either the first modal (*might not could*), the second modal (*might couldn't*), or even both modals (*might not*

couldn't) occasionally may be followed by the negative element. As illustrated, the negative *not* is usually uncontracted when it occurs after the first modal, but contracted after the second; patterns like *might not could* and *might couldn't* have precisely the same negative scope and acceptability and appear to have more or less equal frequency.

THE HISTORICAL DIMENSION

While research progressed on MMs in Southern American English in the 1970s and 1980s, a complementary literature on MMs arose in another part of the English-speaking world where MMs are known, Scotland and Northern England (e.g. Miller and Brown 1982, MacDonald 1981). Feagin 1979 had first assembled most of the existing, rather disparate evidence on MMs in varieties of English in the British Isles, the West Indies, and the United States, but her data from Scotland were confined to the handful of citations from two historical sources, *Scottish National Dictionary* and *English Dialect Dictionary*. More recently three papers (Fennell 1993, Mishoe and Montgomery 1994, and Montgomery and Nagle 1993) have drawn the Scottish and American strands of research together and, by comparing and contrasting the attested MMs in these two regions of the world where they are most vigorously attested, have shown that a connection between MMs in these distant locations can be convincingly posited. There are both considerable, though by no means complete, syntactic similarity with American MMs on the three counts above (see Montgomery and Nagle 1993 for a syntactic comparison) and a straightforward and sufficiently plausible sociohistorical explanation of their migration from Scotland to Ulster to the American South in the 17th and 18th centuries to presume a historical connection (which is supported by the commonality of other grammatical features; see Montgomery 1991).

On the other hand, the dissimilarities between MMs occurring in Scotland/Northern England and the American South argue for their continuing evolution, probably in both places, after they reached North America in the 18th century. Because a narrower range of MMs has been observed in the British Isles than in the American South, because many observed combinations in SAE were not anticipated by earlier elicitations, and because there exist some differences in negation and question formation, MMs seem to be based on somewhat different syntactic systems in the two places, with the American system having somewhat more flexibility (for further details, see Montgomery and Nagle 1993).

THE VARIATION DIMENSION

Despite these advances, a number of things about the syntactic nature and historical evolution of MMs remain unclear. We know nothing, for instance, about whether MMs relate to other means of expressing multiple modalities in English clauses, such as by adverbs (for example, Are *probably can* and *maybe could* acceptable only to users of MMs? Should they be considered types of MMs?) or by other exponents of modality. Further, the trans-Atlantic case for them cited above is less direct than we would like, on several counts. The inventory of possible combinations hardly represents merely a carryover from Scots (though *might could* is common in Scotland, *will can* and *will no can* are even more so), and despite extensive search of the historical record, MMs are not found in their present-day forms until the latter half of the 18th century (and then only rarely). This is generations after the 17th-century Scottish migration to Ulster, from which province of Ireland at least two-hundred thousand Scotch-Irish (called the Ulster Scots in the British Isles) emigrated to the American Middle and Southern colonies between 1718 and 1775 (Leyburn 1962, Dickson 1988; for further details, see Montgomery and Nagle 1993).

Although this is difficult to confirm with current methods of data gathering, the range of permissible combinations, as well as the very grammaticality of MMs of any type, appears to vary radically between speakers of the same social profile and, as revealed by informal elicitations by this writer, even from siblings raised in the same household. This represents a type of extreme variation rarely, if ever, paralleled by other syntactic phenomena and not easily accounted for syntactically. This variation, as well as the challenge of specifying the precise contexts in which they are most likely to occur, makes it unlikely that we can approach the study of MMs solely as a 'linguistic variable' to determine their social correlates. In short, outstanding issues regarding the syntax and history of MMs are inextricable from an understanding of how they vary from context to context, place to place, and speaker to speaker. This raises the general question: What do we know of their variation?

Research on the regional and social dimensions of MMs has lagged considerably behind syntactic and historical research, in part because it cannot utilize the data gathered by syntacticians (elicitations) or historical linguists (written examples from disparate and unrelated sources). Citations from the historical record are too infrequent and scattered, especially chronologically, to give us insight on these matters. Elicitations may be appropriate for syntactic investigations, happily so if judgments turn out to be consistent across even a small sample of speakers, but they are far too piecemeal to permit generalizations about questions relating to the variation of MMs, such as Who uses them?, Where are they used?, and When are they used? Further, it is doubtful whether elicitations can reveal anything at all about *why* MMs are used. Studies based on observed data have proved more helpful in suggesting the larger social distribution of MMs (Di Paolo 1986, Mishoe and Montgomery 1994) and the pragmatics of their use (Feagin 1979, Dumas 1987, Mishoe and Montgomery 1994). However, a detailed analysis of data from LAGS, because of their unprecedented quantity and the expanse of the project, can tell us more about who uses MMs, where they are used, and to some extent when they are used, than any other source.

THE PRAGMATICS OF MMS

As for *why* MMs are used, which is another way of asking 'What is their most favored context(s)?' or 'What are their pragmatics?', the essay by Mishoe and Montgomery argues that there are several keys to understanding this.

Indirectness is the first key. Syntactically speaking, MMs most often occur in embedded clauses (e.g. 'I was wondering if I *might could* come and talk to you later in the week'; 'I think I *may will* have me a piece of cake'; 'I thought you said we *might could* get some candy?'), which reveals that a speaker chooses a statement or question rather than an explicit imperative (e.g. 'Give me a piece of cake', etc.).

Another key is that MMs nearly always occur in one-on-one interactions, having grammatical subjects in the first person about half the time and in the second person nearly a quarter of the time. MMs are usually employed in face-to-face interactions of certain kinds. For the 189 examples in the Mishoe and Montgomery study for which the information was available,[3] 139 MMs were used in what can best be described as one-on-one negotiations, 114 between family members and friends and 25 between strangers, the latter occurring usually in service encounters ('The only thing I *might would* have like that is an egg-shell mattress'; 'If you like it, I *might can* sell it'). Of the 50 used with more than one other person present, 42 came in a setting with family and friends, as around the supper table or in a group setting by one individual to fellow church members ('One of our goals *might ought to* be to encourage nonmember involvement'; 'Are there any other prayer concerns that you *may would* want to share?') Further evidence of negotiation comes from the variety of hedges, mitigations, and expressions of politeness that co-occur with MMs, in addition to the inherent mitigation which modals express, in the form of such qualifying adverbs as *maybe, maybe + just, possibly + just, probably*, and *even*.

With these characteristics of the social and grammatical contexts of MM use identified, it becomes clear that speakers often employ them in situations of caution and sensitivity, in which they are concerned about the 'face' of both themselves and others (for an extensive discussion of the concepts of 'positive face' and 'negative face', see Brown and Levinson 1978).

Finally, Mishoe and Montgomery argue that understanding the pragmatics of MMs provides a good explanation for the scant citations until a rather recent date (the turn of the 20th century, when dialectologists began systematically observing local language and submitting word-lists to *Dialect Notes*, the early publication of the American Dialect Society). MMs cluster in certain types of interactions (subtle give-and-take negotiations and sensitive face-saving situations in which highly conditional and indirect speech takes place) that are rarely found in the written record of the language, even in the dialogue of the most 'realistic' 20th-century fiction. From this, Mishoe and Montgomery posit similar dynamics for MMs in former periods to account for their nonappearance; in other words, the absence of evidence for them in writing does not constitute evidence of their absence in the language. It is their pragmatic restrictions rather than registral salience or stigma, that most likely militates against their showing up in literature or formal records today and, most likely, in earlier eras as well. MMs may well be a speech-based grammatical feature on which the historical record is silent, because of the nature of the historical record and for principled reasons, not because of the nonexistence of the pattern. They are not unique in this regard.[4]

LINGUISTIC ATLAS INVESTIGATIONS

There can be no doubt about elusive, pragmatically governed structures like multiple modals being highly challenging to study and time-consuming to collect. The Mishoe and Montgomery corpus draws from nearly a decade of observation. Even though we now know a good deal about their pragmatics and though some social information on each user of an MM in the aforementioned corpus is available, the distribution of such speakers is quite skewed, reflecting largely the types of individuals with whom the observers had contact (in this case, middle- and working-class whites in certain localities of North and South Carolina). Such an accumulation of examples can tell us little about the comparative likelihood for different social groups to use MMs or in turn give us insight on their social status. For this a more systematic gathering of data across social categories is desirable. A broader collection across speakers would enable us to examine who uses MMs, when, and where. If there were some way to hold a social context relatively constant for a cross-section of speakers, we might begin to answer such questions.

This is where data from linguistic atlas investigations become potentially indispensable. MMs have been an object of interest for American atlases since the mid-1930s, when Hans Kurath and his associates designed the questionnaire for the Linguistic Atlas of the South Atlantic States,[5] a regional component of the Linguistic Atlas of the United States and Canada that was soon merged with its northern counterpart, the Linguistic Atlas of the Middle Atlantic States. Fieldwork for the combined LAMSAS was conducted largely in 1930s/40s. Subsequently, Allen's (1973-76) Linguistic Atlas of the Upper Midwest (LAUM), with interviews done in the 1950s/60s, and the Linguistic Atlas of the Gulf States (LAGS), conducted from 1968 to 1983, were also concerned with collecting MMs, either by seeking them directly (e.g. having speakers complete a sentence prompt) or by observing speakers using them, in order to discern their regional distribution.[6]

Atlas interviews involved substantial contact, on the average five to six hours, between a trained fieldworker and a speaker from a chosen community, affording considerable opportunity for the fieldworker either to listen for or to seek MMs. The interview situation involved two strangers who more often than not were a generation apart, rather than the type of interaction between familiars or family members cited above as apparently most encouraging MM use, but the roles were constant across the gamut of interviews and presumably afforded some consistency in the type(s) of interaction between the participants. The lengthy interview format also permitted the fieldworker to note a great deal of social and personal information about the individual, and this is preserved in an obligatory account (written by the fieldworker for LAMSAS and LAUM; for LAGS, by a scribe in the editorial office) describing the informant and characterizing the conduct of the interview; these accounts are found in the handbooks to various regional atlases and on the prefatory pages to the field notebooks themselves. In fact, we know far more about atlas informants than those for other American linguistic surveys of any type. Just as important for our purposes, LAGS provides more voluminous natural data on MMs themselves than any other single source, because they were largely observed from conversation rather than being elicited.

The three regional atlases collected the types and tokens of MMs listed in table 1. From these atlas data MMs appear to have, or at least to have had, quite an extensive distribution. However, before examining this more closely, it is important to consider in some detail the nature of linguistic atlas data, especially for LAMSAS and LAGS.

Much has been stated in the sociolinguistic literature over the past 30 years about the nonrepresentativeness of linguistic atlas informants

Table 1. Types and tokens of multiple modals
in three regional atlases

	LAMSAS	LAUM	LAGS
Different Types of MMs	5	1	25
Total Number of MMs	499	7	490
might could	455	7	223[7]
might can	11	0	56
might would	2	0	44
may can	30	0	10
used to could	N/A	N/A	83
Others	1	0	74

Other type in LAMSAS, with frequency: *might will* (1)

Other types in LAGS, with frequencies:

can might (1)	*might should* (1)
could might (1)	*might used to* (1)
could used to (1)	*might will* (2)
may not ought to (1)	*ought to could* (1)
may would (4)	*shouldn't have ought to* (3)
might better (3)	*shouldn't ought to* (6)
might have could have (3)	*shouldn't oughtn't (to)* (1)
might have could (1)	*used to would* (19)
might have used to (3)	*used to wouldn't* (12)
might have would have (2)	*would might* (1)
might ought to (6)	*would use to* (1)

(see Montgomery 1993:264ff. for a synopsis and evaluation of this discussion). European atlases, as well as earlier American ones such as those for New England and the Middle and South Atlantic States, concentrated on interviewing so-called NORMs (non-mobile, older, rural males; see Chambers and Trudgill 1980:33–35), data from whom were collected primarily for historical purposes, such as to suggest a general picture of variation of an earlier time and to provide points of comparison for later investigators. Most atlas workers have been quite explicit in acknowledging the limitations of atlas data for drawing hard-and-fast conclusions, although the temptation to make social general-izations from them has often not been resisted by non-atlas researchers and, it must be admitted, by some atlas personnel as well. Although unqualified and incautious statements of the form 'feature x is used in area y but not in area z' or 'feature x is used by lower-class speakers but not upper-class ones', which are based on atlas material collected from older individuals a half-century ago, are still encountered in the literature, citing evidence from earlier atlases as synchronic is not appropriate.[8] For MMs in LAGS this appears to be far less of a problem, at least for the present day, given the recentness of their collection and the fact that they appear as likely to be used by younger speakers as older ones, but it must always be borne in mind that atlas data at best provide a broad and tentative, rather than a definitive, outline of usage.

Among the three aforementioned regional atlases, data from LAGS are the most interesting and the most valuable for three principal rea-sons. First, LAGS interviewed a far wider social spread of speakers; these approximated in some respects the demography of the region and are unprecedented in linguistic atlas work. More than a fifth of primary informants were blacks: 197/914 (21.6%). Nearly half were women (423/914, 46.3%, compared to 30.7% for LAMSAS, for instance), and the imbalance toward older individuals was not nearly so extreme as for previous atlases. More than half of the primary informants were classified as middle class (514/914, 56.2%), slightly less than a third (295/914, 32.3%) as lower class, and a ninth (105/914, 11.5%) as upper class. Of the primary informants, 63.7% (582/914) were over 60 years old, 24.5% were between 31 and 60, and 11.8% were 30 or younger. Since previous projects had interviewed few speakers under 60, the far greater variety of LAGS speakers, especially across age groups, prom-ises a fuller, more satisfying, and probably more reliable view of the social distribution of MMs as of the 1970s. The relative recentness of LAGS data offers to help us see whether MMs represent a Southern linguistic shibboleth whose currency may index the distinctiveness of the region's speech. If they are used by younger Southerners as much as older ones, this argues for the continuing integrity of SAE. That MMs have been cited as a marker of Southern speech can be easily attested,[9] but does this match reality?

Second, LAGS collected far more syntactic data than previous atlases, and these came largely from conversational segments, sometimes extensive, of interviews. Most MMs gathered by LAGS have the status of naturally occurring forms whose full syntactic contexts are cited in both the LAGS protocols and the LAGS *Concordance*. The taping of all interviews, which produced more than five thousand hours of recordings, allowed informants to use them spontaneously and freed fieldworkers from the inherent difficulty of framing a prompt to elicit an MM.

By contrast with LAGS, LAMSAS did not record interviews, except for a few of the very latest ones, and therefore could not rely on having conversational data from which to extract data such as grammatical patterns from a tape later on. Because LAMSAS required fieldworkers to transcribe material on the spot, its citations of MMs exist as bare forms with no larger syntactic context. LAMSAS did collect slightly more MMs (499 to 490 for LAGS), but these normally came from either a sentence-completion prompt or a direct query about usage,[10] and LAMSAS fieldworkers added the special code 'c' (= conversational) to forms that arose in conversation rather than being directly solicited. In this regard, one must carefully distinguish the practices of the two principal fieldworkers for LAMSAS, Guy S. Lowman and Raven I. McDavid, Jr. The latter far more often relied on conversation in his interviews than the former. The *Handbook of the Linguistic Atlas of the Middle and South Atlantic States* offers a succinct contrast (Kretzschmar et al. 1994:126):

> [Lowman] was a meticulous observer of fine phonetic distinctions, notably in vowels and the quality of /r/ . . . He observed fewer lexical variants than some other investigators, paid less attention to word meanings, and recorded relatively few forms from free conversation. Working very fast, he suggested rather frequently.
>
> . . . When [McDavid] could not get a natural response, he would often leave the item blank; on the other hand, he recorded a very large number of conversational responses, especially for grammatical forms.

A comparison of the MM data these two men collected is telling. Of the 95 MMs McDavid gathered in South Carolina, 36 were labeled as conversational. Of Lowman's 138 in North Carolina, only five were; of his 106 in Virginia, none were. In one stretch of 46 interviews in North Carolina, Lowman transcribed *might could* for 43 speakers, a uniformity of response that can be explained only as suggested forms. This fact does not invalidate LAMSAS data nor argue that Lowman's informants were insincere or ingenuous, but it does mean that we can probably conclude little more than that these speakers were familiar with the usage. It is doubtful that we can assume that they distinguished their own usage from that found in their communities. Lowman's primary interest, as indicated in the handbook sketch, was vocalic phonology. It must also be pointed out that worksheet item 58.7 for both LAMSAS and LAGS was designed to collect at least three different things: multiple modals, the phonetic form of /aɪ/ in *might*, and variation between *might* and *mought*, the latter an old-fashioned form of the modal (Lowman records *mought* half as often as *might* in North Carolina and Virginia).

LAGS for the most part avoided investigating MMs directly, but they often arose in conversation. Fieldworker reports indicate that speakers most often used a MM after the interview was completed and the fieldworker was negotiating his/her departure and the possibility of returning or making other contacts. One fieldworker, Guy Bailey (personal communication), indicates that he often left the recorder running deliberately until the very last moment (i.e. as long as possible after formal questioning was done) in order to record this negotiation.[11] In any case, inclusion of complete sentential contexts in the LAGS *Concordance* reveals that LAGS MM data come from free-conversational segments of interviews. This both increases their validity and opens a number of possibilities for syntactic and other analysis of these data. A preliminary assessment of them indicates close conformity to the syntactic profile, as discussed in section one, known to characterize MMs generally. For example, by far the most common MM in LAGS is *might could*, and ten of the eleven negated MMs with initial *might* or *may* have either *not* after the first modal or *n't* after the second. On a number of bases then we can therefore argue the validity of MMs in LAGS as representing naturally occurring data.

Third, as a further consequence of recording all interviews, LAGS collected 25 different combinations (31 if negative patterns are counted separately), as compared to five (no negatives) by LAMSAS and one by

LAUM. The variety of MMs collected by LAMSAS is not surprising; these are almost precisely those listed in the LAMSAS worksheets as the patterns for which fieldworkers were to take note or about which they could inquire (these most likely only began to suggest the range of combinations actually existing):

[58.7]   I might could (do it   /future? past?/
           *might, mout, may can, might can, may could
                         (Davis, McDavid, and McDavid 1969:58)

For LAUM, only limited information on the item is available, because Allen (1975:46) indicates that it was 'added to the [Upper Midwest] worksheets near the end of the Minnesota fieldwork . . . to ascertain the spread of *might could*, which in the East occurs in the South and South Midland and also in the Pennsylvania German part of central Pennsylvania'.

Perhaps it will be useful to synopsize our qualitative assessment of LAGS data with reference to MMs. Researchers must always be careful to describe exactly what types of data are to be found in linguistic atlases and to be cognizant of the type of sample they are drawn from—one that is deliberately skewed toward older speakers who are chosen according to the judgment of the fieldworker to fit predetermined categories. Atlas data can be used for only descriptive, rather than inferential statistical comparisons; that is, to make statements about the LAGS sample rather than any larger population. Since atlas interviews took place between strangers, as a rule they were not uninhibited. There is probably not a complete correspondence between the proportion of speakers using a form during interviews and the proportion actually using MMs. This pertains not only to linguistic features having social stigma or salience; prime opportunities for occurrence of many forms may not have arisen.

For MMs, LAGS data can tell us only certain things. They cannot indicate definitively whether any given speaker does or does not use MMs unless we know that they were asked item 58.7 (and then we must trust speakers' self-reports on their usage as reliable), or that they had every opportunity to use a MM. Heavily constrained, as outlined earlier, by the interpersonal pragmatics of the situation, MMs thus differ from other features sought by atlases such as post-vocalic *r* or the choice of relative pronouns. Consequently, it is doubtful that atlas data can more than give us an outline of the prevalence and distribution of MMs, and it is inappropriate to employ atlas MM data to make inferential statistical statements about their increase or decrease for the South in general, or for any subregion thereof (as, for example, Tillery and Bailey 1990 have done).

REGIONAL DISTRIBUTION OF MMS IN LAMSAS

Other than scattered anecdotal mention in the literature (Carr 1905:87, Payne 1909:349, Kroll 1925:45, etc.), the earliest discussion of MMs, and certainly the first attempt to offer a general statement about them, is found in Atwood's *A Survey of Verb Forms in the Eastern United States* (1953:35), which used the unpublished field notebooks for LAMSAS. Atwood summarizes the geographical range of *might could* in the Atlantic states, calling MMs primarily a Southern and South Midland pattern and speculating about the reason for its occurrence into southern Pennsylvania:

> The phrase *might could*, in the context 'I (might could) do it (future)', is recorded . . . in the M. A. S. [Middle Atlantic States] and the S. A. S. [South Atlantic States].
> The isogloss of this form is peculiar in that it not only indicates a typical South and South Midland form, but shows the form to be current in the German area of Pa. as well.
> . . . Type I informants offer this form with hardly any exceptions, and it is also used by from two thirds (Va.) to practically all (N.C.) of Type II informants as well. Cultured informants as a rule avoid the construction; there are very few instances of it in this type. (Atwood 1953:35)

A close examination of Atwood's map (1953:figure 31) and an analysis of LAMSAS Pennsylvania informants indicate that he was most likely mistaken: *might could* occurred not only in the core German area of southeastern Pennsylvania around Lancaster County but also farther north and west of this, as well as in two pockets of southwestern Pennsylvania. These areas were heavily settled by Scotch-Irish emigrants from Ulster in the 18th century. In the LAMSAS field records, 21 Pennsylvania speakers are reported to use *might could*. While eight of these are cited as having German ancestry, six had Scotch-Irish ancestors, and four had both Scotch-Irish and German foreparents; the ancestry of four speakers was not cited (McDavid, Kretzschmar, and Hankins 1982–86). Not only is the geographical distribution closely consistent with the settlement of the Scotch-Irish, but language contact between them and Pennsylvania Germans has been demonstrated on a number of counts, with the latter preserving lexical and phonological archaisms from Ulster (Reed 1953). In any case, the suggestion of a German source for MMs cannot be supported by what is known of Pennsylvania German, which has not yielded evidence of such a construction (Marion L. Huffines, personal communication). Moreover, positing a Scotch-Irish origin of MMs provides an account of their spread from Pennsylvania into the South Atlantic states that is both unified and consistent with settlement history.

Table 2 provides a state-by-state breakdown of MMs in the Middle and South Atlantic States, as collected by LAMSAS. Since LAMSAS was largely conducted in the 1930s and 1940s, this table indicates that among predominantly older speakers two generations ago MMs occurred as far north as southern New Jersey, though there was far greater evidence of them in the Southern and South Midland regions. This distribution probably reflects greater frequency and social spread of use, as well as fieldworker practice to investigate them more regularly farther south. From LAMSAS evidence and the variety of other citations of MMs in the literature, we would expect them to be found throughout the LAGS territory.

THE REGIONAL DISTRIBUTION OF MMS IN LAGS

In geographical terms MMs are distributed more or less evenly throughout the LAGS data, as seen in table 3, which presents their frequency in each of the 16 sectors of the eight-state region surveyed by the project, and in table 4, which shows the number of different combinations occurring in each sector (since different numbers of speakers were interviewed in each sector, the figures in table 3 cannot

Table 2. Multiple modals in the middle and south Atlantic states
(n = number of speakers interviewed)

	might could	might can	might would	may can	might will
New Jersey (n = 47)	3	0	0	0	0
Pennsylvania (n = 158)	21	0	0	0	0
West Virginia (n = 111)	4	0	0	0	0
Ohio (n = 9)	1	0	0	0	0
Kentucky (n = 17)	9	0	0	0	0
Delaware (n = 14)	4	0	0	0	0
Maryland (n = 59)	31	1	0	1	0
Dist. of Col. (n = 2)	0	0	0	0	0
Virginia (n = 147)	95	4	0	7	0
N. Carolina (n = 150)	130	0	0	8	0
S. Carolina (n = 144)	87	1	0	7	0
Georgia (n = 98)	65	5	2	6	1
Florida (n = 9)	5	0	0	1	0
TOTALS	455	11	2	30	1

be compared directly). In the data, MMs occurred most often in Lower Georgia (61 tokens) and slightly more often in the lower half of the South than in the upper half, according to *LAGS Volume Five: Regional Pattern* (Pederson, McDaniel, and Adams 1991:6). Still, if we examine the number of different combinations in each of the 16 LAGS sectors, MMs hardly appear to occur very disproportionately in any one part of the region.

Table 3. Incidence of multiple modal tokens by LAGS sector (n = 490)[12]

Arkansas	West Tenn	Middle Tenn	East Tenn
38	8	15	29
West Louis	Upper Missi	Upper Ala	Upper Georgia
44	24	17	49
Upper Texas	Lower Missi	Lower Ala	Lower Georgia
46	41	29	61
Lower Texas	Gulf Miss/East Louis	Gulf Ala/West Flor	East Florida
15	32	16	26

Table 4. Incidence of multiple modal types by LAGS sector

Arkansas	West Tenn	Middle Tenn	East Tenn
11	7	5	12
West Louis	Upper Missi	Upper Ala	Upper Georgia
11	12	7	14
Upper Texas	Lower Missi	Lower Ala	Lower Georgia
14	10	9	12
Lower Texas	Gulf Miss/East Louis	Gulf Ala/West Flor	East Florida
7	8	6	8

A visual impression of the distribution of the four most common MMs is provided by figures 1–4, which display on computer-generated maps of the region the geographical distribution of these forms. (For more on the computerized research capabilities of LAGS, see Montgomery, 'Treasury', this volume.) The map for *might could* in particular suggests the greater tendency, as stated above, for MMs to occur in the Lower South.

Figure 1. LagsMap for *might could*

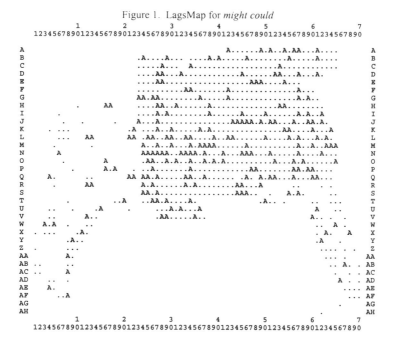

Figure 2. LagsMap for *might can*

```
                1         2         3         4         5         6         7
        1234567890123456789012345678901234567890123456789012345678901234567890
A                                                   ...................A.            A
B                             ............  ..........................A....         B
C                             ...........  .........................              C
D                             ..........      .A.....................              D
E                             ...........  ....................              E
F                             ...........  ...............A.....A           F
G                             ......A...  ....................              G
H               .        ..   ...........  .........A.........              H
I                             .............AA.............A..........       I
J                    .    .       .   A .........................A.         J
K         . .A.            AA .....A...A.......A.A.AA.AA         K
L         ...    ..        ..................A...A.            L
M          .        .      .........................A..A         M
N                             ...................................A..         N
O               .        .    ...A....A.A.......A.A........A...         O
P                        ...  .A.....................A.........         P
Q         ..        ..        ....A.A.A.......A.........A.         Q
R          .        ..        ..................  ...  ..         R
S                             ........AA.......       .         T
T               .        ...  ............         .A.  ...         T
U         ..    ..    ..       ...........         ..  .         U
V         ..        ..A        ...A..A....         ..  .         V
W         A..    ..                    A.  .         W
X         . ...    ...                 .  . .         X
Y                 ...A                  .  .         Y
Z         .        ...                 .....  .         Z
AA                 ..                    ...  .         AA
AB        ..        .                    .. A. .         AB
AC        ..        .                    . . . AC
AD        ..    .                    . . . AD
AE        ..                        .... AE
AF         ...                       ... AF
AG                                    .         AG
AH                                               .          AH
                1         2         3         4         5         6         7
        1234567890123456789012345678901234567890123456789012345678901234567890
```

Figure 3. LagsMap for *might would*

```
                1         2         3         4         5         6         7
        1234567890123456789012345678901234567890123456789012345678901234567890
A                                              ...................         A
B                 ........A. .......................A.A....         B
C                 ..........  ......................         C
D                 ..........  ......................         D
E                 ..........  ...A..................         E
F                 .........A.....................         F
G                 ....A.A............................A         G
H          .    ..  ...........  ......................         H
I                 ...........  ......................         I
J          .    .        .     ...........A...         J
K         . .A.          ..................AA....         K
L         ...    .        ...A....A..A...A.......         L
M          .        .     ........A.........         M
N          .            A....A.A...A........A..AA....         N
O          .        .     ...........A.........         O
P                        ...  .A...............A........AA...         P
Q         ..        ..        ....A.................         Q
R          .        ..        .........A...........         R
S                             ........A.......A....   ...A  ..         S
T               .        ...  ...........         ....  .A  ...         T
U         ..    ..    ..       .A........         ...  .         U
V                 ..           ...........         ...  .         V
W         A..    . A.                    .. A         W
X         . ...    ...                 ...  .         X
Y                 ....                  ...  .         Y
Z         .        ...                 .....  .         Z
AA                 ..                    ...  .         AA
AB        ..        ..                    .. ... . AB
AC        ..        .                    . ... . AC
AD        ..    .                    . . . AD
AE        ..                        .... AE
AF         ...                       ... AF
AG                                    .         AG
AH                                               .          AH
                1         2         3         4         5         6         7
        1234567890123456789012345678901234567890123456789012345678901234567890
```

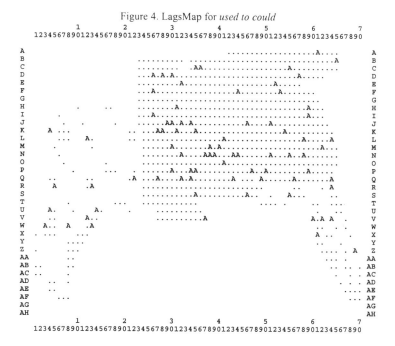

Figure 4. LagsMap for *used to could*

THE SOCIAL DISTRIBUTION OF MMS IN LAGS

As mentioned above, the linguistic atlas interview normally involved gathering a great deal of personal information about each speaker, which in the form of a biographical sketch combined with a synopsis of the interview prefaces each field record (worksheets with transcriptions) and is published if the given regional atlas has a handbook. These accounts, along with their associated community sketches, comprise the bulk of the LAGS *Handbook* (Pederson et al. 1986:81–280), as well as the handbook for LAMSAS (Kretzschmar et al. 1994:165–448). Much of the personal information represents or is reported in terms of standard sociological categories (age, sex, social class, race, size of town/community of residence, level of education, occupational history, ancestry of parents, religious affiliation, etc.). Other information is not so conventional: the length of the interview, the approximate amount of travel, and the reading habits of the speaker, for instance.

Perhaps most interesting is the detailed characterization of the interview, written by the LAGS scribe, noting whether the informant was cooperative, self-conscious, etc., and other points of interest, such as the amount of free conversation. Since every linguistic interview is a unique social encounter between individuals, the *LAGS Handbook* explicitly indicates the general success of each one and the idiosyncrasies and sensibilities of the informant. These accounts make interesting, sometimes humorous reading and remind us of the very personal side to linguistic fieldwork. Since the sketches also identify the fieldworker and the scribe for each interview, researchers can evaluate and compare the strengths and weaknesses of LAGS workers for themselves.

The LAGS informant sketches thus permit classification of speakers in a number of unconventional ways, especially in terms of the interview situation. In the following analysis, the correlation of MMs with five social and three situational variables is examined. These are, respectively, sex, race, social class, decade of birth, level of education, self-consciousness about speech, sex of the interviewer, and length of interview (in hours). For the first two social variables (sex and race of informant), what is far more noteworthy than anything else is the evenness of distribution. The figures are shown in table 5a for *might could*, in table 5b for MMs in general, and in table 6 for the four most frequently occurring combinations.

Table 5a. LAGS speakers using *might could*
by sex, social class, and race

	Female		Male		All Speakers	
	n	%	n	%	n	%
White	76/391	19	90/484	19	166/875	19
Black	24/134	18	22/112	20	46/246	19
TOTAL	100/525	19	112/596	19	212/1121	19
Lower Class	37/160	23	46/193	24	83/353	24
Middle Class	57/299	9	61/340	18	118/639	18
Upper Class	6/65	9	5/61	8	11/126	9
Unassigned	0/1	0	0/2	0	0/3	0
TOTAL	100/525	19	112/596	19	212/1121	19

Table 5b. LAGS speakers using at least one multiple modal
by sex, social class, and race

	Female		Male		All Speakers	
	n	%	n	%	n	%
White	100/391	26	131/484	27	231/875	26
Black	36/134	27	39/112	35	75/246	30
TOTAL	136/525	26	170/596	29	306/1121	27
Lower Class	50/160	31	70/193	36	120/353	34
Middle Class	76/299	25	88/340	26	164/639	26
Upper Class	10/65	15	12/61	20	22/126	17
Unassigned	0/1	0	0/2	0	0/3	0
TOTAL	136/525	26	170/596	29	306/1121	27

Table 6. Incidence of four multiple modals in LAGS
by sex, social class, and race

	Men n = 596		Women n = 525		LowCla n = 353		MidCla n = 639		UpClass n = 126		White n = 875		Black n = 246	
	n	%	n	%	n	%	n	%	n	%	n	%	n	%
Might can	37	6	19	4	24	7	31	5	1	1	41	5	15	6
Might could	112	19	100	19	83	24	118	18	11	9	166	19	46	19
Might would	21	4	23	4	22	6	20	3	2	2	22	3	22	9
Used to could	46	8	37	7	39	11	41	6	3	2	58	7	25	10

Nineteen percent of both white females and white males used *might could*; for black females and males, the figures are 18 and 20 percent. Table 5b shows that for three of these four groups, 26 or 27 percent of those interviewed used at least one MM, while a somewhat higher proportion of black men used at least one MM (35 percent). From this general view of MMs, they appear to be common in the speech of both blacks and whites; table 6 indicates that black informants for LAGS were three times as likely to use *might would* as whites were (9% to 3%), but the other three combinations show near even occurrence across racial groups.

The figures for social class, in the same tables, show a sharper distinction, however. Both women and men display a negative progression from lower class to upper class for both *might could* and all modal combinations (and table 6 shows this same pattern to characterize the usage of *might can*, *might would*, and *used to could*). Lower-class speakers in general were twice as likely (34%) to use an MM as upper-class speakers were (17%); for *might could* the differentiation was sharper (24% to 9%). The obvious implication of this might be that MMs are socially salient and tend to be avoided by members of the upper class, though the relative closeness of percentages for lower and middle classes, especially for *might could*, might suggest otherwise, since middle-class speakers would presumably tend to avoid socially marked linguistic forms as well.

The apparent cleavage between classes is something of a puzzle, despite the statement by Atwood cited earlier that 'cultured informants as a rule avoid the construction', because all other studies have noted that MMs lack social stigma. The earliest statement, from Harry H. Kroll (1925:45) in *A Comparative Study of Upper and Lower Southern Folk Speech*, pertains to *might could* in the South in general: 'This form of the double potential is more or less general, and seems confined to no particular class. It is heard from the mouths of illiterates and graduate students in college'.

Neither Feagin nor Di Paolo found much, if any, social evaluation attached to MMs in Alabama or Texas. Feagin reported that 'the use of double modals has no social evaluation in Anniston. Both school and society ignore them. Most Southerners are not conscious of using them at all' (1979:158). Of the 102 MMs that she observed, 40 were used by upper- or upper-middle-class speakers, 13 by the lower-middle class, 28 by the working-class, and 21 by rural individuals. While these figures probably reflect the nature of Feagin's social contacts as an upper-middle-class speaker herself, they also indicate that such speakers are entirely comfortable with and often do use an MM with another person perceived to be on the same social level. This may provide an explanation for the fact that upper-class LAGS speakers used MMs considerably less often than others. That is, since fieldworkers doubtless were usually members of the middle-class, upper-class informants may have been reticent to engage in the kind of sensitive and deferential give-and-take interactions in which MMs most often occur. This is a reasonable hypothesis, but not one that can be investigated with LAGS data; having individuals with different social profiles interview the same person is one way it could be studied.

From tables 7a and 7b we can consider what the LAGS data may suggest with respect to MMs increasing or decreasing in currency. These tables classify speakers by the decade of their birth, rather than by their age, since they were interviewed over a period of more than a decade. It seems more appropriate to group a 55-year-old person recorded in 1970 with a 65-year-old recorded in 1980 than with a 55-year-old individual interviewed in 1980.

The figures show a fairly even proportion of usage by speakers born from the 1870s through the 1910s, but then a doubling of the proportion of speakers born in the next two decades, for both *might could* and MMs in general. We might be tempted to interpret this as a type of change in progress, even if speakers born in subsequent decades did not appear to bear this out. This would be a strong claim, however, and because of the nature of the data on MMs that LAGS gathered, certainly not supportable by LAGS data alone; the caveat articulated earlier about the reliability of LAGS interviews for telling us that a given speaker uses MMs must be recalled.

If we look at MMs in LAGS in terms of the educational attainment of their users (tables 8a and 8b), we find a fairly even spread across the different levels of education. There appears to be no reason from LAGS to believe that MM use varies inversely with an individual's years of schooling. No less than 13 percent of the speakers at any grade level used *might could* during their interview, and 17 percent of speakers with two or more years of tertiary education (those classified as 'college') used *might could*. The grade-level differential is similar for use of at least one MM.

More than with any other variable, however, one must be cautious in comparing LAGS speakers according to their years of education; this represents an inconstant variable in ways that give comparison across age groups questionable validity. That is, an eighth-grade education in 1900 was undoubtedly quite different from the same 'level' of schooling in 1950; LAGS speakers who were educated at the turn of the century often attended school only three months a year, in contrast to nine months by the 1930s.

Table 7a. LAGS speakers using *might could*
by decade of birth

	Female		Male		All Speakers	
	n	%	n	%	n	%
1870s	1/6	17	0/1	0	1/7	14
1880s	9/28	32	8/48	17	17/76	22
1890s	24/124	19	23/142	16	47/266	18
1900s	19/119	16	28/162	17	47/281	17
1910s	7/80	9	16/87	18	23/167	14
1920s	15/54	28	13/48	27	28/102	27
1930s	12/32	38	6/32	19	18/64	28
1940s	4/30	13	7/30	23	11/60	18
1950s	9/37	24	10/37	27	19/74	26
1960s	0/15	0	1/9	11	1/24	4
TOTAL	100/525	19	112/596	19	212/1121	19

Table 7b. LAGS speakers using at least one multiple modal
by decade of birth

	Female		Male		All Speakers	
	n	%	n	%	n	%
1870s	2/6	33	0/1	0	2/7	29
1880s	9/28	32	10/48	21	19/76	25
1890s	29/124	23	35/142	25	64/266	24
1900s	28/119	24	45/162	28	73/281	26
1910s	10/80	12	27/87	31	37/167	22
1920s	23/54	43	21/48	44	44/102	43
1930s	18/32	56	11/32	34	29/64	45
1940s	5/30	17	8/30	27	13/60	22
1950s	12/37	32	11/37	30	23/74	31
1960s	0/15	0	2/9	22	2/24	8
TOTAL	136/525	26	170/596	29	306/1121	27

Table 8a. LAGS speakers using *might could*
by level of education

	Female		Male		All Speakers	
	n	%	n	%	n	%
None	0/3	0	2/6	33	2/9	22
3rd Grade	8/38	21	14/57	25	22/95	23
4th Grade	3/18	17	9/35	26	12/53	23
5th Grade	4/18	22	4/26	15	8/44	18
6th Grade	7/28	25	5/42	12	12/70	17
7th Grade	8/23	35	5/31	16	13/54	24
8th Grade	14/47	30	16/82	20	30/129	23
9th Grade	4/30	13	4/31	13	8/61	13
10th Grade	5/23	22	7/31	23	12/54	22
11th Grade	21/142	14	23/119	19	44/261	17
12th Grade	14/70	20	8/64	12	22/134	16
College	12/85	14	15/72	21	27/157	17
TOTAL	100/525	19	112/596	19	212/1121	19

Table 8b. LAGS speakers using at least one multiple modal
by level of education

	Female		Male		All Speakers	
	n	%	n	%	n	%
None	0/3	0	2/6	33	2/9	22
3rd Grade	11/38	29	18/57	32	29/95	31
4th Grade	4/18	22	15/35	43	19/53	36
5th Grade	5/18	28	6/26	23	11/44	25
6th Grade	8/28	29	8/42	19	16/70	23
7th Grade	9/23	39	10/31	32	19/54	35
8th Grade	16/47	34	25/82	30	41/129	32
9th Grade	9/30	30	6/31	19	15/61	25
10th Grade	8/23	35	10/31	32	18/54	33
11th Grade	30/142	21	40/119	34	70/261	27
12th Grade	19/70	27	12/64	19	31/134	23
College	17/85	20	18/72	25	35/157	22
TOTAL	136/525	26	170/596	29	306/1121	27

The information routinely provided in the LAGS *Handbook* synopses allows us to obtain a general sense of how at ease and aware of language each speaker was during the course of the interview. Altogether nearly a fifth (215) of all LAGS primary and secondary informants are described in a manner that justifies our classifying them as 'self-conscious' about their speech. For instance, informant 20, a middle-class white man from Cosby, Tennessee, born in 1900, is characterized as 'very careful with certain pronunciations'; informant 164, a middle-class white woman from Savannah, Georgia, born in 1956, as 'self-conscious about grammatical items'; and speaker 778, an upper-class white woman from Shreveport, Louisiana, born in 1896, as 'very conscious of correct speech'. (The fact that these characterizations were written by the small number of LAGS scribes in the editorial office who transcribed the recordings lends a good deal of consistency to them.)

If MMs have some social salience, as is implied by what was seen in tables 5a/5b (that a lower proportion of upper class appear to use them than other speakers), we would expect to find that self-conscious individuals use them less often. However, table 9a and 9b show that this apparently is not true, and it comes as something of a surprise that the trend goes in the opposite direction: both women and men who were self-conscious about their speech or concerned about their grammar and pronunciation use *might could* more often that those who were not. The same is true for MMs in general (table 9b), although for men this does not hold.

While the proportion of self-conscious speakers who use *might could* or MMS is not significantly greater than the proportion of those who do not, this result does argue against MMs having any detectable social markedness and for situational pragmatics having a stronger role in governing the use of MMs than speaker awareness of them.

If the results in tables 9a and 9b represent a surprise, the patterning of data according to the sex of the interviewer is perhaps the most striking of all. For both men and women and for both *might could* and MMs in general, speakers were nearly twice as likely to use an MM when being interviewed by a female, as seen in tables 10a and 10b.[13] This pattern is clearer and more consistent than for any other variable examined in this study; though not shown here in tabular form, the two-to-one ratio holds for other social categories of the speaker as well,

Table 9a. LAGS speakers using *might could*
by self-consciousness about speech

	Female		Male		All Speakers	
	n	%	n	%	n	%
Not self-conscious	69/387	18	96/519	18	165/906	18
Self-conscious	31/138	22	16/77	21	47/215	22
TOTAL	100/525	19	112/596	19	212/1121	19

Table 9b. LAGS speakers using at least one multiple modal
by self-consciousness about speech

	Female		Male		All Speakers	
	n	%	n	%	n	%
Not self-conscious	94/387	24	150/519	29	244/906	27
Self-conscious	42/138	30	20/77	26	62/215	29
TOTAL	136/525	26	170/596	29	306/1121	27

including race and social class. If MMs occur in LAGS interviews in the kinds of social transactions outlined earlier in our discussion, these figures indicate that both men and women are more sensitive to the face of women they are speaking with than to that of men. In other words, they are more polite. Perhaps this is hardly a surprise, but to find supporting quantitative evidence across such a broad territory for over a thousand speakers enables us to state it with some authority. In addition, it gives our intuitions about what choices speakers make in interactions a satisfying confirmation.

Table 10a. LAGS speakers using *might could*
by sex of interviewer

	Female		Male		All Speakers	
	n	%	n	%	n	%
Male Interviewer	24/199	12	46/327	14	70/526	13
Fem. Interviewer	75/322	23	64/263	24	139/585	24
Undetermined	1/4	25	2/6	33	3/10	30
TOTAL	100/525	19	112/596	19	212/1121	19

Table 10b. LAGS speakers using at least one multiple modal
by sex of interviewer

	Female		Male		All Speakers	
	n	%	n	%	n	%
Male Interviewer	33/199	17	75/327	23	108/526	21
Fem. Interviewer	101/322	31	93/263	35	194/585	33
Undetermined	2/4	50	2/6	33	4/10	40
TOTAL	136/525	26	170/596	29	306/1121	27

Finally it is important to examine the distribution of *might could* and MMs according to the length of LAGS interviews, as displayed in tables 11a and 11b. It would be reasonable to expect that grammatical forms like MMs, since they were often collected from the free conversation segments of interviews, were more likely to occur the longer the interview—that the opportunity to use an MM thereby increased. At the very least, the possibility of this must be discounted if we wish to consider the data in tables 5–10 to be meaningful. As we can see in tables 11a and 11b, however, the length of interview has very little correlation with the use of MMs. Twenty percent of speakers inter-viewed from 3:30–4:29 (three-and-one-half to four-and-one-half hours)

Table 11a. LAGS speakers using *might could*
by length of interview (in hours)

	Female		Male		All Speakers	
	n	%	n	%	n	%
0–1:29	3/17	18	3/35	9	6/52	12
1:30–2:29	5/47	11	7/65	11	12/112	11
2:30–3:29	10/81	12	3/66	5	13/147	9
3:30–4:29	18/98	18	23/108	21	41/206	20
4:30–5:29	27/114	24	24/102	24	51/216	24
5:30–6:29	23/91	25	23/99	23	46/190	24
6:30–7:29	3/34	9	14/52	27	17/86	20
7:30–8:29	9/29	31	8/38	21	17/67	25
8:30+	2/14	14	7/31	23	9/45	20
TOTAL	100/525	19	112/596	19	212/1121	19

Table 11b. LAGS speakers using at least one multiple modal
by length of interview (in hours)

	Female		Male		All Speakers	
	n	%	n	%	n	%
0–1:29	6/17	35	7/35	20	13/52	25
1:30–2:29	7/47	15	12/65	18	19/112	17
2:30–3:29	12/81	15	4/66	6	16/147	11
3:30–4:29	27/98	28	29/108	27	56/206	27
4:30–5:29	36/114	32	38/102	37	74/216	34
5:30–6:29	29/91	32	33/99	33	62/190	33
6:30–7:29	6/34	18	21/52	40	27/86	31
7:30–8:29	10/29	34	13/38	34	23/67	34
8:30+	3/14	21	13/31	42	16/45	36
TOTAL	136/525	26	170/596	29	306/1121	27

used *might could*, as did those interviewed for eight and a half hours or more. Twenty-five percent of those whose interviews were less than an hour-and-a-half[14] used an MM, which is virtually the same as for speakers altogether. MMs were collected in many of the shortest interviews.

CONCLUSION

This paper has had three purposes: 1) to show the richness of linguistic atlas data on multiple modals, 2) to demonstrate how these data can be analyzed in terms of social and situational variables, and 3) to add to our general knowledge about multiple modals.

If part of the quest of sociolinguistics is to discover the strongest correlates between linguistic phenomena and social categories and to see how these correlates make sense in terms of our knowledge of how humans relate to one another as social beings and in terms of general sociolinguistic theory, LAGS data in particular are strategic in confirming that MMs are best described as an interactional linguistic feature.

It would be reasonable to expect epistemic modal verbs like *might* and *may* to occur more frequently in situations in which speakers are tentative about making a proposition or careful not to offend or to overstep their privileges; multiple modals, which almost always have one of these epistemics as their initial element, would seem to be structures tailor-made for such uses. If the sex of the interviewer is the social variable which correlates most strongly and consistently with MM use, this indicates that speakers, more than anything about who they are themselves, are aware of their interlocutor and make linguistic adjustments based on who that person is. As social beings who shift and adjust our speech every day according to our audiences and tasks, this comes as no surprise. But it is welcome to find confirmation of this, as this paper shows, even from a linguistic atlas project whose primary aim was to collect speech from older speakers to use as a historical baseline for future study.

NOTES

1. In this paper 'multiple modal' is used in preference to the more common term 'double modal' for two reasons: combinations of three modals have occasionally been observed (e.g. *might should ought to*), and the designation 'multiple' is more consistent with one conclusion reached by Mishoe and Montgomery 1994, that syntactic constraints on modal combinations are not so strict as earlier studies claim.

2. Both Coleman and Boertien report apparent exceptions to this involving MMs with *ought to* as the final element (*might ought to, should ought to*, etc.), permitting a form like *She might ought to ==> Might she ought to*. This probably tells us more about the status of *ought to* than anything else.

3. Forty-seven examples were collected in 1981–82 by Gail Skipper, a graduate student at the University of South Carolina. These could not be assessed, because she left the university sometime before analysis of them was begun.

4. Other features include double negatives, the negator *ain't*, and perfective *done*.

5. The item was added between the composition of the preliminary worksheets for the South, circulated by Kurath in 1933, and the final draft of the worksheets for the South Atlantic States, completed in 1935. It became item 58.7 for both LAMSAS and LAGS.

6. It is not clear whether the Linguistic Atlas of the North Central States collected MMs. LANCS surveyed Michigan, Ohio, Kentucky, Indiana, Illinois, and Wisconsin.

7. This indicates the total number of occurrences of *might could* in the LAGS data (including negative forms and multiple citations for some speakers). It therefore differs from the figure 212 used in tables 5a–10b, which refers to the number of speakers using *might could* at least once.

8. For example, Atwood's summary statement about which social classes of LAMSAS speakers use MMs, a statement Wardhaugh (1992:137) still apparently relied on: '[I]n the southern and south midlands [sic] dialects of the United States, a form such as *you-all* is found in use among all social classes, where *I might could* and *a apple* are found in use only among speakers in the low and middle classes'.

9. Two cases will illustrate. Lewis Grizzard (1987:53) in his 'The Compleat Southerner: A Refresher Course in the Essentials' cited *might could* as one of six 'Phrases and Constructions Southerners Should Know and Use'. More recently, *might could* was used 18 times in the best-selling novel *The Guns of the South* (1992) by Harry Turtledove, a native of Southern California, although largely in ways unlike its pragmatics as outlined in Mishoe and Montgomery 1994.

10. Raven McDavid's approach to this item was as follows: 'Suggesting the possibility of being able to do something, you say, "I'm not sure, but I____." Or, you say, "If it quits raining by Thursday, I ____ get the yard work finished"' (Pederson et al. 1972:158).

11. Given the pragmatics most often surrounding the use of MMs (i.e. that they are most often used in sensitive or tentative negotiations), it seems entirely reasonable for them not to occur as often in conversational sociolinguistic interviews as researchers had once expected. For example, Wolfram and Christian 1976, a large-scale sociolinguistic study conducted in southern West Virginia, reported only marginal usage of MMs and concluded that 'the variety of [Appalachian English] that we consider in this study exhibits many other characteristics of other southern varieties, but it does not appear to share in the usage of double modals to any significant degree . . . The scarcity of the examples might indicate that the usage is receding in this area, but the evidence is uncertain' (90–91). Most likely it was the infrequency of situations in which an interviewer threatened the face of the interviewee and, especially, in which negotiation was going on that accounts for the scarcity of MMs they noted in West Virginia, at least on the recorded portions of the interviews. In the interviews for Montgomery 1979, collected in East Tennessee in an area where the author had frequently heard MMs, only four instances occurred during his more than 40 hours of recordings. On the basis of such limited observed data one would have been tempted to conclude that in Appalachian English the modal combinations were either marginal and indistinct in function or were

recessive in use. In the course of concluding his interviews, however, Montgomery noticed that informants used more MMs (usually *might could*) in the brief period of the few moments in which he turned off the recorder and prepared to leave than in the more than 40 hours of recorded interviews.

12. Figures in table 3 cannot be directly compared across the 16 LAGS sectors, for two reasons. One is that different numbers of speakers were interviewed in each sector. The other is that the figures in the tables do not represent the number of speakers using an MM; that is, some speakers used more than one. Percentages of speakers in each sector using an MM can therefore not be computed.

13. All LAGS interviewers are identified by initials in the handbook sketches and listed in the preface to the section by these initials. Because ten interviews were conducted by individuals with names like *Terry* or *Chris* that could have belonged to either a male or a female, these are classified as 'undetermined' in tables 10a/10b.

14. Speakers who were interviewed for under three hours or with whom less than about eighty percent of the survey items were covered were usually classified as secondary informants.

The Chattahoochee River: A Linguistic Boundary?

Edgar W. Schneider

For about three decades, it has been one of the generally shared assumptions of American dialectology that a primary dialectal division runs along the lower course of the Chattahoochee River, which for the most part also constitutes the state line between Georgia and Alabama. Using data from Lee Pederson's Linguistic Atlas of the Gulf States (LAGS), I wish to challenge this assumption. In the first section of this paper, the background and emergence of this traditional notion will be discussed. Subsequently, the data and methodology used to test this assumption will be outlined. In the main part of the paper, I will present lexical data which are relevant in this matter, and finally, the results will be summarized.

It has been customary to relate dialect differences to their possible origins in the history and, in particular, the settlement pattern of an area. In the present case, this is also necessary, of course; but it is helpful only to a limited extent, because we have to take into consideration two alternative accounts of the linguistic and cultural constitution of the area under discussion, and there is historical evidence and support for both. Simplifying the matter quite radically, we can call them the 'Division Model', which is the claim that in fact there is a significant difference between the states of Georgia and Alabama in terms of their population structure, and the 'Homogeneity Model', which is the belief that at least the southern parts of Georgia and Alabama are more or less culturally identical, both being shaped by the traditional coastal southern plantation culture. Note that this issue concerns only about the lower two-thirds of both states; we are not talking about their northern parts and the difference between highland and piedmont on the one hand and lowland and coastal plains on the other; this is noncontroversial. The Homogeneity Model rests upon statements such as 'the Cotton Belt of western Georgia, Alabama, Louisiana, Mississippi, and eastern [sic]

Tennessee was settled very largely by the cotton-growers of the tide-water of Virginia and the Carolinas' (Kurath 1928:392). On the other hand the Division Model is supported by the fact that

> English-speaking inhabitants of eastern Georgia and adjacent parts of the Carolinas did not . . . push west into the Gulf Coastal Plain even though that direction of advance looks easy on the maps . . . If one seeks to explain the relative slowness of this westward advance, he must weigh these restraints at least: Hostile Indian tribes had to be defeated and forced to give up the land. Besides, there may have been no real pressures of population in eastern South Carolina and Georgia for persons to find a new land. Further there were variable combinations of natural barriers—southward flowing rivers to be crossed with great difficulty, and the presence of piney woods, a sign of soil unsuited to the familiar crops. (Wood 1971:2, 4)

Basically, there is reason and logic to both assumptions, for in historical terms they roughly reflect two subsequent stages in the westward expansion of European settlement. The Division Model reflects the pre-1800 situation: Georgia was colonized very early (for example, Savannah in 1733, Augusta in 1735), and it was one of the founding states of the Union, while Alabama was settled only after the turn of the 19th century, and gained statehood in 1819. According to this view, the roots of the state of Georgia lay in an older, aristocratic South Atlantic plantation culture, while a significant portion of the settlers of Alabama were ultimately Scotch-Irish in descent, represent-ing the mountain rather than the coastal plantation culture and coming to the state through the great valley of the Appalachians, which extends from Pennsylvania in a southwesterly direction. In Alabama and the Gulf region, this stock of people merged with settlers of a different origin. In the 19th century, mainly after the invention of the cotton gin, people from Georgia and the Carolinas moved straight westward and thus expanded the plantation culture—which is the basis for the Homogeneity Model.

It is not only the coexistence of these alternative explanations, but also the subsequent settlement streams of different origin, that should prevent us from an overly simplistic understanding and explanation of the cultural and linguistic constitution of the area. Even within the two explanatory phases, things are not as simple as they might seem to be. Even within state boundaries, settlement patterns and communication lines are far from simple and in accordance with the above outline, as the excellent account of the history of the area in the *LAGS Handbook* (Pederson, McDaniel, Bailey, and Bassett 1986:43–58) tells us. For example, the pre-Revolutionary War settlement of Georgia was heavily concentrated in the eastern part of the state, and by 1800 it was only the area east of the Oconee River that was colonized. Roughly twenty years later, settlement in Georgia had extended somewhat further to the west, roughly to the Ocmulgee River, but certainly not to the western half of the state, while in Alabama it was basically the western half of the state which by that time had been permanently colonized. Western Georgia and eastern Alabama, the area around the Chattahoochee River, was actually the last part of the region that was opened to civilization. In addition, the influx of Appalachian settler streams not only affected Alabama and the western Gulf States, but also concerned the state of Georgia to a significant extent. Wood (1963:map 4) showed that a set of Midland words penetrated central Georgia southward, roughly between the Ocmulgee and Flint Rivers. So, settlement history accounts for the cultural diversity of the area, but it does not strongly support the assumption of a sharp division along the Georgia-Alabama state line.

The classic studies which established dialect areas in the United States, Kurath 1949, Atwood 1953, and Kurath/McDavid 1961, are based upon the Linguistic Atlas of New England and the Linguistic Atlas of the Middle and South Atlantic States, the latter of which extends no further westward than eastern Georgia. Therefore, these books have nothing to say on the present topic of investigation. The only statement that is vaguely relevant concerns the borders of the Midland speech area: 'Its limits in the southern portion are likewise difficult to fix, since the Pennsylvania-derived populations of w. Va., w. N. C., and s. W. Va. were subjected to southern cultural and linguistic influence' (Atwood 1953:39).

The putative dialect boundary which is the topic of this paper was proposed by Gordon Wood on the basis of his lexical analysis of eight southern states, as published in Wood 1963 and, more extensively, Wood 1971. Since Wood's study was the first and for almost twenty years the only publication that suggested a dialect structure of the

Southern United States, it turned out to be highly influential. Wood established four primary subdialect areas in the South, namely Coastal Southern, Mid Southern, Gulf Southern, and Plains Southern, and he claims that the line which marks the boundary of what he calls Coastal Southern sets off the southern lowlands from the Mid Southern speech area in the mountains, roughly follows the southern boundary of the Appalachian mountains in a southwesterly direction, and then turns south in western Georgia: 'As the isoglosses move westward, they converge and then turn south. Generally the boundary follows the valley of the Chattahoochee River as it flows west and south. This river line and part of the political boundary of Georgia coincide with the boundary of coastal Southern' (Wood 1963:246; see map 1 below). Later on, he repeats: 'Coastal Southern has a western boundary along the Chattahoochee River in Georgia' (Wood 1963:255).

Map 1. Wood's coastal Southern

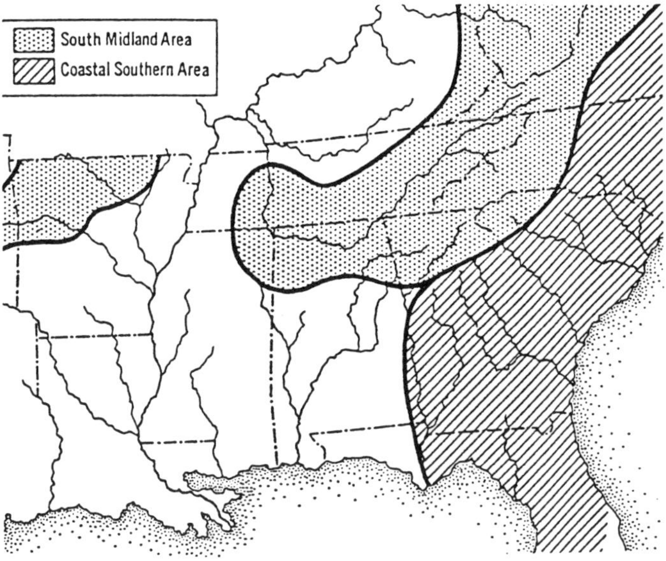

Detail from *American Speech*, "Dialect Contours in the Southern States," by Gordon R. Wood. Copyright © 1963 by The University of Alabama Press. Used by permission.

The evidence which Wood presents for this assumption is not very strong, however; in fact, Wood 1963 presents hardly any detailed evidence at all. Maps 3 to 8 in his article mark the spread of various words in Georgia in the east and Mississippi and Arkansas in the west. Apart from the fact that these are only composite maps which show figures but not precise distributions of words, ignoring all methodological problems involved in such a procedure (see Schneider 1988), the only evidence that is presented in favor of this so-called 'significant boundary in the South' (1963:246) is a list of eight words which are said to form an isogloss bundle along this line: *lightwood, low, tote, co-wench, snap-beans* or *snaps, harp* or *mouth harp, turn of wood,* and *fritters* (246). Wood 1971 (figure 13, p.29) has a map to substantiate the claim of this division, yet again this map has only very general and rough indications of numbers of 'boundaries', and these numbers are surprisingly low: The three categories are '1–2 boundaries', '3–4 boundaries', and '5 or more boundaries'. Again, a list of words is offered which are said to form boundaries in this area, which include, in addition to some of the aforementioned ones, *fire dogs, salad, spider, whicker, fireboard, battercakes, press peach, clabbered milk,* and *rock fence*; these are said to 'come together to form a composite zone of composites shaped vaguely like a tree. The trunk is fairly compact in southwest Georgia; further north its branches diverge east and west' (Wood 1971:29).

Recently, the dialectal division of the United States was refined, modified, and extended to the Pacific Coast by Craig Carver 1987, whose studies are also based exclusively on lexical material. In his summarizing conclusion, Carver accepts the Chattahoochee line as a first rate linguistic boundary, distinguishing between a 'Lower Atlantic South' area in the east and a 'Delta South/Alabama' area to the west (Carver 1987:246–48). If we go into details to see what kind of data this assumption rests on, however, we find again that the evidence for this boundary is extremely weak. The southern speech area is constituted by a set of several so-called 'layers', which consist of groups of regionally distinctive words whose extension is determined by a certain number of these words being found in an area. There are as many as nine layers, or maps, which are relevant in this region, and seven of these do not indicate any trace of a dialect difference along the Georgia-Alabama state border. These are: the 'South II Layer' (Carver 1987:101, map 4.5), the 'South-and-West Layer' (116, map 4.8), the 'Delta South Layer' (139, map 5.5), the 'Lower South Layer' (145, map 5.8), the 'Upper South Layer' (166, map 6.2), the 'Inland South Layer' (169, map 6.3), and the 'Midland Layer' (175, map 6.5). In the case of the 'Atlantic South Layer' (128, map 5.2), there is a tertiary boundary in this area, yet it runs to the west of the Chattahoochee River and encompasses parts of southeastern Alabama. Carver's claim of a primary boundary along the river rests solely upon a single map, the 'South I Layer' (98, map 4.3), apparently in addition to historical considerations and the example of Wood, both of which he refers to (100). However, a closer look at this map, which is reproduced here as map 2, reveals that there is very little justification for this solid line, which, incidentally, is located right in the center of the 'South I Layer' area and does not extend further to the north or to the south. There are three localities east of this line in western Georgia which have as many as 47 and twice 52 'South I' words. The localities west of this line, in eastern Alabama, have values between 23 and 33 such items, and throughout the rest of Alabama and Georgia the figures given are mostly in the twenties and lower thirties, thus not much different at all. Considering that the South I Layer consists of 78 lexical items, these values are not impressively high anyway. Finally, it might be worth considering that two neighboring localities in the southern corners of both states, on both sides of the Chattahoochee River, have almost identical values: 32 in Georgia, 34 in Alabama, so the separating line vanishes immediately north of these places.

My suspicion as to the inappropriateness of the claim of a primary dialect division along the Chattahoochee arose when I prepared a paper that used data from the states of Georgia and Alabama to exemplify methodological principles employed in the division of dialect boundaries (Schneider 1988). The expected boundary did not emerge; rather, I came to suspect that 'the area around the lower course of the river has a certain degree of individual identity, for a number of forms seem to form a pattern in a corridor from south to north, with occasional extensions to the east or west' (Schneider 1988:190; cf. 207, map 12). Thus, I felt that it might be worth investigating this question in greater detail.

Map 2. Carver's 'South I layer' with the Chattahoochee boundary

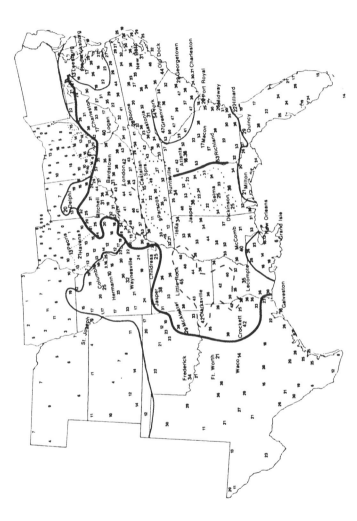

From *American Regional Dialects: A Word Geography*, by Craig M. Carver. Copyright © 1987 by The University of Michigan. Used by permission.

Thanks to Lee Pederson, who launched and directed the project with remarkable efficiency and energy, we now have the appropriate tool to study all sorts of questions concerning the linguistic geography of the Southern United States, the Linguistic Atlas of the Gulf States (LAGS). Within just two decades, this project has provided us with an immense amount of extremely valuable material. To see whether there is in fact a linguistic boundary along the Chattahoochee, we can now simply compare Linguistic Atlas records from both sides of this river, that is, from the states of Georgia and Alabama.[1] This is what I have done for the present paper. To accept a distribution as 'a linguistic boundary', I propose that we should have either a solid isogloss bundle, that is, at least a handful of distributions such that a form occurs only on one side of the line but not on the other, or a number of statistically significant quantitative differences such that on one side of the proposed border a given form is found more frequently than on the other to an extent that excludes the possibility of chance.

The amount of data collected for LAGS is so vast that even for limited topics such as the given one a radical selection is necessary; one could easily write a book rather than just a paper on each of the subregions discussed, as Pederson did on East Tennessee (Pederson 1983). Fortunately, he has also given us another ingenious device that can serve as a useful and quite reliable shortcut to a preliminary solution of a variety of questions: the 'idiolect synopses', which are available for all LAGS informants in microfiche form in the *LAGS Basic Materials*. On a single page, the synopsis collects selected phonetic, grammatical, and lexical information that characterizes the speech of one individual and, given the underlying philosophy of the Linguistic Atlas methodology, his or her locality. I have chosen to base the following analyses upon the lexical section of the data collected in these synopses, for two reasons. First, the previous accounts of the area which I am questioning, the ones by Wood and Carver, are also based solely upon lexical data. Second, there are practical space and time limitations to consider. The grammatical material could be analyzed along similar lines, but that would provide enough material for yet another paper. As to phonetics, LAGS contains so much detail that any attempt to systematize and categorize it, even for a limited area, would go far beyond the scope of a paper-length study. The LAGS team itself, with its experience and with access to the computerized database which holds phonetic data coded in Pederson's various schemes (Pederson 1985, 1987), is in a much better position to investigate these matters, should this be desired.

In determining the area to be chosen for investigation, I have excluded roughly the northern one-third to one-half of Georgia and Alabama, because, as outlined above, the present research question relates only to the southern parts where the Chattahoochee constitutes the border, and also eastern Georgia, because due to an overlap with LAMSAS, LAGS is somewhat differently structured there. The Lower Alabama zone of LAGS was chosen as a starting point, and the neighboring grid units of western Georgia were included. So, the area studied here basically consists of the southern parts of the western half of Georgia and all of Alabama, plus the adjacent parts of Florida in the south. More precisely, it consists of the following grid units in the following LAGS sectors (*LAGS Handbook*): in Upper Georgia, X–Z, AA; in Lower Georgia: all west of the line AC–AG–AL; in East Florida: AR–AT; in Lower Alabama: all grid units (BY–CI); and in Gulf Alabama/West Florida: all units (CJ–CN). Within this area, all and only the primary informants of Atlas types I and II (i.e. 'folk speakers' and 'common speakers') were chosen and investigated. A base map of this area was produced which showed the locations under investigation, and for each of the linguistic units considered the responses were mapped by means of a symbolic code of small circles, triangles, squares, etc. Map 3 shows the area studied here, including the divisions into LAGS grid units and into subregions as explained below.

In the presentation of the material and the analysis of possible regional patterns, I will proceed as follows. First, I give a qualitative overview of the major response types and, if possible, a verbal description of their regional patterning. In particular, I will be paying close attention to the question of whether an isogloss can be drawn, that is, whether the various responses can be regionally delimitated, especially along the expected north-to-south boundary. It should be noted that in this area we frequently find fairly small-scale and local distributions, so a statement saying that there are 'no regional concentrations' should be taken to refer to the overall structure but not to exclude the possibility of local clusterings of response types. Second, I will check whether there are quantitative differences between subregions, that is, whether

Map 3. The region under consideration, subregions,
and LAGS grid units studied

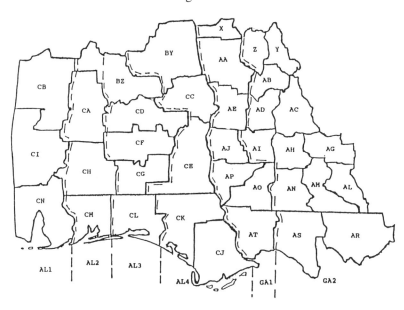

a particular form occurs significantly more frequently in one region than in a neighboring one without having a clearly delimited regional dissemination. For this purpose, I have subdivided the area under investigation into six subregions. Since I am interested primarily in the possibility of dialect boundaries running from north to south, these subregions have been defined such that they all have the shape of vertical corridors extending from the northern to the southern border of the area under investigation. Thus, from the west to the east in their orthographic arrangement corresponding in general terms to their regional location, these subregions are defined as follows in terms of LAGS grid units (the number of speakers per unit is given in parentheses):[2]

AL1: CB, CI, CN. (16)[3]
AL2: locality 260 from BZ, CA, CH, CM. (12)[4]

AL3: BZ with the exception of locality 260, CD, CF, CG, CL. (25)[5]
AL4: BY, CC, CE, CK, CJ. (20)[6]
GA1: X, AA, AE, AJ, AP, AO, AT. (24)[7]
GA2: Y, Z, AB, AC, AD, AG, AH, AI, AL, AM, AN, AR, AS. (38)[8]

It is clear that regions AL4 and GA1 are the ones which deserve closest interest in the given context, being adjacent to the Chattahoochee River on both sides. However, because we do have indications that, possibly due to the southbound progression of settlers from the mountains, there might exist minor north-to-south boundaries in central Georgia and central Alabama (Wood 1963:249, map 4; Schneider 1988:190–91), these subregions will also be compared quantitatively. So, to a certain extent, this study investigates the general question of whether or to what extent lines running from north to south play a role as linguistic separators along the Gulf Coast.

In the following paragraphs, linguistic items will be identified by means of their questionnaire number and citation form as given in the *LAGS Handbook*. For geographical terms, I use conventional abbreviations (AL, GA and FL for the states, s/n/w/e/c for southern, northern, western, eastern, and central sections of the states, respectively).[9]

The quantitative analyses carried out below rest upon the assumption that the nature of the data, especially the existence of multiple responses, requires a 'binomial' analysis (for a discussion, see Schneider and Kretzschmar 1989:130–32), that is, the restriction to the study of the spread of individual forms and their occurrence or non-occurrence in a speaker's set of responses, rather than the simultaneous study of alternative synonyms. Incidentally, the LAGS team also has always followed this principle in their published analyses. The procedure applied here was as follows. In all cases, the frequencies of the principal forms in all six sub-areas (AL1 to GA2) were counted. Depending on the findings, various chi-square tests were carried out to detect significant characteristics of a quantitative nature, such that the numbers of users and non-users of a form in two neighboring areas were arranged in a 2x2 table to be subjected to the test. 'Neighboring areas' is taken to mean either just two adjacent sub-regions (e.g. AL4 vs. GA1, or AL2 vs. AL3), or any clustering of sub-regions on either side of a line, with the only restriction that, of course, only immediately adjacent sub-regions can be joined in a test (e.g. AL vs. GA, or AL1 + AL2 vs. AL3 + AL4). Such accumulations are permitted and conventional in chi-square testing, provided that they make sense—which they do in the present case.[10] In the following text, these tests will be indicated by a shortcut formula which represents the joined sub-regions by a plus sign and the presumed dividing line by a slash. So, for instance, 'AL1 + 2/AL3 + 4 + GA' will be taken to mean that it was tested whether the proportion of users and non-users of a given form in areas AL1 and AL2 taken together was different from the same relationship in the area formed by the merger of sub-regions AL3, AL4, GA1 and GA2. Chi-square (χ^2) will be given (always with one degree of freedom, unless otherwise indicated), and the significance level will be indicated by conventional symbols: '*' means 'significant with an error chance of less than 5 per cent', '**' indicates significance at the less than one per cent level, and '***' that p <.001. 'ns' is to be interpreted as 'not significant' (at the five per cent level).

Since this may seem complicated, let me illustrate the procedure of quantitative testing by a step-by-step presentation of an example, the word *firedogs*. Almost every lexical item is followed by an abbreviated indication of its frequencies in the six subregions, so '*firedogs* (4-3-14-11-13-18)' means that the word was counted with four informants in AL1, three times in AL2, 14 times in AL3, 11 times in AL4, 13 times in GA1, and 18 times in GA2. Given the overall number of speakers per sub-area as indicated above (AL1 16, AL2 12, AL3 25, AL4 20, GA1 24, GA2 38), it follows that, alternatively, it is not listed for 12 respondents in AL1, nine in AL2, 11 in AL3, etc. Testing the distribution with the Chattahoochee River as the dividing line, we get a 2x2 matrix of 32 users and 41 non-users in AL (and wFL) as opposed to 31 users and an equal number of non-users in GA (and eFL). If we calculate chi-square on this matrix, the result is an insignificant .29 ('GA/AL ns'). This is not surprising, because the distribution obviously is such that the form is relatively more infrequent in the western half of AL as opposed to the eastern half of the state and GA. So AL2 vs. AL3 will make a good candidate, but this comparison is of doubtful status, because it violates a restriction postulated by some statisticians in 2x2 tables, namely that the minimum sample size be 40 (e.g. Clauß and Ebner 1978:260). We can join AL2 with AL1 to the west of it, which shares the low value, and AL3 certainly with AL4 and possibly also with the whole of GA, areas which have values in the same range. AL1 + 2 vs. AL3 + 4 yields a table of 7 vs. 25 users but 21 vs. 20 non-users, thus a significant $\chi^2 = 5.36$ (*). Another possibility, in this case with roughly the same result, is AL1 + 2/AL3 + 4 + GA (7:56 vs. 21:51), with $\chi^2 = 5.61$ (*).

(8.3) *andirons*. The form *firedogs* (4-3-14-11-13-18) predominates in particular in the southern half of the area. The delimitation of *firedogs*, while not clear-cut, roughly follows the northern limit of grid units CF–CE–AJ and encompasses a small southern stretch of AD–AC. As shown above, the form is significantly less frequent in AL1 + 2 in the west. In the northern and central portions of AL (or, more precisely, the part of the state considered), *dog irons* (2-4-5-3-0-4) is also strong, but the AL/GA difference fails the significance test by a narrow margin ($\chi^2 = 3.66$ ns). The form *andirons* (2-1-3-1-6-7) is an occasional variant without regional concentration. It seems to be somewhat more frequent in GA but the difference is slight (AL/GA $\chi^2 = 2.60$ ns). Several other forms come up infrequently.

(8.4) *mantel*. No clear isoglosses are possible. The main forms are *mantel* (8-2-8-5-7-12), *mantelpiece* (4-3-5-2-6-15), *mantelshelf* (1-0-1-4-0-3), *mantelboard* (1-4-5-3-3-3), and *shelf* (1-1-2-2-3-0), all without regional concentrations.[11] None of the quantitative tests was significant.

(15.3) *milk gap*. The form *cow pen* (2-6-13-7-5-5) predominates throughout AL, especially in the central and southern portions of the region, and wFL, but turns up in GA and eFL as well. Quantitatively, the Chattahoochee can be shown to be a dividing line (AL3 + 4/GA $\chi^2 = 9.01$ **; AL/GA $\chi^2 = 7.13$ **). There are many other expressions for the same item, for example, *lot* (AL twice, GA four times) and *break* (only GA but only three times).

(16.6) *rock wall*. The main choices, besides several others, are *rock fence* (3-1-7-1-3-7), strongest in central AL, and *rock wall* (0-0-2-3-4-3), relatively more common in GA but fairly infrequent. No major concentration can be discerned, nor are any of the quantitative distributions significant.

(19.5) *paper poke*. Again, there are no clearly delimited areas. *Paper bag* (7-3-10-6-6-13) is fairly general, but *paper sack* (2-2-8-2-7-6) and *bag(s* = 2-3-1-5-1-8) are also widespread and have local but no large-scale areal concentrations. The form *sack* (0-2-3-3-5-5) leans toward the eastern part of the area, but the tests are all insignificant.

(19.7) *tow sack*. The predominant item all over the area is *croker sack* (9-9-17-11-12-13), without significant patternings. The variant *croker bag* (0-0-3-2-6-12) is distinctively eastern, being occasional in eAL and wFL and frequent in GA and eFL. The tendency can be demonstrated even within GA (AL + GA1/GA2 χ^2 = 6.55 *; although GA1/2 ns), but both the Chattahoochee line (AL/GA χ^2 = 10.16 **; AL3 + 4/GA χ^2 = 3.96 *) and the internal divisions in AL (AL1 + 2/AL3 + 4 + GA χ^2 = 5.81 *; AL1–3/AL4 + GA χ^2 = 6.72 **) can be shown to be significant. There are a large number of occasional variants.

(20.5) *harmonica*. Most generally, we find *harp* (7-8-21-14-19-20) throughout the area, although the term is particularly frequent in the southern and central part of AL and wFL and less common in wAL (AL1 + 2/AL3 χ^2 = 4.30 *; AL1 + 2/AL3 + 4 + GA ns). *Mouth harp* (2-2-0-1-1-9) occurs most frequently in eGA and eFL (AL + GA1/GA2 χ^2 = 6.79 **; AL/GA ns) and is scattered elsewhere. The form *harmonica* (5-1-1-2-3-3) was registered repeatedly in Mobile, AL, and is scattered elsewhere; three more items are isolated.

(22.5) *seesaw*. The regular lexeme is *seesaw* (13-11-18-16-17-25) everywhere. *Ridy-horse* (0-0-3-2-2-6) is fairly frequent in FL and parts of AL, and especially in GA close to the FL border. Three more words turn up only occasionally.

(24.3) *flambeau*. Again, the mapping shows one predominant response, *flambeau* (2-4-15-11-11-18), one fairly common alternative without regional concentrations, *torch* (3-1-0-3-3-4), and a set of a few others of which there are only isolated instances. However, there is a clear quantitative difference in the frequency of *flambeau* when we compare the western and the eastern halves of AL (plus wFL = AL1 + 2/AL3 + 4 + GA χ^2 = 6.89 **; AL1 + 2/3 + 4 χ^2 = 7.85 **).

(24.6) *pirogue*. In this case we can observe very clear regional preferences of a quantitative nature, although, qualitatively speaking, it is nowhere possible to draw an isogloss around the spread of any one item. Given the main research question of this paper, the form *bateau* (0-0-7-8-15-6) is particularly interesting because it actually has the Chattahoochee as the center of its distribution, a joining force, as it were. It can be found to the east and west of the river but not in wAL and hardly at all in eGA, and this pattern is far from a chance result: both the western boundary of its spread (AL1 + 2/AL3 + 4 + GA χ^2 = 11.18 ***; AL1–3/AL4 + GA χ^2 = 6.99 **) and its weaker presence in the eastern part of GA + eFL as opposed to the one adjacent to the Chattahoochee are highly significant (GA1/GA2 χ^2 = 12.32 ***). In eGA and cAL, *rowboat* (2-0-8-1-1-7) is strong. None of the possible clusterings of sub-areas reaches the significance level (although AL3/AL4 misses it by a narrow margin and would satisfy a ten per cent level of error chance), but the overall distribution is apparently not a chance product (a 4x2 tabulation of AL1 + 2/AL3/AL4 + GA1/GA2 yields χ^2 = 8.74, * at 3df). The form *fishing boat* (1-2-2-3-1-2) occurs along the southernmost part of the area, in particular in seAL and the easternmost section of wFL. Another form that has a highly significant distribution in terms of the east/west contrast is *skift* (6-2-0-1-1-1), which is concentrated in wAL (AL1 + 2/AL3 + 4 + GA χ^2 = 16.40 ***, AL1/AL2–4 + GA χ^2 = 16.68 ***, AL1/AL2–4 χ^2 = 9.21 **), although it is also scattered in eFL, sGA and sAL. In addition, the map registers many other, rarer variants.

(37.1) *pulley bone*. The form *pulley bone* (6-6-19-14-11-25) is the regular one throughout the area, although it is less frequent in the western half of AL (AL1 + 2/AL3 χ^2 = 4.69 *). This may be a consequence of the fact that *wishbone* (8-4-2-2-5-3) occupies a compact area in swAL in Mobile and around Mobile Bay as far east as the western-most bit of wFL, a concentration which—despite scattered occurrences elsewhere—renders the overall identity of wAL significant (AL1 +

2/AL3 + 4 + GA χ^2 = 13.11 ***; AL1/AL2–4 + GA χ^2 = 10.51 **; AL1/AL2–4 χ^2 = 7.46 **). A few more variants are isolated.

(45.3) *flitters*. *Pancake* (8-6-10-8-4-15) is fairly general, while the other main forms display regional tendencies without a clear division. An isogloss could be drawn along the Chattahoochee, because all localities west of it in AL have *pancake* but none of the adjacent ones in GA do, the local alternatives being *battercakes* and *fritters*, once *flitters*. *Battercakes* (3-0-3-3-8-11) is much more regular in GA than in AL (AL/GA χ^2 = 5.77 *). *Flapjacks* (1-1-5-1-1-0) is concentrated in ecAL, and while its distinctness from wAL cannot be determined on statistical grounds, the division in the east is noncontroversial (AL3/AL4 + GA χ^2 = 7.00 **). In two more cases, frequencies are low and the distributions are quantitatively insignificant, but regional preferences of *hotcakes* (1-1-2-3-0-2) for AL and *fritters/flitters* (1-2-2-2-6-3) for GA and eFL can be suspected.

(47.1) *souse*. In this case, fairly clear regional delimitations can be described, although the boundaries do not have a north-south extension. *Hoghead cheese* (6-4-3-2-1-13) has a strong concentration in swAL, on both sides of the Mobile Bay and the part of FL next to its western border, and also in seGA and eFL, an area roughly delimited by grid units AS–AN–AH–AG. This implies that it is less common in the central portion around the Chattahoochee, with the cut-off being significant on both sides (GA1/GA2 χ^2 = 5.97 *; AL1 + 2/3 + 4 χ^2 = 4.98 *; AL1 + 2/AL3 + 4 + GA1 χ^2 = 8.69 **). The form *press meat* (0-0-2-0-4-5) is almost restricted to the three grid units X, Z, and AA in nwGA, which renders the comparison of both states distinctive (AL/GA χ^2 = 4.87 *). *Souse meat* (0-3-4-3-3-8) concentrates both in neAL (grid units BZ and BY) and in cGA (grid units AJ–AE–AD–AC) and is scattered elsewhere. *Hoghead souse* (2-1-1-0-2-2) occurs mostly in nwAL and eFL. In addition to these more or less localized forms and two other, idiosyncratic ones, we have the most frequent and predominant one, *souse* (6-3-12-11-10-6), which, however, is significantly less frequent further to the east, in GA (AL + GA1/GA2 χ^2 = 7.86 **; AL/GA χ^2 = 4.00 *).

(48.1) *cottage cheese*. The generally dominant form is *Cottage cheese* (4-6-11-11-8-16). There are a few isolated others; the only one which is somewhat frequent is *cream cheese* (5-0-0-0-0-0), used by five informants in Mobile, AL. The statistical testing of this pattern is not permitted; tests for *cottage cheese* are insignificant.

(50.3) *mush*. *Mush* (7-7-8-7-6-12) is the most frequent form, to be found in local clusters but without overall regional tendencies. In addition to several infrequent possibilities, there are two forms which are more than occasional and display small-scale local concentrations. One is *cush* (0-2-4-2-3-3), which occurs in swGA (the very northern edge of the area under consideration in GA) ncAL, and with fair frequency in the central corridor of AL3 and adjacent parts of AL4. The chi-square test is ineffective in all cases.

(54.3) *clingstone (peach)*. The main boundary runs in an east-to-west direction: *press (peach* = 4-5-16-6-7-13) occurs in the southern part of GA, in eFL and wFL, and in most of AL except the northeastern corner. Its counterpart *plum peach* was recorded five times but only in the north, especially in the corners of the area considered, grid units X in GA and BY in AL. However, there is also a significant difference in terms of the east-to-west distribution of *press (peach)*: it is strongest in AL3, with a significant frequency difference distinguishing it from the neighboring areas on both sides (AL1 + 2/AL3 χ^2 = 4.18 *; AL3/AL4 χ^2 = 6.57 *; AL3/AL4 + GA1 χ^2 = 6.42 *; AL3/AL4 + GA χ^2 = 7.08 **). A variety of other expressions have also been recorded in the area, but they are all rare.

(54.4) *freestone (peach)*. *Clear seed* (2-6-17-9-9-20) predominates throughout the area, although it is significantly less used in the western half of AL than in AL3 (AL1 + 2/AL3 χ^2 = 6.73 **). *Freestone* (2-0-2-4-3-4) shows up in scattered fashion, and there are almost a dozen other items which are rare.

(54.7) *peanuts*. The standard item *peanuts* (5-5-2-7-9-14) is fairly common everywhere except AL3, where it is recorded but significantly less regularly than east and west of this corridor (AL1 + 2/AL3 χ^2 =

4.32 *; AL3/AL4 + GA1 χ^2 = 5.26 *). *Ground peas* (1-0-4-5-5-6) is the local form in a small area on both sides of the Chattahoochee (in grid units CE–AJ–AP) and can be occasionally found elsewhere, too, especially in GA. The word *pinders* (2-4-10-3-4-6) is strongest in wFL and sAL (though not in immediate proximity to the Chattahoochee), where it occupies a territory between grid units CL and CF (AL3/AL4 + GA χ^2 = 5.27 *), and it can also be found in sGA and eFL. *Goobers* (5-1-7-1-5-7) has its greatest density in n, nw, and wAL, nwGA, and ceGA, that is, in a way, along the outskirts of the area studied here. The two other options, *goober peas* and *ground goobers*, show just a single instance each.

(55.3) *tommytos*. The map displays a large number of items without noteworthy concentrations, with a single exception. The lead form *tommytos* (4-8-8-7-0-3) is concentrated in swAL and wFL and occurs throughout the state of AL but is exceptional in GA; the difference between the states is highly significant (GA/AL χ^2 = 18.23 ***).

(55A.4) *green beans*. The dominant form, *snap beans* (12-10-14-8-17-24), is almost the only one throughout eFL and GA with the exception of the three northernmost grid units, but it has more competitors in AL, although the difference is insignificant. It seems that *string beans* (2-1-6-5-1-4) reaches into the area from the north, showing up in GA only in the northeastern corner (plus two isolated instances further south) but extending in AL especially in the central corridor down to the southern state line; there is even one attestation in wFL. *Green beans* is rare but has a local concentration in the se corner of AL, fairly close to the Chattahoochee.

(59.3) *woodpecker*. *Peckerwood* (5-5-8-7-4-7) and *woodpecker* (7-4-10-8-11-19) are the dominant forms throughout the area, with the former being comparatively stronger in AL, and the latter in GA (although it is also common around Mobile Bay, in wFL and parts of seAL and cAL). In the case of *peckerwood*, this preference is significant (AL/GA χ^2 = 3.86 *). With one exception close to Mobile Bay in swAL, *woodchuck* (1-0-1-1-0-4) is located only in FL, with a strong pocket especially in the easternmost section of the area. The form *yellowhammer* (1-0-3-0-3-

3) turns up repeatedly but is scattered all over the area. Finally, there are a few more occasional forms.

(60.5) *red worm. Earth worm* (8-4-9-9-7-20) is the most common form everywhere, with a variety of others interspersed. The expression *red worm* (1-4-10-3-2-3) also has attestations in all parts of the area, but it is most frequent in AL, especially the central corridor of AL3 (AL3/AL4 + GA χ^2 = 10.46 **). In Mobile, AL, the local form is *worms*; elsewhere, this is very rare, as are all other forms.

(60.7) *terrapin*. Again, the main division runs east-to-west, with *gopher* (8-10-15-10-11-18) being the southern, lowland variant, and *terrapin* (2-0-6-5-6-8), plus a few infrequent alternatives, dominating in the northern part of the area, roughly coming down to the line AI–AJ–CD. There is no evidence for north-to-south distinctions.

(60.8) *crawdad. Crawfish* (13-8-19-13-14-26) occurs throughout the area; *crawdad* (3-1-2-1-2-1) and a few others are scattered variants. There are no distributional patterns of any kind.

(60A.4) *dragonfly*. This represents a classic and well-known case of a clear division running east to west between an upland and a lowland word: *snake doctor* (1-2-6-4-4-6) is located to the north, in my area almost exclusively in the northernmost grid units, while *mosquito hawk/skeeter hawk* (12-7-12-11-8-23) is the lower southern designation for the insect. The standard lexeme *dragonfly* occurs at several localities throughout the area but is quite rare. North-to-south distinctions do not play a role.

(60A.9) *chigger*. Only two forms have been registered in the area: *red bug*, the main form everywhere, and *chigger*, for which only five occurrences were recorded in different locations. As there are practically no alternatives, counts and calculations would not make much sense here.

(82.5) *serenade*. The word *serenade* (3-2-11-7-6-17) predominates everywhere. *Shivaree* was registered in Mobile, AL, and a few times in scAL and elsewhere. Several other words have been noted without greater frequency. Rates of significance were not calculated in this case, because the unusually high number of missing responses, in particular in certain areas such as GA1, might distort the proportions considerably, as these cases would be counted as 'non-users' in the given rationale.

(95.7) *lagniappe*. A fairly large number of response types have been registered. The most frequent of these are *bonus* (0-3-3-3-4-5) and *gift* (2-1-1-0-2-3), without regional concentrations. Again, I have refrained from calculating significance because of a large number of missing responses.

On the whole, we have to conclude from the foregoing discussion that there are hardly any clear qualitative distinctions (i.e. isoglosses) to be discerned in this area under study. In addition, the few dividing lines that were found tend to have an east-to-west rather than a north-to-south course. This would mean that there is no serious supportive evidence for the assumption that the Chattahoochee River constitutes a dialectal boundary. On the other hand, the quantitative comparisons carried out have repeatedly yielded results that would argue against such a negative conclusion. The methodology employed above has its shortcomings, of course; in particular, one may argue that the division of the area into six vertical corridors is somewhat artificial. The procedure also necessarily entails a certain level of abstraction, as small-scale, local structures are not considered in their own right but may determine a difference on a superordinate, more general level. On the other hand, it excludes the possibility of biased preconceptions; it investigates the existence, importance, and strength of speech boundaries running north to south in this area in general; and it develops and applies a novel and fairly simple way of significance testing in the comparison of neighboring linguistic areas.

To get an overview impression of the strength of north-to-south divisions in this area, the results have been summarized as follows. Table 1 lists all the items which displayed statistically significant distributional differences between neighboring vertical corridors in the above descriptions. The strength of the division (i.e. the degree of

Table 1. Significant quantitative boundaries in the area

LAGS Item	AL1	AL2	AL3	AL4	GA1	GA2
firedogs			*			
cow pen				**		
croker bag		*	**	**	*	
harp			*			
mouth harp					**	
flambeau		**				
bateau		***	**		***	
skift	***	***				
pulley bone		*				
wishbone	**	***				
battercakes				*		
flapjacks			**			
souse				*	**	
hoghead cheese		**			*	
press meat				*		
press (peach)		*	**			
clear seed		**				
peanuts		*	*			
pinders			*			
tommytos				***		
peckerwood				*		
red worm			**			
sum of asterisks	5	21	12	11	9	
total significant items	2	12	7	7	5	

significance) is indicated by the number of asterisks. For each word, only one division between adjacent zones can be entered, irrespective of whether this line proved a significant separator also with other combinations of adjacent zones, but the strongest one found between any two neighbors will be chosen. Thus, this is to be interpreted as

'Between zones X and Y there runs a quantitative boundary of statistical strength Z that separates adjacent areas of any size on both sides'. The numbers and weights of significant differences can then be added up. Note that this notion of a 'quantitative boundary', being solely based on frequency differences (i.e. tendencies and usage preferences rather than clear-cut limits) is a useful but much weaker delimitator than the conventional 'isogloss'.

The table indicates that on the basis of the lexical level and the limited amount of material studied there is certainly sufficient justification to assume a dialectal boundary that separates an eastern/South Atlantic sub-area from a western/Gulf region. However, the boundary cannot be understood to be clear-cut, to follow a single line; rather, a broad zone of gradually changing lexical choices, a series of minor steps, can be observed. If one really felt the need to pinpoint the more or less exact location of the boundary, one would find that a stronger separating force stretches from north to south through central Alabama rather than coinciding with the AL-GA state line and the Chattahoochee River. (For a sketching of such a boundary using LAGS data from throughout Alabama, see Fitts, this volume.) Thus, there is hardly any support for the demarcation proposed by Wood and taken over by Carver. The lexical items which Wood says his proposal rests upon cannot be shown to constitute isoglosses in the LAGS material (see note 9), and it should be noted that even the north-to-south divisions which I have established rest upon the weaker requirement of quantitative preferences rather than qualitative all-or-nothing differences. It appears that among the two fundamental approaches to the linguistic and cultural constitution of southern Alabama and Georgia outlined in the introduction the Homogeneity Model is more important as a baseline, with the Division Model being constrained in its impact to areas further to the north and reduced here to the role of fairly weak lexical intrusions.

These results, and many other, more important ones, have been made possible only by the steady, energetic, organized and innovative labor of Lee Pederson. While others have made more noise by proclaiming some short-lived theory, this modest personality has quietly both carried on the tradition of American dialectology and revolutionized the field by introducing innovative techniques and modern technology, and he and his team have amassed enough material for generations of scholars to work on. Since Hans Kurath, no single scholar in American dialectology has achieved so much.

NOTES

1. Volume 5 of *LAGS* recognizes secondary boundaries between subregions roughly in this area, namely between Eastern and Western Piedmont, Eastern Plains and Black Belt as subregions of the Plains, and Eastern and East Central Piney Woods, respectively.

2. For reasons of simplicity, the labels ignore the fact that the southernmost grid units of AL2, AL3, AL4, GA1 and GA2 are in fact parts of Florida.

3. The speakers are LAGS informants 406, 407, 408, 449, 450, 451, 472, 473, 474, 477, 478, 479, 480, 481, 482, and 483.

4. LAGS informants 400, 401, 402, 403, 405, 446, 447, 448, 467, 468, 469, and 470.

5. LAGS informants 394, 395, 396, 397, 399, 415, 416, 417, 420, 421, 434, 435, 436, 438, 439, 440, 441, 442, 444, 445, 462, 463, 464, 465, and 466.

6. LAGS informants 390, 392, 393, 410, 411, 423, 424, 426, 427, 428, 430, 431, 432, 433, 459, 460, 461, 453, 454, and 455.

7. LAGS informants 116, 117, 139, 140, 142, 143, 169, 172, 192, 193, 194, 221, 222, 223, 224, 225, 215, 218, 219, 220, 239, 241, 242, and 243.

8. LAGS informants 119, 121, 122, 134, 135, 136, 138, 145, 146, 148, 149, 150, 165, 166, 167, 182, 183, 184, 186, 187, 188, 189, 190, 203, 204, 205, 206, 207, 208, 210, 211, 212, 213, 234, 235, 236, 237, and 238.

9. Note that I take these regional terms to relate only to the area under consideration, which excludes the northern parts of both states and eastern Georgia; thus, when I talk about 'nGA' in this paper, in general terms this refers to north-central GA.

10. This relatively simple test is sufficient and adequate for the purpose and the data of this study. Recent years have seen the development of considerably more sophisticated statistical techniques of analyses and considerations on their applicability. For further details, see Kretzschmar 1992, 1996a, Girard and Larmouth 1993, Davis and Houck 1996, and Kretzschmar and Schneider 1996.

11. As mentioned above, Wood (1971:29) lists *fireboard* among the words that display an isogloss along the Chattahoochee, thus contributing to the constitution of the Coastal Southern-Gulf Southern division. There is no support for such an assumption in this material: the form is very rare (three

instances in GA, one each in AL and wFL) and displays no evidence at all of a regional concentration, let alone an isogloss-like arrangement. Incidentally, the present materials permit Wood's claims to be tested for a number of the other forms which he lists as well, e.g. *fire dogs*, *snap beans*, *(mouth) harp*, *press peach*, *battercakes*, etc. In no case does a clear isogloss emerge, and only rarely can these claims be supported by a quantitative difference (as in *battercakes*).

Dialect Boundaries in Alabama: Evidence from LAGS

Anne Malone Fitts

When I moved from Pensacola, Florida, to Dothan, Alabama, as a child, I had to learn to avoid stepping barefoot on sand spurs instead of on rockachaws, as we called the porcupine-like grass seeds in Pensacola. That, along with a few pronunciations we were teased about and the Dothan expression 'riding on the bus' instead of 'in' it, was my introduction to dialect differences. Other dialect puzzles soon entered my life. What, I wondered on a fishing trip, was the difference between the dragonflies I read about in books and the mosquito hawks near my Pensacola home? Later I forgot these dialect questions until the regional contrast between mosquito hawks and snake doctors was mentioned in a linguistics class.

In the early 1970s, I began field work for the Linguistic Atlas of the Gulf States (LAGS) to gather material for a dissertation on Alabama dialect. I taped nine interviews, each five to six hours in length, with informants who were natives and life-long residents of their communities, and I laboriously transcribed them in the narrow phonetic script I learned from studying tapes and transcriptions made by Raven McDavid. It was a wonderful experience. I met a one-hundred-year-old woman who remembered living on virgin land between Prattville and Clanton ('You could see for miles'). An old man in Clanton startled me by announcing, 'I'll show you the oldest pair of pants in Alabama', and sending his daughter to fetch a child's pair of short pants. His sister had grown and picked the cotton, ginned and carded it, spun it, dyed it, woven it, and made it into that pair of pants for him. I learned that pioneer life in some parts of Alabama was only as far back as the turn of the century.

My understanding of sociolinguistics expanded when I interviewed two old women in Prattville. The old white woman, retired from the farm, would use standard verb forms picked up from her educated new neighbors, then self-consciously 'correct' the forms to nonstandard ones of her rural years. The old black woman would give the nonstandard verb forms of her neighborhood, then correct to the standard forms she was taught as a child by her school teacher papa, a former slave and early graduate of Alabama State University ('Papa used to make us correct each other,' she said.)

My own adventures resulted in a long hiatus in work on my dissertation, and when I returned to it, the LAGS fieldwork was complete and six of my interviews were included among the 129 primary interviews conducted in Alabama and neatly entered on microfiche cards in the LAGS *Basic Materials* (Pederson et al. 1986). I decided to discover what the atlas revealed about the regional boundaries of words in Alabama, especially whether the dialect patterns that Kurath 1949 had found in the Atlantic states held up to any extent in Alabama, the goal of the present paper.

Previous researchers have consistently found dialect boundaries in Alabama although they have disagreed about their location and nature. In her 1966 dissertation, Virginia O. Foscue drew the first general dialect boundary, interpreting responses to a mail questionnaire on Alabama vocabulary based on LAMSAS worksheets. A study of the settlement history of the state guided the selection of her 25 communities, each providing two native white informants, one elderly and provincial, one younger and more educated. Foscue, who planned her work as a preliminary study for a linguistic atlas, drew a boundary line from Lanett in the eastern piedmont to Livingston in the western Black Belt (see map 1, from Foscue 1971:41). Also using the short atlas worksheets was Lawrence M. Foley in his dissertation study on the speech of Tuscaloosa County (Foley 1969/72). Foley not only analyzed an historically important county in depth, but he provided the first analysis of regional black speech in Alabama, including five black speakers among his 27 native informants.

Based on research conducted in the 1950s, Gordon Wood in early publications mapped selected individual items such as *plum peach* vs. *press peach* (Wood 1961:12), and later formulated a general boundary somewhat different from Foscue's in his *Vocabulary Change: A Study of Variation in Regional Words in Eight of the Southern States* (1971). Wood analyzed results from a mail survey distributed in Alabama by

Map 1. Foscue's Alabama dialect boundary

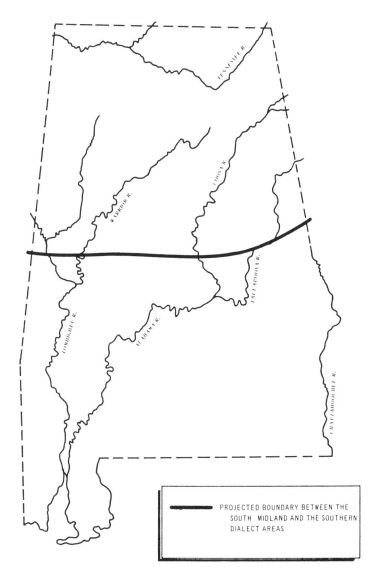

From *A Preliminary Survey of the Vocabulary of White Alabamians*, Publication of the American Dialect Society, by Virginia Foscue. Copyright © 1974 by the American Dialect Socity, published by University of Alabama Press. Used by permission.

students in University of Alabama language classes. He gathered many more responses than Foscue did, but gave little care to insure that informants were native and lifelong residents of their communities. Wood marked the northern fourth of Alabama as belonging with most of Tennessee in the territory he called Mid Southern and the rest of the state as belonging to a large region called Gulf Southern (1971:358); thus, his boundary ran somewhat north of Foscue's (see map 2).

In 1987 Craig Carver published conclusions similar to Wood's. His study, *American Regional Dialects*, was based on data collected for the *Dictionary of American Regional English*, which contains 21 complete interviews in Alabama with a much longer questionnaire since *DARE*'s purpose was a dialect dictionary rather than an atlas (see Hall, this volume). Carver separates off the northern tier of counties, dividing the state into Upper South and Lower South. Like Wood, he places Georgia in a region separate from Alabama, with only the southernmost Alabama county included in what he designates the Atlantic South. While earlier studies determined their boundaries through isogloss bundles, Carver devised an approach based on multiple layers that 'describes the dialect of a specific area in terms of the relative degree to which it participates in the lexicons of the layers that overlap its area' (1987:18) and to which it is representative of the region being determined. Carver's layer maps show very few regional terms in a large area in the middle of Alabama, a fact he attributes to the state's 'late settlement' (1987:158). By 1820, however, Alabama was already a more populous state than Mississippi, and most of the region that shows little distinctive dialect was settled ahead of neighboring regions of Mississippi and Georgia (Fitts 1989:12). A more likely explanation of Carver's finding is that the DARE informants for mid-Alabama were younger, more urban, and more educated than those in surrounding areas showing more dialect terms (Fitts 1989:13), and the often-obsolescent terms were more frequently retained by the oldest, most rural, and least educated informants.

Of the various dialect research projects, LAGS offers the most thorough coverage of Alabama as well as continuity with the information gathered in the Atlantic states by the Linguistic Atlas of New England and the Linguistic Atlas of the Middle and South Atlantic States. In the *LAGS Regional Pattern* (Pederson, McDaniel, and Adams

Map 2. Wood 's 'redefinition' of Southern

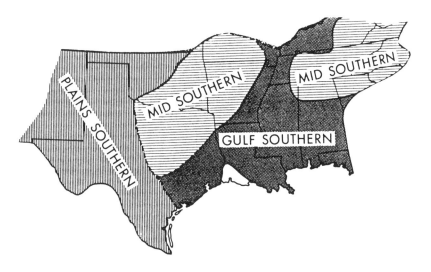

Detail from *Vocabulary Change* by Gordon R. Wood. Copyright © 1971 by Southern Illinois University Press. Used by permission.

1991), LAGS data are used to show how speech patterns from the South Atlantic states follow the natural geography of the Gulf States, with settlers generally adhering to familiar terrains: the highlands, the piedmont, the plains, the piney woods, or the coast. Still deserving an answer, however, is the question of what the LAGS vocabulary in Alabama suggests about the major Southern dialect boundaries drawn by Kurath, Wood, and Carver and, in Alabama, by Foscue.

I find that the vocabulary in LAGS supports a dialect boundary in Alabama that closely follows the one drawn by Foscue 1966, 1971. In discussing my findings, I shall generally use Carver's terms for regions—Inland, Upper South, Atlantic South, and Lower South—rather than Kurath's corresponding terms—Midland, South Midland, and Southern—because Carver's terms more accurately designate the geography of the dialects. Words not covered by Kurath 1949 (and therefore not having a label of 'Midland' or 'Southern') are categorized according to their patterns in LAGS.

It is interesting to see that many of the words in the South Atlantic states with especially sharp isoglosses on the maps in Kurath 1949 also have strong patterns in Alabama. Generally, terms more common in the mountains of the South Atlantic states are more common in North Alabama, sometimes traversing the state in the southwesterly direction taken by the mountains, which come down from the northeast to end south of Birmingham. Words confined generally to the coastal regions of the South Atlantic states are more common in South Alabama and sometimes also in the eastern Alabama Piedmont, with only one, *cooter* (for a type of turtle), being rare in Alabama but fairly common in Georgia. This probably means that the cooter itself is rare in Alabama, just as the gopher turtle is rarely mentioned north of its territorial boundary just below the center of the state (Fitts 1989:62). The pattern of words investigated by Kurath for the Atlantic states follows in Alabama the tendency of settlers to migrate to land similar to that which they left, as the volumes of LAGS often show with boundaries so roughly following divisions of physical geography.

Word distribution in LAGS data from Alabama closely reflects the settlement history. For example, maps for the coastal terms *piazza* 'porch', *flambeau* 'homemade bottle lamp', and especially *bateau* 'rowboat' closely follow the pattern of predominantly Georgian settlement of the piedmont and the eastern half of southern Alabama. (Maps for these three and all other terms mentioned herein can be found in Fitts 1989, but space permits the reproduction of only a few maps here.) When I asked the county agent office in Prattville to help me find informants in Autauga County, the secretaries said to be sure to ask about *piazza*. They were often told to just put any deliveries 'on the pizer'. The maps for Inland *French harp* 'harmonica', *back stick* 'large back log in a fire', and the expression *want off* 'want to get off' reflect the southwesterly path of settlers from the mountains of the Carolinas and Virginia through North Georgia and Tennessee, in that these terms occur as far south as the piedmont in East Alabama and extend sometimes to Choctaw County just below the Black Belt in western Alabama.

Other terms common to the mountains or spreading westward from the Virginia Piedmont or North Carolina occur across northern Alabama, e.g., *bawl* of a calf, *nicker* of a horse, *plum peach* 'cling peach', *snake doctor* 'dragon fly' (map 3), *fire board* 'mantel', and *tow sack* 'burlap sack' (map 4). Terms from the coastal South extend across southern Alabama, e.g. *whicker* of a horse, *spider* 'three-legged skillet', *press peach* 'cling peach', *mosquito hawk* 'dragon fly' (map 3), *pinders* 'peanuts', *cat squirrel* 'gray squirrel', and *wiggler* 'earthworm'. The spread of population up the rivers from Mobile as far as Montgomery and Choctaw County is reflected in the distribution of *gallery* 'porch' and *hoghead cheese* 'congealed loaf made from boiling the hog's head'.

Other isoglosses follow the same general pattern of Inland and Upper South words being more common in North Alabama, and Atlantic and Lower South words being more common in South Alabama. However, LAGS finds some of Kurath's Southern words and Craig Carver's Lower South words throughout most of the state. *Croker sack* 'burlap sack' occurs in all but the northeast and northwest corners of the state. *Bream* 'blue-gill fish' and *collard greens* are common in all but the northernmost tier of counties. Some contrasting terms for the same items overlap broadly. Most LAGS respondents in Alabama knew both Lower South *red bug* and Inland *chigger*, Lower South *light bread* and Inland *loaf bread*, and Lower South *earthworm* and Upper South *red worm*, and many claimed to use the paired terms interchangeably.

But according to LAGS, the farther north one goes, the more apt Alabamians were to say *red worm*, *loaf bread*, and *chigger*, and the farther south one goes, the more apt they were to say *earthworm*, *light bread*, and *red bug* (map 5). Most Alabamians also were equally familiar with *skillet* and *frying pan*, but if only volunteered responses to questions (as opposed to those suggested by the fieldworker) are considered, Alabamians showed a preference for Inland *skillet* in the same northeast to southwest pattern as that of *French harp* mentioned earlier.

The words used for calling cows illustrate the gradual transition from one dialect region to another across the middle of the state. Elizabeth Dearden in her 1943 dissertation on South Atlantic states vocabulary pointed out that in general, 'calls with *co-* are eastern [coastal] and calls with *sook* are western [inland]' (115). In Alabama calls with *sook* are northern and northeastern, occurring from north of the Piedmont in the East to just north of the Black Belt in Bibb County; and calls with *co-* are southeastern (*co-et*, *co-ee*, and one *co-wench*), occurring from the

Map 3. Alabama LAGS responses for *dragonfly*

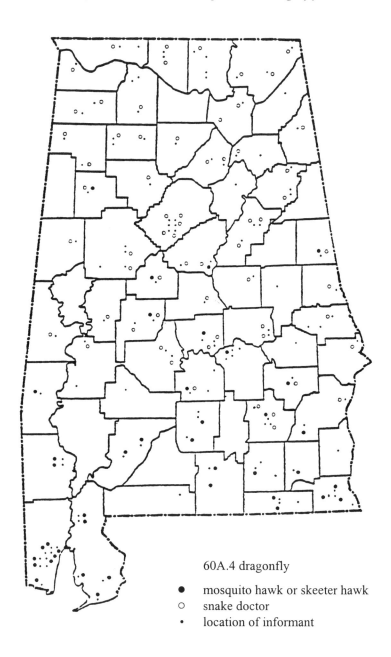

60A.4 dragonfly

●   mosquito hawk or skeeter hawk
○   snake doctor
·   location of informant

Map 4. Alabama LAGS responses for *burlap sack*

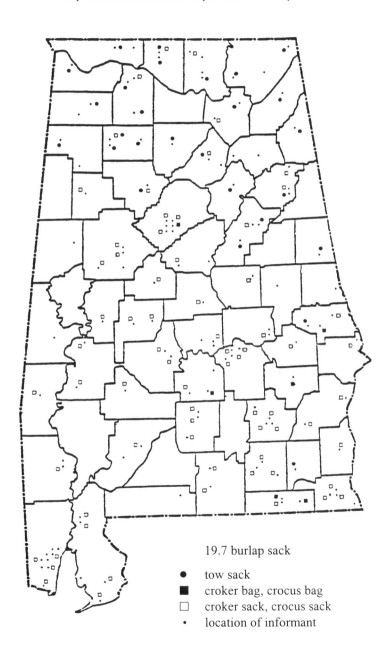

19.7 burlap sack

●   tow sack
◼   croker bag, crocus bag
□   croker sack, crocus sack
·   location of informant

Map 5. Alabama LAGS responses for *red bug*

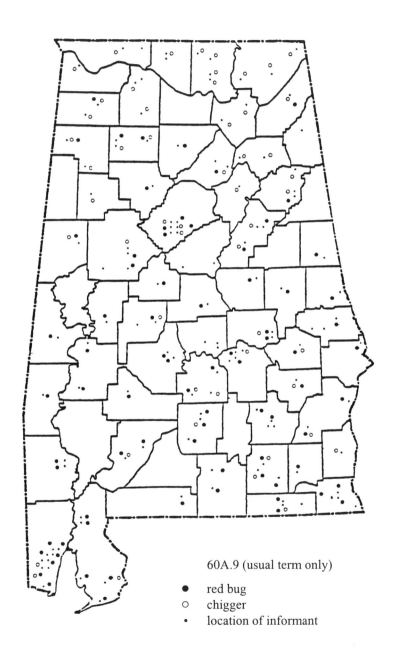

60A.9 (usual term only)

- ● red bug
- ○ chigger
- · location of informant

southern Piedmont to the northwest Florida border. Between the two areas, the common call is *soo*, probably a corruption of *sook* by analogy with *soo pig*.

Although those who came from the mountains farther east most often settled in northern and western Alabama, quite a few upland settlers came to the hilly land below the Black Belt, the Chunnenuggie Ridge and the Southern Red Hills or Piney Woods (see map 6). Butler County was first settled by a caravan of people from South Carolina who named their new town after their hometown of Greenville. Terms for 'mantel' reflect this history. The mountain term *fire board* is volunteered only in North Alabama, especially in the northwest, but in South Alabama the hybrid term *mantel board* often occurs, especially in Butler County, where all three informants volunteered it and two agreed to having heard *fire board*.

Other Inland terms also occur infrequently in South Alabama. A *turn of corn* for the amount that would be ground at one time comes from the mountains and Virginia Piedmont; it is common in North Alabama but is also scattered across South Alabama. *Green beans* for the beans that are eaten in the pod occurs as the primary term several times in the Wiregrass, although Southern *snap beans* occurs more commonly there.

Despite the overlapping and the sometimes gradual transition in the LAGS data between competing terms, it is possible to draw a boundary generally separating North and South Alabama speech. Two kinds of maps combining the regional terms show similar results: layer maps showing how many Upland (Inland plus Upper South) and how many Coastal (Atlantic South and Lower South) terms each informant used; and a map of isogloss bundles (maps 7–9). Because the inventory of terms used for creating the layer maps includes some rare words, I have used a figure of one-third or more of the listed terms to establish either dialect as predominant in a given community, i.e., nine or more of the 27 Upland words, or 17 or more of the 50 Coastal terms (see tables 1 and 2 for the lists of words, along with the LAGS worksheet number, the item elicited, the response in question, and the number of occurrences of that response in Alabama compared to the total number across the Gulf States).

The area in which worksheets usually report 17 or more of the 50 Coastal South words is considered to belong to that dialect. The area in

Map 6. Geological features of Alabama
(Hilly lands below the Black Belt)

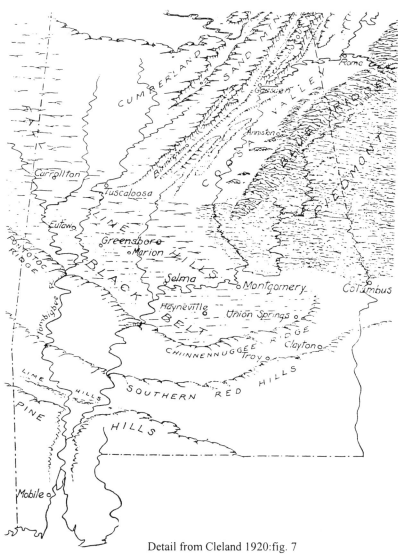

Detail from Cleland 1920:fig. 7

which worksheets usually report 9 or more of the 27 words listed for the Upland South is considered to belong to that dialect region, even though the speaker may actually report more words (but a percentage smaller than 33%) of the 50 listed for the Coastal South. In West Central Alabama, where it happened that the informants used fewer of the regional terms considered, the proportions are still revealing. The Pickens County informant with 7 Upland words and 8 Coastal words gave a higher percentage of Upland words, whereas the Sumter County informant immediately to the south, with 3 Upland and 11 Coastal terms, gave a higher percentage of Coastal words.

The map of isogloss bundles (map 9) reveals a virtually identical pattern, though perhaps showing more clearly the transition between dialect regions. Foley's 1969/72 study of Tuscaloosa County and Faneuf's early study (1939) of Lee County using an atlas questionnaire corroborate the LAGS results very closely. Frequently the isoglosses of competing terms overlap, and the map of isogloss bundles shows the gradual transition between North Alabama and South Alabama speech effectively.

However, even if LAGS data suggest boundaries, the regional dialect mapped here reflects the heritage of the state rather than actual present-day speech. All of the terms discussed were used more frequently by speakers over 65 than by those under 65. A steady urbanization has affected even rural Alabama. A couple of the informants I interviewed who were born by or before 1900 had grown up in pockets of pioneer territory in the state where they lived in log cabins, made their own soap, candles, and cloth, and washed their clothes in a wash pot. When I practiced my first LAGS interview back in 1970, the informant, a friend born around 1940 on a farm in South Alabama, was unfamiliar with many of the farming terms sought by LAGS. Not only has the 20th century's rapid technological progress made many words obsolete, but often even regional plant and animal words are being replaced by book words. As one young informant put it, 'Snake doctor is what I called it before I knew it was a dragon fly'.

Map 7. Upper and Inland South layer

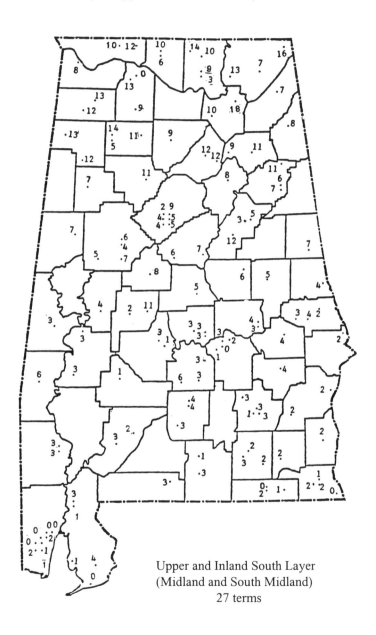

Upper and Inland South Layer
(Midland and South Midland)
27 terms

Map 8. Words from the Coastal South

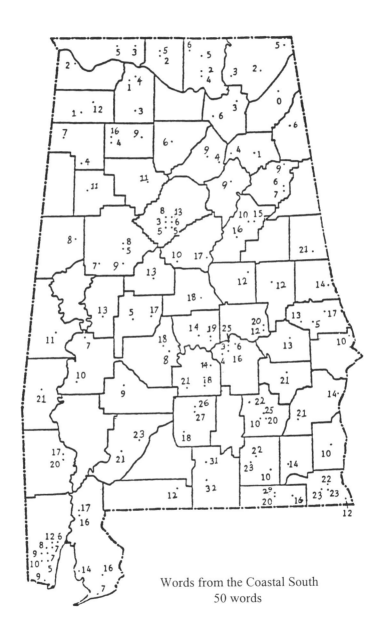

Words from the Coastal South
50 words

Map 9. Isogloss bundles with boundary drawn

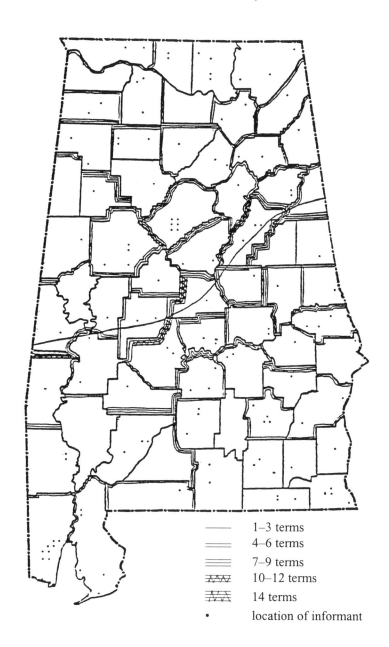

——	1–3 terms
≡	4–6 terms
≣	7–9 terms
全个	10–12 terms
全个	14 terms
•	location of informant

Table 1. Words of the Upper and Inland South

LAGS worksheet page #	item	word	number of occurrences in AL/LAGS
8.3	andirons	dog irons	40/283
8.4	mantel	fire board	14/69
8.5	backlog	back stick	20/129
15.6	barnyard	barn lot	10/73
16.6	stone wall	rock wall	20/121
17.5	frying pan	skillet only	42/180
19.5	paper bag	poke	6/109
19.7	burlap sack	tow sack	27/315
19.8	amount ground at once	turn of corn	21/139
20.5	harmonica	French harp	29/292
21.6	plow types	bull tongue plow	3/46
		turning plow	27/46
33.3	mongrel	cur dog	23/222
36.2	cry of a calf	bawl	24/210
36.4	horse sound	nicker	21/243
37.5	call to cows	sook	23/194
44.3	loaf bread	loaf bread	39/137
44.5	corn bread (baked pone)	corn dodger	14/42
45.3	pancake	flitter	6/73
47.1	boiled, congealed	press meat	13/64
	hog's head meat	souse meat	43/201
47.6	curdled milk	clabber(ed) milk	33/65
54.3	cling peach	plum peach	23/96
55A.4	green beans	green beans	25/328
60.5	earthworm	red worm	50/234
60A.4	dragon fly	snake doctor	63/276
60A.9	red bug	chigger	52/407
85.4	want to get off	want off	20/112

Table 2. Words from the Coastal South

LAGS worksheet page #	item	word	number of occurrences in AL/LAGS
5.7	(going to) clear up	fair, fair off, fair up	35/95
8.3	andirons	fire dogs	43/210
8.6	kindling	lightwood, lighterd	59/192
		fat wood	6/35
		fat pine	8/41
10.8	porch	piazza	21/50
		gallery	28/180
17.5	frying pan with legs	spider	14/79
19.7	burlap sack	crocus/croker bag	6/58
		crocus/croker sack	70/355
19.8	amount of wood you can carry	turn	37/83
21.6	plow types	turn plow	9/54
		sweep	9/60
		middle buster	10/143
23.5	grindstone	grind(ing) rock	36/195
24.3	makeshift lamp	flambeau	37/153
24.6	rowboat	bateau	23/118
31.7	byway	farm-to-market road	15/53
32.1	throw	chunk	25/161
36.2	cry of a calf	blate	42/236
36.3	moo	low	56/277
36.4	horse sound	whicker	19/77
		bray	17/57
37.2	pig or cow liver and lungs	haslet	14/96
37.5	call to cows	co-ee, co-et, co-wench or co-up	19/48
44.3	loaf bread	light bread	70/482
44.5	cornbread (cornmeal dumpling)	corn dodger	10/33

47.1	congealed, boiled	souse	52/296
	hog's head meat	hog's head cheese	44/312
47.2	liver sausage	liver pudding	12/103
47.6	curdled milk	clabber	69/463
50.3	cornmeal mush	gruel	15/54
		cush	10/65
54.3	cling peach	press peach	29/117
54.7	peanuts	ground peas	35/73
		pinders	17/96
55A.4	green beans	snap beans	55/402
55A.5	greens	collard greens	63/229
59.6	gray squirrel	cat squirrel	22/160
59.9	blue-gill fish	bream	63/277
60.3	spring frog	rain frog	27/130
60.5	earthworm	earthworm	55/385
		wiggler	29/100
60.6	turtle	cooter	3/61
60A.4	dragon fly	(mo)squito hawk	39/242
60A.9	red bug	red bug	79/429
64.1	grandfather	Big Daddy	9/15
64.2	grandmother	Big Mamma	6/20
80.4.	sick at his stomach	sick on his stomach	11/81

Still, along with regional computer jargon yet uncharted, some of the old regionalisms remain, even some that LAGS tried to capture but couldn't. When I explained what I was studying, a friend who worked with rural black people in Wilcox and Monroe counties asked if I had come across *na'n* for 'nary a one'. No, I had not, although the question was in the worksheets, and there were occurrences of [nær] and [ær] as in 'nare a cent less', 'without aer a post in it' and even one *narun* from a black informant. But the further reduction to *na'n*, a process of shortening found commonly in black speech and, by extension, southern speech generally, was perhaps too casual a form to be caught in the relatively formal atmosphere of a LAGS interview. However, it still exists, for one of the two conversations I heard it in was with an African-American teenager from Selma I was tutoring.

Alabama speech may no longer have the colorful variety that older Alabamians remember, but it may still have distinctive features, including a noticeable difference between the northern and southern portions of the state. Of the 23 Alabama LAGS informants aged 36 or under at the time of the interviews in the 1970s (i.e., all informants born after 1940), none mentioned *bateau* or *cur dog* or *pinder* or a *turn of corn*, and none called cows by *sook* or *co-et* or hastened horses with *come up*! However, eight mentioned *lightwood* or *lighterd*, five said that cows *low*, 15 referred to *snap beans*, 16 to *clabber* or *clabbered milk*, six to *tommytoes* for miniature tomatoes, and nine to *snake doctors*. Since *collard greens* are as popular as ever, it is not surprising that 12 referred to them and 13 mentioned *souse* or *souse meat*, still sold under those names in Alabama groceries. Relatively younger speakers in North Alabama used the terms *tow sack* and *red worm* and *chigger*, while younger informants in South Alabama mentioned *croker sack* and *wiggler* and *red bug*. Five of the seven younger informants in the area settled predominantly from Georgia were familiar with *ground peas*, and six with the term *cracker* as applied to people. Finally, the four younger interviewees from the area around Mobile still referred to *hog head cheese*, to the *gallery* of a Victorian house, and to *mosquito hawks*. Indeed, the distinctive features of Alabama vocabulary have not yet disappeared.

Analytical Procedure and Three Technical Types of Dialect

William A. Kretzschmar, Jr.

It has always been a great curiosity to me that dialectologists have never agreed among themselves on a common definition of dialect for analytical purposes.[1] There have been attractive political and perceptual definitions, say the distinction between the French of Paris and other varieties which are dialects because not Parisian, or the assertion that certain people speak a dialect because they themselves, or others, perceive and say that they do (e.g. Davis 1983:1–3). However, political and perceptual definitions do not help dialectologists who wish to describe varieties within the speech of a region by analysis of evidence from that region. Analysis, as opposed to collection and mere description of data, demands an attempt at technical definition in order to identify just what the analyst should look for in the data, so that the analyst can devise methods of finding it. Taking my lead from Saussure, I would like to suggest that three kinds of dialects, based on the logic of the common procedures necessary for dialect study, can be valid goals of analysis, and that any analysis of dialect should identify what its goals are. I shall call these three procedurally differentiated dialect types, to be explained below, ATTRIBUTIVE, BLIND, and DERIVED. Distinguishing between these three can reveal the ambiguity or show argument at cross purposes in several prominent existing analyses of dialect, and the same distinctions show the promise of the procedures used for Lee Pederson's LAGS volumes.

Pioneering linguistic geographers such as Wenker, Gilliéron, and Kurath were most concerned with gathering information about particular linguistic features, and then with full and fair presentation of their evidence. Their goal was the production of an atlas; their graphic method was to plot particular occurrences of linguistic forms, in all their phonetic differentiation, at particular geographic points. Kurath later shifted to the creation of list manuscripts in which particular linguistic forms were not actually shown on maps, but the effect was the same: association of a speech form with a place. The method here, as Pederson (1990–95:36–37) describes it, is 'a logically ordered and systematic approach that begins with common sense, proceeds through deductive cycles, and concludes in enumeration. It conducts research in a geographic context, but its research concerns a few words of a language, not the language itself and its universe of discourse'. Pederson goes on to suggest that to name this research 'linguistic' geography may raise expectations that were never envisaged for these projects—viz. that an atlas survey will somehow treat the language as a whole—and he prefers 'word' geography as a term to describe the variation at the word level that such surveys were designed to study. In Pederson's LAGS and in our work on LAMSAS (Kretzschmar, McDavid, Lerud, and Johnson 1994), age, sex, and many other categories have joined geography as potential categories for association with linguistic forms at the word level. None of this primary and secondary work, first collecting data about the linguistic forms specified in a questionnaire and then plotting the particular occurrences of linguistic forms in association with geographic locations or other points of categorization, has said anything about dialects. Certainly traditional word geographers have had their own ideas about dialects, but those ideas were not supposed to interfere in the processes of collection and full enumeration.

Analyses of the information that has been collected require further reflection about what we mean by the term *dialect*. Many people have accepted a general definition that dialects, in the words of W. Nelson Francis (1983:1), 'are varieties of a language used by groups smaller than the total community of speakers of the language'. Perceptual and political factors often lead to a belief in the reality of discrete dialects: exclusive groups of speakers kept separate from one another by geographical (e.g., rivers, mountains, oceans), social (e.g., age, sex, race), or political (e.g., national, ethnic) boundaries. As early as the time when Gilliéron's atlas was still new, however, Saussure admitted the attractions of such a conception of dialect but had to disagree with it because of the evidence:

> The current practice, which differs from ours, is to picture dialects as
> perfectly defined linguistic types, bounded in all directions and covering

distinct zones placed side by side on a map. But natural dialectal transformations produce entirely different results. As soon as we studied each phenomenon separately and determined its spread, our old notion had to give way to the new one: there are only natural dialectal features, not natural dialects; in other words, there are as many dialects as there are localities.

The notion of natural dialects is therefore incompatible with the notion of fixed well-defined zones. This leaves us with two choices: 1) we may define a dialect by the totality of its characteristics—which involves choosing one point on the map and encompassing only the regional speech-forms of a single locality, since the same peculiarities will not extend beyond this point; or 2) we may define a dialect by one of its characteristics, and simply map the spread of this characteristic—which obviously is an artificial procedure since the boundaries that we mark off correspond to no dialectal reality. (1959[1915]:201–02)

Saussure's point here is that it is not so easy to find groups of speakers so naturally separate as we might wish them to be.[2] Instead, he asserts, we must rely on procedure, the investigator's decision either to define a dialect by nominating a place, or to define a dialect according to the area of use of a linguistic feature. Saussure continued his argument with discussion of isoglosses and what we have come to call bundles of isoglosses. He posited two points, A and B, separated by such a bundle:

The two points . . . obviously have some divergencies and constitute two rather clearly differentiated forms of speech . . . A dialect is defined, roughly speaking, by a sufficient accumulation of such concordances [of isoglosses]. Their foundations are social, political, religious, etc., matters which do not concern us at the moment but which veil, without ever erasing completely, the basic and natural fact of differentiation from zone to zone. (203)

Saussure's remarks maintain a strong distinction between a 'dialectal feature' or 'characteristic' and the notion of 'natural dialect'. The former is in practice the artifact of a dialect survey—Saussure mentions Wenker and Gilliéron—one of those (word-level) linguistic features chosen for investigation in a survey. He denies that nature is so neat as to allow 'distinct zones', but he allows the 'artificial procedure' of mapping separate dialect features. When the investigator can build a 'sufficient accumulation' of dialect features for an area, that inventory of features constitutes, 'roughly speaking', a dialect. This kind of dialect is not the 'natural dialect' that Saussure rejected, but instead an indication or measure of the natural differentiation that one may expect to find between any two localities or zones (cf. the comments of Gaston Paris, as quoted in Francis 1983:2). Saussure does not, after all, refuse to acknowledge that localities have different speech habits, and he does admit that two localities can have 'two rather clearly differentiated forms of speech'; he just refuses to say that speech differences between two localities constitute two 'natural dialects' if, to pursue the implication of the argument, that assertion is taken to indicate self-consistent and mutually exclusive identities in real terms of two linguistic systems. He believes his view to be well supported by nonconcurrent distribution of dialect features, the result of historical forces.

It is important to note that the practical result of each of Saussure's choices for naming a dialect, either the conjunction of areas of occurrence for a number of dialect features or specification of a locality to 'encompass' its regional speech forms, is a list of particular features. Saussure does not recommend comprehensive description of the language of a locality; he wants a list of dialect features known to be used in the locality, exactly parallel to the list for an area that could be created from co-occurrence of dialect features.

Either way, he presupposes a dialect survey that has searched for information about particular features, and a list that in itself constitutes the inventory of features shared (to some extent) by the speakers who live in the area specified. Such an artificially generated inventory would mirror the complete inventory and arrangement of linguistic features that would compose a natural dialect, if a natural dialect could exist.

A natural dialect, as we might define one in a Saussurian way, must in theory depend on a common inventory and system of features (or signs), and in practice in natural language that commonality never occurs because of linguistic continua created by historical processes. Since there are no natural dialects, the inventories constitute dialects because we so name them, and they are useful because they help us to conceive of the 'basic and natural fact of differentiation from zone to zone'. Thus the dialects that we can name, and any dialect boundaries that we assert, are arbitrary and conventional as opposed to natural:

> The dividing lines between languages, like those between dialects, are
> hidden in transitions. Just as dialects are only arbitrary subdivisions of the
> total surface of language, so the boundary that is supposed to separate two
> languages is only a conventional one. (1959[1915]:204)

Dialect boundaries, whether constituted selectively by a single isogloss
or by assembling bundles of isoglosses, are not transitional—isoglosses,
after all, are quite real and sharp, derived from data (see Kretzschmar
1992)—but should rather be thought of as conventional because they
indicate a merely conventional entity, a dialect, and not a division
between (unreal) naturally occurring distinct varieties. To say that
'dividing lines . . . are hidden in transitions' is actually to say that there
are no 'natural' dividing lines between linguistic systems, that natural
language and dialect are characterized by continual transitions.
Differences in the inventory of dialect features at different locations
make dialect for Saussure a term with only local reality by convention,
according to the two options he provides for creation of lists of dialect
features. While Saussure concentrated on the areal boundaries in
common use in his time, his characterization of all linguistic boundaries
as 'conventional' applies directly to the modern designation of social
categories, to the arbitrary dividing lines between social classes or
educational levels or any other artificially created groupings, and so his
ideas apply to social as well as regional dialects.

All this is significant for dialectologists both as general guidance
about the nature of dialects and for particular specification of dialect
types. If we believe Saussure, and in my view there is every reason to
believe him, we should abandon the idea that we are looking for self-
consistent and mutually exclusive natural dialects, no matter how
attractive the political or perceptual notions, and instead recognize that
we are creating abstractions, called dialects, that help us to model and
thus to understand real regional and social variation in language. Insofar
as we rely on survey instruments designed to study particular linguistic
features, we should abandon any idea that we can talk about all-
encompassing dialect-qua-language and should instead take Pederson's
advice to limit our assertions to the word-level features we have
collected. To drop constraints on consistency and exclusivity immediately points toward current work on social networks (e.g. Milroy 1987,

Eckert 1989), and toward the idea that individuals can participate simultaneously in several groups and show linguistic characteristics associated with more than one group. Dialect is thus associated with groups of speakers as such groups may be defined by arbitrary and conventional dividing lines, especially as the dialect features of a dialect can be shown to contribute to group identity, and individual speakers 'speak a dialect' only insofar as, and to the degree that, they adopt the linguistic behavior of a group. Milroy and Eckert consider networks and interactions in groups of only a few people, and can demonstrate linguistic effects even at this micro level, and so their work forces us to think even about very small groups rather than just about dialects as they are traditionally conceived for large groups. The association of abstract dialects with groups thus frees individual speakers from having to speak the same way all the time because they are 'speakers of a dialect', an implication of the traditional model, and allows them instead to act as we know they act: to vary their linguistic behavior according to circumstance, and according to how they are (or wish to be) aligned with different groups.

Moreover, we can identify two different procedural senses of the term *dialect*, corresponding to the two choices outlined by Saussure. For the first sense, call it ATTRIBUTIVE DIALECT, we predefine a locality or category of speakers and seek to describe the dialect features of that locality or category, as we have evidence about particular features from our survey instrument. The second procedural sense of dialect, call it BLIND DIALECT, begins with the linguistic features that result from a survey designed to cover a large region or large group of people, as in the regional projects of the American Linguistic Atlas. Similarities in the distributions of features may reveal unforeseen correspondences between features and areas or social groups and thus suggest dialects. One and the same survey might be used for both purposes; the difference between attributive and blind dialects is a difference in procedure, subsequent to the collection of the data about particular features. Attributive procedure begins with the area or category and then matches dialect features to it; blind procedure begins with dialect features and matches areas or categories to them.

Both kinds of dialect require a notion of sufficiency: what constitutes sufficient evidence and elaboration, in practice, to describe attributive

dialects or, on the other hand, what number of correspondences constitutes enough shared dialectal features, with what degree of precision
in areal or social identification, to define blind dialects. How long must
the list of features be? Exactly who is supposed to be using them? In
practice different investigators will necessarily choose, and later
disagree about the validity of, different levels of sufficiency in the
participation of speakers in particular groups and for the elaboration
required for inventory. For instance, recent debate about African-
American English (including the convergence/divergence controversy)
has been handicapped because different kinds of speakers have been
identified as members of the group—only young people, both old and
young people, speakers from different cities or regions—though newer
terms, with more limited and specific group identifications, may
improve matters (see Butters 1989). Even if the speakers of African-
American English are agreed upon, there will still be the question of
how many dialect features are required to show sufficient linguistic
differentiation from other groups. The logical arrangement of the two
types of dialect, however, should not be in dispute. Blind dialects are
quite different from attributive dialects, because the investigator begins
with language in blind dialects and with location or category in
attributive dialects.[3]

Both kinds of dialects may be divided or combined, but conversion
between types is restricted. One may convert a particular blind dialect
into an attributive dialect: once an area has been defined by conjunction
of isoglosses or other linguistic measurements, one can make a list of
all the dialect features known (through a survey) to be used in the area.
Attributive dialects are not convertible into blind dialects—having
predefined an area or category and made a list of dialect features for it,
one may not then turn around and define the area again from the
features on the list. One ought not claim, for instance, that one has
discovered the special features of the dialect of New York City (i.e.,
those features that distinguish the city's speech from that of other
places) just because one has made a list of dialect features for New
York City. On the other hand, one might well plot a number of dialect
features and notice that several of them were peculiarly associated with
New York (i.e., those features that distinguish the city's speech from
that of other places), and then go on to add to that list other dialect

features in use in the city. Further, it is possible to subdivide either an attributive dialect or a blind dialect, or to combine dialects of either type into larger entities, so long as type distinctions and one-way convertibility are observed. One might, for instance, wish to subdivide an attributive North American dialect of English into United States and Canadian components, or one might wish to combine a set of features associated with a lower-class blind dialect with the set associated with a lower-middle-class blind dialect, to yield a larger set associated with a 'working'-class population. Divisions and combinations that do not violate the logic of the types are possible because neither attributive dialects nor blind dialects are natural; their artificial boundaries, whether regional or social, whether predetermined or observed from occurrences of features, always require decisions from the analyst, and different valid and sufficient judgments are possible.

Let us turn now to the work of Kurath to consider his methods in light of our new technical distinctions for dialect. Kurath's classic methods, as described in *Studies in Area Linguistics* (1972), appear to be inductive, in accordance with our theory for discovering blind dialects. He would select those items from his survey which show 'fairly clear-cut dissemination patterns' (24); in our terms, he begins with language and selects forms in order to observe areas in which speakers use them. He further asserts that 'one finds that in some parts of the area [heteroglosses] run in bundles of various sizes—closeknit or spaced. These bundles show the location of major and minor dialect boundaries and thus indicate the dialectal structure of the total area' (24). Again in our terms, Kurath uses bundles of heteroglosses to group speakers according to shared inventories, and he decides what bundles are sufficient to constitute major and minor boundaries. There is some reason to suspect, however, that Kurath did use another method to define groups of speakers, settlement history. In his *Word Geography* he states that

Each of these [original American colonies] had a life of its own for several generations and had closer ties with the mother country across the sea than with its sister colonies on this side of the Atlantic. When the several colonies finally established physical contact with each other, each one of them must have possessed distinctive social and cultural characteristics, including a dialect of its own—a unique blend of British types of speech, supplemented in its vocabulary by borrowings from the Indians or from Dutch or German neighbors. (1949:1)

This talk about the origins of American English dialects must lead us to speculate about how much influence his knowledge of settlement history might have had on Kurath when he judged the 'clear-cut dissemination' of items and when he assessed the sufficiency of number and definition of his bundles of glosses. Kurath's treatment of American English dialect areas in *Studies in Area Linguistics* (1972:39–57) contributes to this ambiguity when he frequently says that dialect areas 'reflect' settlement history. One must wonder whether, for Kurath, settlement history defines dialect areas, and the items merely reflect the definition. There is no accusation of dishonesty here; in terms of procedural definitions of dialect, defining a group of speakers before establishing an inventory for an attributive dialect is just as good a method as using an inventory of features to define an area for a blind dialect. If it is true that considerations external to the inventory of forms were an influence on him, then Kurath might have been guilty of shifting between or mixing attributive dialects, predefined groups of speakers, and blind dialects, where the definition of groups of speakers should emerge from the evidence. In fact the conjunction of dialect areas with settlement areas is just what we would expect anyway, but a mixed approach can lead to mixed expectations.

It may have been just such mixed signals that Uriel Weinreich and Samuel Keyser responded to. In his landmark article promoting the notion of system in dialect study (1954), Weinreich pointed out that identical inventories may hide differences in paradigmatic or syntagmatic arrangement of features, and that differences in inventories have systematic consequences. What Weinreich does not say is when these considerations become relevant. In each of his examples he presupposes a body of evidence—notably the low-front vowels in *man*—and so his arguments must be relevant only when we have already established inventories, such as the inventory for his attributive dialect of selected speakers in the case of the low-front vowels. Weinreich's discussion of low-front vowels hinges on whether or not a dialectologist has considered vowel length as a distinctive factor in the system of an attributive dialect; this is essentially a theoretical question—whether dialectologists can identify and record all of the features of inventory that might yield distinctions—and only secondarily a question of the use of features to discriminate between dialects. Dialectologists will indeed fail to distinguish two blind dialects on the basis of length if their sampling does not consider length; some similar losses are to be expected in any survey, for no sampling method is perfect, and there are features we strongly suspect of marking dialectal differences, such as some suprasegmentals or kinesics, that we have had no good way to sample. If we assume that dialectologists are capable of sampling length, and if we put the best possible face on Weinreich's argument, that length is in free variation among one subgroup of his chosen speakers and is distinctive among another subgroup—so that the inventories of both subgroups appear the same—then it is true that analysis of system can reveal the existence of something like blind dialects.

We should not, however, use the term BLIND DIALECT for these subgroups, because their definition results entirely from description of systems, and is therefore conditioned if not determined by the particular sampling instrument and by the particular method of description employed. An appropriate name for this kind of dialect might be DERIVED DIALECT: given both an inventory of dialect features and a locality or category of speakers, subgroups of speakers may be derived on the basis of separate syntagmatic or paradigmatic systems of features observed to exist with the common inventory. Derived dialect logically follows attributive dialect, just as attributive dialect follows blind dialect. Just as one can convert a particular blind dialect to an attributive dialect by means of further study, one can convert a particular attributive dialect to a derived dialect with further study, now in analysis of different systems, paradigms, or frequencies of occurrence, given an identical inventory (for further discussion of the interpretation of frequency differences, see Kretzschmar 1992, 1996b). The process, however, is not reversible, and the separate step between blind and derived dialects for study of attributive dialect is probably advisable, because of the risks of working from the more limited inventory of a blind dialect. Weinreich is perfectly justified in promoting the notion of system in dialectology, but only, even in his own examples, posterior to the initial collection and enumeration of data and to definition of a blind or attributive dialect.

Samuel Keyser's argument was in some ways parallel to Weinreich's when, in his review (1963) of Kurath and McDavid's *Pronunciation of English in the Atlantic States*, he attacked the phonemicization practices of *PEAS* and used rule ordering in a generative subsystem to account for the diphthongs in *five*, *twice*, *down*, and *out* for informants from Charleston, SC, New Bern, NC, and Winchester, VA. For generating the observed pronunciations from an underlying form, he proposed two rules with differing applicability (310):

Rule 1 ɑ → ɐ before a vowel followed by a voiceless consonant.
Rule 2 ɑ → æ before **u**.

As table 1 shows, Rule 1 operates for Charleston, Rule 2 for New Bern, and both rules in order for Winchester. Reversing the order of the rules also predicts an observed pronunciation for an informant near Roanoke, VA.

Table 1. Phonological rules generating PEAS vowel variation

Location	Observed Pronunciation				Operative Rules
	five	twice	down	out	
Charleston, SC	[ɑ˚ɪ]	[ɐɪ]	[au]	[ɐu]	R1
New Bern, NC	[a˚ɛ]	[a˚ɛ]	[æ˚u]	[æu]	R2
Winchester, VA	[ɑ˚ɛ]	[ɐɪ]	[æ˚u]	[ɐu]	R1 + R2

(adapted from Keyser 1963)

Keyser then speculated about dialect areas:

Let us suppose that Rule 1 arose in South Carolina and that, through dialectal diffusion, it began to travel northward, stopping finally at the northern periphery of the Virginia Piedmont. Let us also suppose that Rule 2 arose in the Upper Potomac Valley, and, through dialectal diffusion, began to migrate southward through the entire Virginia Piedmont area and beyond into New Bern. Given this migration, it follows that the area between, i.e., the area which was essentially overlapped by the two movements, would be characterized by Rule 1 (acquired when Rule 1 moved northward from South Carolina) followed by Rule 2 (acquired when Rule 2 moved southward from the Upper Potomac). And we have seen that the area marked by Rule 1 followed by Rule 2 is precisely the one which lies between South Carolina and the Upper Potomac, i.e., the Virginia Piedmont.[4] (1963:311–12)

With this procedure Keyser predefined a group of speakers, from one segment of the Atlantic States region as represented by his sample informants, an attributive dialect; he then predicted the inventories for two diphthongs in three subregions on the basis of system. This is manifestly not what Kurath and McDavid were trying to do; they were looking for blind dialects across the entire region, presumably without predefinition. To the extent that the review is not simply a disagreement about phonemicization theory,[5] parallel to Weinreich's discussion of vowel length, Keyser did not address dialect in the same sense as Kurath and McDavid took it, and the review argues at cross purposes. Whether or not Keyser's generative subsystem actually accounts for the diphthong inventory of the informants he selected (see Davis 1983:138–39), and regardless of the potential of Weinreich's ideas, in our terms their arguments do not appear to match their tools to specific critical tasks adequately.

The interest of both structural dialectology and generative dialectology in derived dialects should not obscure the difference between the two approaches. As Petyt has remarked (1980:173),

> What traditional and structural dialectology have in common is the fact that they both concentrate mainly on the *data* of the different dialects. This is where the approach of generative dialectology is claimed to differ: it focuses not so much on the data, the actual forms, as on the grammars of dialects—the *rules* which generate these forms . . . [L]inguists of this school hold that when the grammars of different dialects are compared, it is normally the case that they will have the same underlying forms and a majority of the same rules.

The structural approach observes an identity of inventory, in practical terms, and the generative approach posits an identity of underlying forms which, through ordered rules, accounts for differences in surface inventory. The status of the inventory of underlying forms raises its own questions of the order of procedures for generative dialectology, as pointed out by Thomas 1967: if the validity of the inventory of under-lying forms results from a comparison of the systems of different dialects, the generative dialectologist should begin there, but in fact that has not been the case in practice. In the terms presented here, it is not significant whether the common inventory of underlying forms is drawn from one or another of the dialects to be described, or from neither one, but it is highly significant that the inventory of underlying forms for the group of speakers in an attributive dialect be clearly stated and defended, including description of an underlying system, before description of the ordered rules which predict surface dialect features.

A more straightforward development of what I would call derived dialects has been carried out by William Labov. In a continuing series of publications (Labov, Yaeger, and Steiner 1972, Labov 1981, 1991), he has described three dialects of English characterized by chain shifts, systematic vowel rotations, called respectively the Northern Cities Shift, the Southern Shift, and the Low Back Merger. These dialects do not compete with regional dialects identified by Kurath and others, even though they are described (and two of them are named) with regional attributes:

> It's not a question of identifying dialects or dialect regions: that's what comes out of the work of Kurath and McDavid, Orton and Dieth, the LAGS, and so on. A dialect region seems to me well defined by a confluence of lexical, grammatical, and phonological evidence. The overall patterns of chain shifting give us a way of thinking about what's happening in the long-range development of sound change. Some of these patterns run across dialect regions, but for the most part, they coincide and confirm them . . . This identification of similar patterns of chain shifting that cover vast regions is not conceived as a challenge to the earlier establishment of dialect regions. The similarity between the Southern States version of the Southern Shift, and the processes operating in the south of England, South Africa, Australia and New Zealand is obvious, but once more, there is no suggestion that in some way Australian English and Philadelphia represent the same dialect! (Labov, personal communication)

Furthermore, Labov has argued that while the dialect areas identified with linguistic atlas methods seem well justified, 'the list of differences between these dialects has a miscellaneous character with little relation to phonological or grammatical theory' (1991:2), and that 'radical rotations of vowel systems, and not differences of inventory ... account for the greatest differences between vowel systems, and for problems of crossdialectal comprehension' (1991:3). Labov's approach, designed specifically for the theoretical and practical problems with which he prefers to work (e.g. the question of lexical diffusion as opposed to regularity of sound change, in Labov 1981), is to measure with acoustical phonetic equipment modern reflexes of words from the Middle English short *a* and short *o* classes, primarily, as a way to observe systems of sound change in progress. He studies a single attributive category of speakers:

> [The interviews] are heavily concentrated in that section of the upper working class that shows the most advanced forms when sound change is in progress; for the most part urban; and with a strong focus on spontaneous speech that is so heavily involved with emotion and interaction that the constraints of the interview situation are lowered. (Labov, p.c.)

Interviews under the same conditions for class and residence have been collected in cities around the US and around the world. When the results support the identification of three types of vowel systems, each system then defines the subgroup of speakers who use it. The fact that the geographic locations of these dialect subgroups may be seen in many places to correspond with blind areal dialects based on word and phone inventories in Atlas-style analyses thus may constitute independent confirmation of the approaches: Labov's and Atlas-style procedures can be seen to be complementary because the relation between them may be explicitly specified, unlike the case for Keyser's review. The fact of these parallel results is valuable because it may help to relieve worry about excessive dependence of derived dialects on the theory or research methods that allowed them to be described, in this case the manner in which generalizations are made on and from F1/F2 plots, and the particulars of membership in word classes (Romaine 1982).

Let us review one further reaction to Kurath. In his *American Regional Dialects*, Craig Carver prefers the 'participation method' to Kurath's heteroglosses. Given a body of evidence from the *DARE* corpus, Carver began as Kurath apparently did: he selected only those items which to him showed 'unequivocally regional distributions' (1987:17). He then segregated the items into lists, called 'layers', apparently because the regional patterning of the separate items on each list appeared to him roughly to coincide. For each list, he then counted the number of items possessed by each of the informants in the survey, plotted the counts on a map at the location of each informant, and drew boundaries to enclose locations where informants' inventories included some particular number of the items. The method renders areas for each list with high numbers, but also areas with lower numbers, creating a sort of gradient. Carver's approach, in our terms, uses linguistic forms alone to select groups of informants; he concentrates exclusively on blind dialects. However, his participation method, in reaction against the sharpness of isoglosses (12–13), conceals just what blind dialects should consist of: inventories of shared dialectal features. Since his maps show only numbers and not the presence or absence of particular linguistic forms from the lists, Carver does not directly compare inventories of informants; we cannot know whether his numbers show any coherence in inventories, that the same linguistic forms occur frequently within an area, or whether the numbers arise from dissimilar inventories (for a model that does consider coherence of inventories, see Babitch and Lebrun 1989). For that reason, in our terms we also cannot rely on boundaries drawn with absolute participation numbers—we have no assurance that the boundaries reflect any single linguistic form or combination of forms.

For example, Carver's analysis, in opposition to Kurath's 1949 formulation, 'argues against the existence of a separate Midland dialect region, since the divide [between Carver's North and South I layers] would cut directly across the region's center. At the same time it argues that the Lower North [another layer] is a major region, distinct from the North and South because of its strong mixed and transitional nature' (99). The North layer is based on 82 items, with boundaries (evidently) drawn in order to separate places with 30 or more responses matching the list, 25 to 29 responses, 20 to 24 responses, 10 to 19 responses, and under 10 responses. The South I layer contains 78 items, with lines drawn in order to separate places with 30 or more matching responses, 20 to 29 responses, and 19 or fewer responses. The Lower North layer has 53 items, with lines separating places with 10 or more matching responses, 5 to 9 responses, and 4 or fewer responses. The argument above is based on the rough complementarity of the areas with 30 or more matching responses for the North and South I lists (about 3/8 of each list); the Lower North has a core area with at least 10 of 53 items. Unfortunately we have no way of knowing whether the communities that had 30 or more matching responses mainly shared the same 30, or whether any single response from the list was widely or little known in the region; we can wonder whether some of the core Lower North communities with 10 or more of 53 items had very many responses in common at all. Whatever one may think of Kurath's Midland area, it was certainly described according to an incompatible procedure, and Carver seems to be arguing at cross purposes with it (a similar assessment might be made of the regression analysis of Davis and Houck 1992).

It has not been my intention in these examples to find fault with dialectologists or their work, but only to test an ordered technical definition of dialect against actual projects. What we have not seen so far is a straightforward attributive approach, and that is a particular strength of the work of Lee Pederson. The difficulties suggested so far have all come from the wish of analysts to 'discover' dialects, to make the language yield up its relation to geography and culture through induction. I believe in the possibility of the kind of induction that leads to blind dialects, but the procedure can certainly be methodologically difficult (see, e.g., Schneider and Kretzschmar 1989). Pederson has preferred to demonstrate time and again the efficacy and usefulness of attributive dialect study. His book on East Tennessee folk speech (1983) is a classic example of the construction of an inventory of dialect features for a predefined place and category. Pederson's work on LAGS, particularly as exemplified in the fourth volume, *Regional Matrix*, breaks new ground for the attributive approach: he provides the means for attributive study of a wide range of localities and categories from the LAGS region. Three earlier articles (Pederson 1986b, 1988, McDaniel 1989) describe in some detail the foundations of the LAGS mapping styles and matrices, information treated more briefly in *LAGS: Volume 4*. Pederson's three matrix formats, sector totals, social totals, and area totals, and two mapping formats, LAGS maps and code maps, define a set of attributive localities and categories in terms of which the dialect features of the project can be plotted, some 10,000 features in the published volumes. Over 400 LAGS maps and over 6500 sector total matrices appear in *LAGS: Volume 4*, with full enumeration of the other maps and matrices in volumes 5, 6, and 7. Pederson has not produced lists of features for particular localities or categories, but his maps and matrices will enable readers to make their own lists. Moreover, the extent of data collected for LAGS and reported in these volumes is so tremendous that there is great potential for readers also to describe derived dialects out of the attributive dialects for which they may choose to compile lists. For instance, there seems to be a fine opportunity here to confirm and to extend those studies that suggest that speakers of African-American English and Southern White English may have similar inventories of dialect features but significantly different frequencies of occurrence for some features, and thus be distinguishable as derived dialects.[6]

The predefinition of Pederson's areas and categories is selective but broad. There are 16 sectors, the boundaries of which are largely based on state boundaries and pragmatic divisions of states into smaller units (e.g. East, Middle, and West Tennessee). These are not the areas of blind dialects, identified through language, but arbitrary regional subdivisions of quadrants. There are 33 areas for the area totals, based on physical geography of the region, drawn from six principal land and vegetation regions: highlands, piedmont, coast, plains, piney woods, and delta categories (*LAGS Volume Five: Regional Pattern*). Boundaries here are not arbitrary in the same sense as sector boundaries, but their rationale comes from the land, not from language. The social total matrix (*LAGS Volume Six: Social Matrix*) offers nine social categories, with 24 divisions: two divisions for race, two divisions for sex, three divisions for each of two age categories, and so on. Social boundaries are sometimes simply binary, like sex, and sometimes controversially arbitrary, like social class. They are all, however, generated by criteria other than language. The mapping styles seem a little more open ended. There are nine different combinations of social categories among the code maps, and each map plots 18 divisions. LAGS maps plot dialect features by individual informant, so it is theoretically possible to recover inventories by informant from them. These maps recapitulate the procedure of earlier dialectologists by associating a particular linguistic form with a place, but they also do more. The 18 symbols used on the code map show selected social characteristics of the informants who used the forms, and Pederson includes in the volume a set of overlays that show the sectors and areas, attributive categories (overlays are also included with the later volumes). In short, he has provided interpretive tools for plotted data that lead directly back to the matrix totals and to the predefined categories. Speech forms, places, and attributive categories are all associated together at the same time on the same map. The procedure specially enabled by Pederson's methods is the study of attributive dialect, not just of one place or category but of any of many of possible localities or categories according to readers' interests.

That Pederson has chosen just the boundaries he has for the presentation of LAGS dialect features shapes the possibilities for analysis offered to readers, as appropriate for attributive analysis. Other boundaries might be devised, coded, and implemented by anyone who wanted to return to the original data of the LAGS computer files (Pederson has arranged publication of the data in several ways without attribute marking), but general readers will profit from the range of options for localities and categories that Pederson has already provided in the matrix and map volumes. The presentation of so many separate features as they occur in so many categories will present opportunities, not limitations, to most readers. Pederson's approach does not mix procedures or work at cross purposes, either with previous dialect analysis or with itself. Nothing in the matrices or maps is ambiguous or unexplained. Pederson's processing of the LAGS data is the result of an honest choice. It is not the only possible choice, but it is what it is. We can only hope that dialectologists, whether they choose to pursue blind or attributive or derived dialects, will be as straightforward in the logic of our common procedures.

NOTES

1. I would like to thank Edgar Schneider, Universität Regensburg, John Kirk, The Queen's University of Belfast, and Ellen Johnson and Rafal Konopka, members of the LAMSAS staff, for their assistance in the development of ideas

for this essay. An earlier version of this paper was read at the MLA annual meeting, 1988. I do not mean to minimize definitions and discussions of dialect since Saussure (or to trivialize his own, although a brief discussion like this one cannot avoid oversimplication), many of which are well summarized in Chambers and Trudgill 1980, Petyt 1980, Davis 1983, Francis 1983 (among others), and variation theory more generally. This essay attempts a rather pragmatic methodological argument, not a comprehensive definition.

2. In this he may be seen to anticipate modern unease with the notion 'speech community' (see, e.g. Romaine 1982, Fasold 1990:40–42).

3. John Kirk has suggested to me that politically or perceptually defined dialects, let us call them CULTURAL DIALECTS, ought to be set out explicitly as part of this schema, if only to differentiate them from the technical types presented here. Cultural dialects, then, do have artificial boundaries but no valid or sufficient judgments should (or can) be made to justify them because they are not defined on the basis of particular evidence: name a cultural dialect, and it exists. When people talk casually about dialects, very often they are talking about cultural dialects, not one of the technical types. When people, even in casual conversation, can cite particular evidence (e.g., that Boston is a different place linguistically because people say that they 'pahk a cah', or that they have only heard the word *bubbler* in Wisconsin and nowhere else), then they begin to talk about attributive and blind dialects.

4. Keyser actually presented alternative proposals, only one of which is discussed here. He also noted that he was not confusing diachronic with synchronic analysis: 'The ordering [of a set of rules] is clearly synchronic, but that does not preclude the possibility of drawing diachronic conclusions based upon that ordering' (1963:312n10).

5. That is the motivation for much of Keyser's review. One may recover a sense of the ferment of the time on this matter from the footnotes at the beginning of Stockwell 1959, which itself offers a proposal.

6. Frequency differences may also be used as part of a blind-dialect procedure, as Kretzschmar 1992 shows. I am not aware of a good discussion of the effect of differential frequencies of occurrence for dialect features, especially grammatical forms, in analyses of paradigms and other linguistic systems. Labov 1981 is a landmark article in its treatment of frequency differences and theories of sound change.

More Indexes for Investigating Chicago Black Speech

†Michael I. Miller

The dynamics of Chicago's black speech entail common but striking sociolinguistic processes, including assimilation of one regional dialect to another, relic formation, local innovation, status stratification, and age-grading, at least. Among current social developments, William Julius Wilson (1978, 1988) has documented how escalating black poverty since 1970 has led to increased class stratification and intensive ghettoization. One goal of the Sociolinguistic Survey of Chicago, the intensive survey of black and white speech patterns in the city conducted three decades ago by Lee Pederson (1965), was to explore the linguistic consequences of these ongoing social developments. However, the present paper is methodological rather than explanatory and describes some quantitative analytical techniques. The characteristics of Chicago black speech to be described are well known, thanks to Pederson's research, but I hope the methodological suggestions made will bring out some details in a new light.

LINGUISTIC INDEXES

Sociolinguists have been constructing 'indexes' ever since William Labov and Lee Pederson pioneered their use in the sixties (Pederson 1966 was first to use the term). Typically, linguists construct an index by counting the number of times a feature could occur in the natural flow of speech versus its actual occurrence. This linguistic index can then be compared with other nonlinguistic data, such as social status, age, or ethnicity. An advantage of this approach is that it uses more or less 'natural' data; a disadvantage is that the data are uncontrolled.

In the case of postvocalic /-r/, for example, we know that 'a much lower incidence of constriction occurs after rounded stressed vowels'

(Pederson 1966:5) than after unrounded vowels. In a 'natural' stream of speech, linguists seldom control for this variable and so produce unreliable results. That is, the words a speaker happens to use randomly entail front or back vowels with accidental predominance of one or the other type depending, for example, on the topic of conversation, so the index score for this variable shifts randomly and produces unreliable results.

The examples from Pederson's research to be discussed all derive from controlled interviews which examine preselected variables and ignore all other features within the stream of speech. The resulting data are neither better nor worse than the data obtained from free conversation. However, the sources differ from free conversation, and that fact influences results.

An Index of Postvocalic /-r/ in Chicago

In an earlier paper (Miller 1988b) I described how a linguistic index could be combined with a social status index using linear regression techniques. To make its point, my earlier paper relied on a plot and associated statistics similar to the one shown in figure 1 below. The data for this plot came from Pederson's survey of Chicago black speech, which was supervised by Raven I. McDavid, Jr. In addition to the regression line's flat slope, the most significant fact of this plot is the correlation of .43 and the R-square of .18. In other words, while there may be a correlation between social status and the articulation of postvocalic /-r/ in Chicago's black community, the correlation is not terribly great. The R-square indicates that if you tried to guess how a black person would articulate /r/ following a vowel based solely on knowledge of his or her social status, you would be right only about 18% of the time. On the other hand, people with lower social status do tend to have lower scores on the linguistic scale than people with higher social status: the L's all cluster below 60, for example, while the H's and M's seem to split evenly above and below that point.

Other Chicago Indexes

Though these data are interesting, to say that language, particularly articulation of postvocalic /-r/, varies with social status is not news. We need to do more than prove irrefutably that a few pronunciation features

Figure 1. Social status with r-index by class

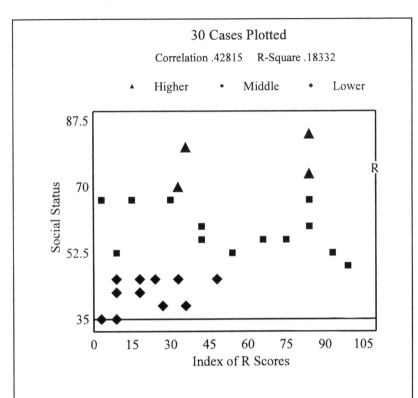

relate more or less to social status. And for this purpose, in addition to information on postvocalic /-r/, Pederson provided information about several other elements of Chicago black speech. These aspects of the linguistic system (see table 1) include (1) constriction of postvocalic /-r/ following both rounded and spread vowels; (2) height of articulation of the onset of /aɪ/ in words like *five* and *wife*; (3) presence or absence of an off-glide with the vowel of *cut* in words like *shut* and *husband*; (4) consonant loss such as the final stop in *chest* or the medial stop in *candles*; (5) consonant phoneme incidence, such as fricative versus stop as the initial in *this* or labial versus dental as the final in *mouth*; (6) systematic alternation in stressed vowel incidence, such as the vowels of *bet* or *bat* in words like *married* and *parents* or the vowels of *law* or *father* in words like *palm* and *wash*; (7) nonsystematic alternation in vowel incidence such as the stressed vowel of *aunt* or the unstressed vowel of *yellow*; (8) lexical differences, such as *faucet* versus *hydrant*, *pipe*, and *spigot*; and (9) preterites and participles like *drive* and *write*. Though not inclusive, these lists slice into the linguistic system at crucial points and provide a convincing cross-section of everyday speech.

Table 1. Linguistic features and items investigated

Feature	Items
1. constriction of postvocalic /r/	beard, careless, thirteen, furniture, Birmingham, four, fourth, horse, hoarse, chair, morning, mourning
2. onset height of /aɪ/	five, nine, twice, dining, China, spider, wife, right, tired, climbed, might
3. offglide with /ʌ/	shut, brush, touch, onions, husband, son, judge, pus, nothing, something, hundred, once
4. consonant loss	help, vegetables, forehead, hundred, good, tube, umbrella, chest, left-overs, fifth, ninth, joints, bag, yeast, caught, candles, Louisiana
5. consonant incidence	February, grease, greasy, this, wash, with, mouth, without, fourth, rinses, chimney, Birmingham
6. systematic stressed vowel alternation	dairy, married, kerosene, parents, hoarse, mourning, tomorrow, borrow, palm, wash, water, laundry, haunted
7. nonsystematic vowel alternation	deaf, rather, aunt, shut, brush, soot, roof , window, widow, yellow, tomorrow, tomato, Saturday, genuine
8. lexical differences	faucet, kerosene, yolk, cobweb, chest, got, sick, stamp, bulge, afraid, aunt
9. verb forms	drive, sit, swim, begin, dive, kneel, climb, eat, drown, bite, eat, write, drink, do

Building an Index from Categorical Data

Furthermore, though categorical from a word-by-word point of view, all of Pederson's data can be converted to proportional indexes or even to a single index. For example, table 2 reorganizes the data on nonsystematic incidence of both stressed and unstressed vowels in the 14 words listed for linguistic feature seven in table 1.

Table 2: Incidence of Inland Northern vowels in Chicago black speech

Item	Frequency (30 tests of item)			Percent Inland North
	Inland North	Other	(Missing)	
1. roof	22	6	2	79
2. brush	23	7	0	77
3. deaf	22	8	0	73
4. shut	21	8	1	72
5. widow	20	9	1	69
6. window	18	9	3	67
7. Saturday	17	13	0	57
8. rather	13	12	5	52
9. tomorrow	15	14	1	52
10. genuine	13	14	3	48
11. soot	14	16	0	47
12. tomato	10	19	1	34
13. yellow	8	22	1	28
14. aunt	6	24	0	20

The most common Inland Northern pronunciations, as established by Pederson's *The Pronunciation of English in Metropolitan Chicago* (1965), are /rʊf/, /brʌš/, /dɛf/, /šʌt/, /wɪdou/, /wɪndou/, /sætɚdei/, /ræðɚ/, /təmarou/, /ǰɛnjuɪn/, /sʊt/, /təmetə/, /jɛlou/, and /ænt/. Adoption of typical Inland Northern pronunciations varies in Pederson's sample from a high of nearly 80% for *roof* (indicated in the far right column) to a low of 20% for *aunt*, often pronounced with the vowel of *father* in Chicago's black community.

These data are categorical rather than linear. The resulting indexes differ sharply from those typically used in the Labovian paradigm. We are not saying that any given person or group was likely to pronounce *roof* like a white native Chicagoan 79% of the time, merely that 79% of the people Pederson interviewed (and by implication, something like 79% of the black population) typically used the Inland Northern pronunciation of *roof*; conversely, only 20% said *aunt* with a low-front vowel. We ignore stylistic variation.

However, as with postvocalic /-r/, we can still build a linguistic index for these words simply by adding the total number of Inland Northern usages for each informant and dividing by the total number of usages observed for that informant. That is, we count the actual number of Inland Northern usages versus the possible number in the speech of each person and convert the result to a percentage. In this case, we are saying that in this general area of linguistic usage—nonsystematic incidence of stressed and unstressed vowels—any given individual's usage varies from a specific low proportion to a specific high proportion. Table 3 below shows explicitly how this works out in each case for the sample we are working with.

Here the indexes range from a low of 8.33% for informant 30 at the bottom (who, confusingly, pronounced *aunt* in the typical Inland Northern way) to a high of 92.31 for informant 21 (who used a nonlocal pronunciation only for *aunt*). In addition to our categorical data for each informant, we now have another scale. Since this scale differs from purely categorical frequency counts and looks like an interval scale—misleadingly so—we can use it for a variety of analytical techniques that we can't use when we are dealing with purely categorical data.

Michael I. Miller

Table 3. Data matrix: Inland Northern vowel incidence

Words Investigated

Case no.	d e a f	r a t h e r	a u n t	s h u t	b r u s h	s o o t	r o o f	w i n d o w	w i d o w	y e l l o w	t o m o r r o w	t o m a t o	S a t u r d a y	g e n u i n e	Index
1	1	0	0	1	1	1	1	1	1	1	1	0	0	1	71.43
2	1	1	0	1	1	1	1	1	1	1	1	1	1	0	85.71
3	1	1	0	1	1	1	1	0	1	0	0	1	0	1	64.29
4	0	1	0	1	1	1	1	1	1	1	1	1	1	0	78.57
5	1	1	0	1	1	1	1	9	1	0	0	0	1	9	66.67
6	1	1	0	0	0	1	1	1	1	0	1	0	1	0	57.14
7	0	1	0	1	1	1	1	9	1	0	1	1	0	1	69.23
8	1	0	0	1	1	1	1	1	1	1	1	1	1	0	78.57
9	1	9	0	1	0	1	1	1	0	9	0	1	0	0	50.00
10	0	0	0	0	0	0	1	0	9	0	0	0	1	1	23.08
11	1	1	1	9	1	1	9	1	0	0	1	0	0	0	58.33
12	1	0	0	1	1	0	1	1	1	0	1	0	1	0	57.14
13	1	1	0	1	1	0	1	1	1	1	1	1	1	1	85.71
14	1	0	0	1	1	1	1	1	0	1	9	0	0	0	53.85
15	1	9	0	1	1	0	1	1	1	0	1	0	0	9	58.33
16	1	0	0	0	1	0	9	9	0	0	0	0	0	1	25.00
17	1	0	0	0	0	0	0	0	0	0	0	0	1	1	21.43
18	0	0	1	1	1	0	0	0	1	0	0	0	1	0	35.71
19	1	0	1	1	1	0	1	0	1	0	0	0	1	0	50.00
20	0	0	0	0	1	0	0	0	1	0	1	0	0	1	28.57
21	1	9	0	1	1	1	1	1	1	1	1	1	1	1	92.31
22	1	1	0	1	1	0	1	1	1	1	1	1	1	1	85.71
23	1	1	1	1	1	0	1	1	1	0	1	1	1	1	85.71
24	0	9	0	1	1	1	1	1	1	0	1	0	1	0	61.54
25	1	1	0	0	1	0	1	1	1	0	0	0	1	0	50.00
26	1	0	1	1	1	1	0	1	0	0	0	0	0	1	50.00
27	1	1	0	1	0	0	1	1	1	0	0	0	0	0	42.86
28	1	1	0	0	1	0	1	0	0	0	0	0	0	1	35.71
29	0	0	0	1	0	0	0	0	0	0	0	9	1	0	15.38
30	0	9	1	0	0	0	0	0	0	0	0	0	0	9	8.33

NOTE: 1 = Typical Inland Northern Usage; 0 = Atypical Inland Northern Usage; 9 = Missing Data. The formula for computing the vowel index is (SUM (DEAF TO GENUINE) / R) x 100, where R = Response Count, or the sum of 1's and 0's.

SOME USES OF LINGUISTIC INDEXES

For example, we can use indexes like these to make broad descriptive statements about our target population's language, to investigate the effects of social phenomena like class stratification, urban migration, and cultural isolation, and to identify specific problems that justify further research.

Comparing Mean Index Scores

As an illustration, we know that several processes influence the distinctive characteristics of Chicago black speech, including age-grading, relic formation, and local innovation, as mentioned earlier. However, much variation from Inland Northern norms and within the black community can be attributed to importation from other regional dialects and differential adoption of Inland Northern speech habits. By constructing composite index scores we can estimate which features of Inland Northern speech have been most thoroughly adopted in the black community and which features of extraregional speech have been preserved. Table 4 illustrates one way to compare indexes like these.

Table 4. Descriptive statistics for nine Chicago indexes

Index	mean	Std.Dev.	Minimum	Maximum	N
1. cons. incid.	95.72	7.17	66.67	100.00	30
2. consonant loss	61.06	19.66	18.75	100.00	30
3. verb forms	58.41	26.74	11.11	100.00	30
4. lexical	57.52	20.56	10.00	90.00	30
5. non-sys. vowel	54.88	23.14	8.33	92.31	30
6. sys. vowel	51.32	17.75	23.08	78.57	30
7. /-r/ constric.	39.61	30.57	0.00	100.00	30
8. /ʌ/ offglide	39.34	28.46	0.00	91.67	30
9. /aɪ/ onset hgt.	34.20	33.99	0.00	90.91	30

This summary lists the mean index scores (based on typical Inland Northern pronunciations), standard deviations, minimums, and maximums for each of the nine linguistic features listed on table 1. Table 4 suggests that nearly all black people in Chicago use the regionally standard consonant forms, since the mean index score for variation in consonant incidence is 95.72 with a small standard deviation. Though pronunciations like *mouf* and *dis* stereotype black speech in Chicago, they seldom occur in fact. On the other hand, black people in Chicago have been slow to adopt typical Inland Northern /r/, /ʌ/, and /aɪ/ pronunciations. These features tend to distinctively mark black speech in Chicago, but they are obviously Southern imports rather than spreading new formations. This analysis also suggests that if we want to identify the features that distinguish Chicago black speech most clearly from Chicago white speech, we would look to the pronunciations of words like *beard*, *husband*, and *wife* rather than to the pronunciations of words like *mouth* and *chest* or to the forms of verbs.

Investigating Class Stratification

These index scores also permit the analysis of class stratification within Chicago's black community. Table 5, for example, breaks the composite scores down by social class and reorders the index sequence by the mean scores of the highest social class. This table also includes the results of an F test for each index and two correlation statistics: R-square and ETA-square.

Table 5. Summary of index means, F test, R-square
and ETA-square by class

Index	Social Class			F	SIG	R^2	ETA^2
	high	middle	lower				
1. vb forms	95.71	67.01	38.33	17.7250	.0000	.5677	.5677
2. cons. inc.	93.91	97.96	94.04	1.1272	.3387	.0100	.0771
3. n-sys vwl	83.79	64.31	36.55	7.9592	.0000	.5639	.5709
4. cons. loss	81.26	69.46	46.43	12.2350	.0002	.4577	.4754
5. lexical	77.50	61.79	47.09	4.8640	.0157	.2647	.2649
6. /aɪ/ onset	71.79	43.79	13.05	8.2091	.0016	.3778	.3781
7. sys. vwl	63.73	59.42	39.41	7.6845	.0023	.3203	.3627
8. /-r/ cons.	59.09	53.44	19.78	6.8374	.0040	.2906	.3362
9. /ʌ/ offgl.	40.91	42.86	35.35	.2205	.8035	.0101	.0161

This is a complex table, but the salient points are these: First, verb forms and nonsystematic vowel alternation, rows 1 and 3 on the table, appear to be effective diagnostics for class stratification within black speech. The scores for R-square and ETA-square suggest this interpretation most clearly. ETA-square is usually defined as 'the total variability in the dependent variable that can be accounted for by knowing the values of the independent variable' (Norusis 1983:58). Unlike R-square, ETA-square 'does not assume a linear relationship between the variables'. Second, because 'standard' consonants have been adopted throughout the black community, consonant incidence is not socially diagnostic; that is, the F test produces nonsignificant results and the ETA-square is only .0771.

Conversely, because the typical Chicago monophthongal mid-central vowel has not been adopted on a large scale within the black community, this feature is also not socially diagnostic, with a nonsignificant F test and ETA-square of only .0161. In table 4 we saw that verb forms would not be our best choice for distinguishing between black and white speech (assuming the latter represents Inland Northern pronunciation); table 5, on the other hand, indicates that verb forms would be an excellent choice for investigating class stratification within the black community. Similarly, tables 4 and 5 indicate that postvocalic /-r/ may be a useful feature for distinguishing black and white speech, but it is far from our best choice for investigating class stratification within the black community.

Analyzing Nonparametric Data

An objection to the data presented in table 5 is that the indexes we have been discussing do not represent true interval scales. That is, if one person scores 83 on, let us say, the /aɪ/ scale and another scores 44, it does not make sense to say that the first has precisely 39% more /aɪ/ in his speech than the second. All we can justifiably say is that the first has a score higher than the second. One way to cope with this fact is to treat the scales as rank orderings rather than intervals. In this case, analyses such as the one shown in table 6 below may provide a more accurate view of how the indexes relate to each other. This table reorders the indexes as devices for exploring class stratification. It is probably more reliable. Moreover, the indexes of verb usage and the pronunciation of postvocalic /-r/ appear in similar positions near the top and near the bottom of the list. Consonant incidence and articulation of /ʌ/, though perhaps distinctively marking Chicago black speech, likewise seem not helpful for investigating class stratification within black speech.

Table 6. Kruskal-Wallis one-way ANOVA index mean ranks by class

Index	Social Class			χ^2	SIG	Corrected	
	high	middle	lower			χ^2	SIG
1. vb forms	27.75	18.08	9.15	15.6146	.0004	15.6739	.0004
2. nnsys vwl	27.00	19.23	8.23	18.0234	.0001	8.1211	.0001
3. lexical	24.63	16.85	11.35	7.4958	.0236	7.6455	.0219
4. /aɪ/ onset	24.50	17.69	10.54	9.1161	.0105	9.3876	.0092
5. cons. loss	24.13	19.85	8.50	15.2274	.0005	15.2647	.0005
6. sys. vwl	21.88	19.54	9.50	10.8720	.0044	10.9036	.0043
7. /r/ constr	21.38	19.31	9.88	9.5028	.0086	9.5645	.0084
8. /ʌ/ offgl	15.50	16.46	14.54	0.3102	.8563	0.3115	.8558
9. cons. inc.	12.50	17.77	14.15	1.6323	.4421	2.1928	.3341

Simple Linear Regression

Nonparametric techniques like the one-way ANOVA alone, though revealing, do not permit observations that emerge when we use regression techniques. It can be helpful, sometimes, to treat index scores as points on an interval rather than merely ordinal scale even when we know better. For example, figure 2 below plots the standardized residuals around the regression line for the nonsystematic incidental vowel index we constructed earlier, a technique available for linear regression analysis but not for analyzing nonparametric data.

This plot also lists measures known as Mahalanobis' Distance and Cook's D. The function of Mahalanobis' Distance is to identify cases whose value on the independent variable differs remarkably from other cases. The function of Cook's D is to identify influential points. The Mahalanobis' Distance scores for cases 1 and 21 are significantly higher than the scores for all other cases. Perhaps the social status of these two informants has been overrated. The second measure on this plot, Cook's D, is particularly large for case number 1, who may therefore be unduly influencing the upper end of the scale. These scores warn us not to put

too much faith in conclusions influenced heavily by these two informants' responses.

Figure 2. Casewise plot of standardized residual social status with
nonsystematic incidental vowel index

	-3.0	0.0	3.0	NNSYS VWL		
CASE #	0:.........:.........:0			INDEX	*MAHAL	*COOK D
1	.	* .	.	71.43	4.9604	.3626
2	.	. *	.	85.71	1.5268	.0180
3	.	* .	.	64.29	1.1731	.0176
4	.	. *	.	78.57	1.0137	.0059
5	.	* .	.	66.67	1.0137	.0061
6	.	* .	.	57.14	.3016	.0057
7	.	. *	.	69.23	.1573	.0049
8	.	. *	.	78.57	.0282	.0342
9	.	* .	.	50.00	.0282	.0049
10	. *	.	.	23.08	.0282	.0961
11	.	. *	.	58.33	.0037	.0016
12	.	. *	.	57.14	.0037	.0009
13	.	. *	.	85.71	.0456	.0970
14	.	. *	.	53.85	.2690	.0066
15	.	. *	.	58.33	.3539	.0211
16	.	* .	.	25.00	.3539	.0405
17	.	* .	.	21.43	.4505	.0544
18	.	* .	.	35.71	.5587	.0045
19	.	. *	.	50.00	1.1079	.0337
20	.	* .	.	28.57	1.2743	.0079
21	.	. *	.	92.31	3.6945	.0059
22	.	*	.	85.71	2.6147	.0018
23	.	. *	.	85.71	.7298	.0354
24	.	. *	.	61.54	.1957	.0197
25	.	. *	.	50.00	.5587	.0088
26	.	. *	.	50.00	.6786	.0129
27	.	. *	.	42.86	.8101	.0023
28	.	*	.	35.71	.9532	.0006
29	.	* .	.	15.38	2.0562	.0563
30	.	* .	.	8.33	2.0562	.1263
Case #	0:.........:.........:0			INDEX	*MAHAL	*COOK D
	-3.0	0.0	3.0			

A topic worth further investigation is that the standardized residuals of informants 21 through 30 cluster around the regression line a little more tightly than for informants 1–20. However, Pederson classified 21 through 30 as recent in-migrants, so it seems that the linear regression model for social and linguistic stratification fits newer in-migrants better than long-term Chicagoans. Though counterintuitive, this result may confirm William Julius Wilson's observation that the combined effects of caste and class discrimination tend to isolate long-term black residents more than newer black in-migrants. And this may relate to Wilson's observation that the older black population is not following the traditional path of other ethnic groups in Chicago to economic power and social integration, even though newer in-migrants seem to be doing so.

In any case, both observations—concerning the behavior of longtime versus newer residents and the behavior of people with unusually high social status—confirm the usefulness of regression analysis for sociolinguistic survey research. Of course, parametric techniques are frequently not justified in analyzing survey data of any type. However, as long as we are cautious in our interpretations and careful to find more than one source of evidence to back up interpretations, techniques like regression analysis can be revealing.

Comparing Linear Correlations

Plots like the one at the beginning of this paper illustrate the just-stated point well. We can easily plot the correlation of social status with the vowel index we have been discussing as in figure 3 below.

In this case social status and linguistic index correlate much better than they did for postvocalic /-r/, as table 5 suggested they would. We now have an R-square of .58. However, we should interpret this statistic loosely. The nonparametric ANOVA shown on table 6 in fact confirms that social status and linguistic usage correlate well for these items. However, it may be pushing the analysis beyond credibility to argue for the precise correlation this plot seems to imply. The plot presents a revealing graphic metaphor, and the associated regression analysis can lead to valuable insights. But it seems unlikely that social status and linguistic form covary with great precision. Given this caution, we can still construct indexes for each set of linguistic features and compare

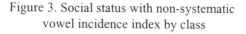

Figure 3. Social status with non-systematic
vowel incidence index by class

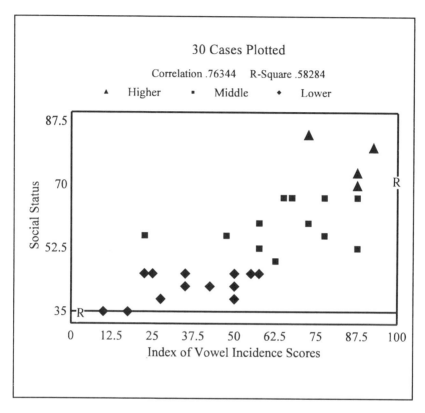

how they correlate with social status using the Pearson R. Table 7 summarizes the results of this procedure. These data suggest that nonsystematic alternation of stressed vowels in words like *aunt* and *roof*, verb forms like the preterit of *drive* and participle of *write*, and consonant loss in words like *chest* and *candle* correlate strongly with social stratification within Chicago's black community. In addition, the lexicon is a neglected feature that can provide a meaningful index of class stratification, though the lexical items Pederson investigated may not have been the best for our purposes. However, articulation of postvocalic /-r/, incidence of consonants in words like *this* and *mouth*, and articulation of the vowel of *cut* are less important correlates of social stratification. This result is similar to the result produced by nonparametric analysis.

Table 7. Summary of index correlations with social status

Index	Correlation	R^2	S.E.	SIG.
1. non-sys. vowel	.76344	.58240	8.61783	.0000
2. verb forms	.68950	.47542	9.66390	.0000
3. consonant loss	.68353	.46721	9.73920	.0000
4. /aɪ/ onset hgt.	.60487	.36587	10.62516	.0004
5. lexical difference	.56603	.32039	10.99956	.0011
6. systematic vowel	.56131	.31507	11.04254	.0013
7. /r/ constriction	.42815	.18332	12.05791	.0183
8. consonant incid.	.12087	.01461	13.24491	.5246
9. /ʌ/ offglide	.08992	.00809	13.28868	.6365

CONCLUSION: FUNCTIONALITY

If we want to contribute substantially to the debate that William Julius Wilson originated, we will need to do more than reiterate the obvious points that language is both socially stratified and changing. Key problems now are identifying structural forces at work and describing the linguistic and cultural consequences of these forces.

For these purposes, the indexes described here can reliably orient our investigation of Chicago black speech. However, these sources of information will need supplementary and supporting evidence drawn from sources as diverse as free conversation and the sorts of postal questionnaires pioneered in the Great Lakes region by Alva Davis in his 1949 dissertation. Without question, Davis' approach to the lexicon can usefully supplement Pederson's oral approach to pronunciation and grammar. But that was a subject for another paper (Miller 1988a). Regardless of the sources of our data, the statistical techniques outlined here provide essential tools for investigating the dynamics of Chicago black speech.

Educational and Gender-Related Differences in the Use of Verb Forms in the South Atlantic States
Virginia G. McDavid

Among the publications dealing with grammatical items in the Linguistic Atlas of the Middle and South Atlantic States (LAMSAS) is E. Bagby Atwood's *A Survey of Verb Forms in the Eastern United States* (1953). Atwood's study considers both geographical and social differences in some 90 items, 56 of them forms of irregular verbs, and concludes that usage for these is more sharply divided along social and educational lines than is true for vocabulary or pronunciation items. Harold B. Allen reaches the same conclusion for the grammatical materials in his *Linguistic Atlas of the Upper Midwest* (1973:2:83). All of my later work with verb forms in the Atlas data bears socio-educational division out (McDavid 1987, 1988a, b, c, 1989, 1990).

However, neither Atwood nor Allen considers the gender of the informant in his analyses, nor did I consider it in my 1956 dissertation *Verb Forms in the North-Central States and Upper Midwest*. The first person to use Atlas data for the study of differences that might be gender related was William R. Van Riper, who offered a paper 'Usage Preferences of Men and Women: *did*, *came*, and *saw*' at the Chicago Conference on Language and Cultural Pluralism in 1977. Van Riper concludes his paper (1977:4): 'If a verb form . . . is strongly supported by school handbooks of usage and by editors of widely-read publications, and if the competing forms are censured by usage handbooks, more women than men in any age group or on any level [of educational attainment] except the highest will favor the supported form; and sometimes this is the case even on the highest level'. Again, my own work with Atlas materials in the Middle and South Atlantic States, in the North-Central States, and in the Upper Midwest tends to confirm Van Riper's hypothesis, as does the present study.

Using data from the LAMSAS, the present study considers differences between men's and women's choices of standard and nonstandard forms of preterit or past participle for eight verbs: the preterits of *blow*, *give*, *run*, and *throw*, and the past participles of *drown*, *tear*, *wear*, and *write*. The South Atlantic territory covered appears as sectors D, E, and F on figure 1. (The divisions are the ones developed by the editors of the Linguistic Atlas of the Middle and South Atlantic States, principally William A. Kretzschmar, Jr., and Ellen Johnson.)

Figure 1. LAMSAS sectors D–F

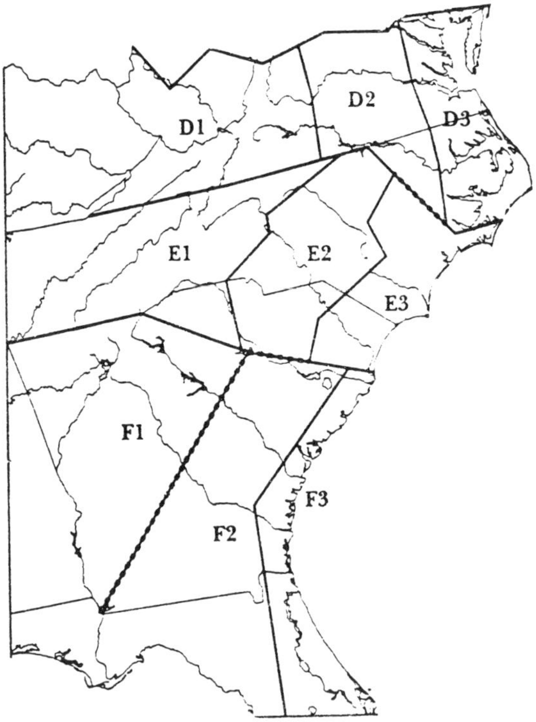

These areas are part of what is often thought of as the South and extend from Virginia and southern West Virginia through the Carolinas and parts of Georgia and Florida. Among the larger cities in the area are Richmond, Roanoke, and Norfolk in Area D; Charlotte, Raleigh, and Asheville, North Carolina, as well as Greenville and Columbia, South

Carolina, in Area E ; and Charleston, Augusta, Savannah, and Atlanta in Area F.

LAMSAS divisions D, E, and F contain a total of 503 informants (see table 1), most of whom were interviewed in the 1930s and 1940s. Not all informants, of course, responded to each item, but because the verbs are such common ones, the percentage of those responding was high. Type I informants—those with a grammar school education or less—comprised 58 percent of the total. The remaining 42 percent were Type II informants—those with a high-school education. The mean age of Type I informants was 73; that of Type II informants was 66.

Table 1. Summary of informants

	Area D	Area E	Area F	Total
Type I	108	94	89	291
Type II	69	75	68	212
Total	177	169	157	503

Sixty-one percent of all informants were males, 39 percent females. Type III informants, those with a college education, are not included here; their usage was almost invariably standard. Tables 2 through 9 present the numbers and percentages of informants using the standard form for each of the eight verb principal parts examined in this study.

The selection of the eight verbs was largely arbitrary. They are common verbs in frequent use, and almost every informant responded to the questions that targeted them. For the most part they have only one nonstandard variant. For the preterit *blew* it is *blowed*; for the past participle *drowned*, *drownded*; for the preterit *gave*, *give* (*gin* is rare and occurs almost always as a form reported for others); for the preterit *ran* it is *run*; for the preterit *threw* it is *throwed*; for the past participle *torn*, *tore*; for the past participle *worn*, *wore*; and for the past participle *written*, *wrote*. Suggested or reported forms are not included, nor have multiple responses been counted.

Seven of the eight verbs (*blow, give, run, tear, throw, wear,* and *write*) are historically strong verbs. For *give, run, tear, wear,* and *write,* the use of the nonstandard form results in the reduction of the number of principal parts from three to two, and in the case of *run*, from two to one. With *blow*, the use of the nonstandard *blowed* is the result of analogy with weak verbs ending in *-ed*. The same is true of *throwed*. With *drown*, the nonstandard two-syllable pronunciation *drownded* represents, at least synchronically speaking, an excrescent *d* sound added to the base *drown*.

In the sections below, tables 2–9 treat each verb in turn, presenting the informants' responses by education level (i.e. informant type) and gender. The individual discussions of the eight verb forms are followed by a summary of usage by informant type and gender. The nonparametric chi-square test was used in analyzing the data for statistically significant results. Parametric tests must assume that the samples analyzed come from normally distributed populations, something that we cannot demonstrate for linguistic atlas data. Since nonparametric tests make no such assumptions, the chi-square test is entirely appropriate.[1]

Preterit *blew*, nonstandard *blowed*

The preterit of *blow* is anomalous among the eight verbs because it is the only one in which the females did not use the standard form more than the males did; the percentages of male and female users of the standard form were the same in each of the three geographical areas (percentages of use of standard form by gender are presented for all eight verbs in table 10 below).

In Area F, the percentage of users of the standard form *blew* was about twice that in the other two areas. The standard form *blew* was used by about one-fourth of all informants in Areas D and E, which include most of Virginia, all of North Carolina, and northern South Carolina; and by about half of them in Area F, comprising southern South Carolina, eastern Georgia, and a small part of northeastern Florida. The difference between Type I and II informants was significant at the .05 level in all three areas. In no area did more than one-third of the Type I informants use *blew*, and in Areas D and E, fewer used it. In Areas D and F more than half the Type II informants used the standard form. Only in Area F did more than half of the informants use the standard form.

Table 2. Preterit *blew*

	Area D		Area E		Area F	
Type I	11/101	**11%**	4/79	**5%**	22/64	**34%**
Type II	36/68	**53%**	26/69	**38%**	34/46	**74%**
Type I Male	10/64	16%	4/50	8%	12/40	30%
Type I Female	1/37	3%	0/29	0%	10/24	42%
Type II Male	16/30	53%	14/38	37%	26/35	74%
Type II Female	20/38	53%	12/31	39%	8/11	73%
All Male	26/94	28%	18/88	20%	38/75	51%
All Female	21/75	28%	12/60	20%	18/35	51%
All M + F	47/169	28%	30/144	20%	56/110	51%

Bold indicates significance at p < .05

Past participle *drowned*, nonstandard *drownded*

The difference between Type I and Type II informants was significant in all three areas. The difference was particularly striking in Areas D and E, where the standard participle *drowned* was used by only one-fourth of Type I informants but by nearly three-fourths of Type II informants. In all three areas the females used the standard form more than the males, but the difference was significant only in Area D. In Area F the proportions were more nearly even.

Preterit *gave*, nonstandard *give*

In all three areas fewer than a third of all informants used the standard preterit *gave*. The difference between Type I and Type II informants was striking and significant in all areas, particularly in Area D, where only three percent of Type I informants were recorded as using only the standard form, but 79 percent of Type II informants were. The percentage differences between all male and female informants were significant and similar in all three areas.

Table 3. Participle *drowned*

	Area D		Area E		Area F	
Type I	24/101	**24%**	10/79	**13%**	31/71	**42%**
Type II	50/67	**75%**	47/67	**70%**	33/44	**75%**
Type I Male	14/63	22%	9/50	18%	19/46	41%
Type I Female	10/38	26%	1/29	0%	11/25	44%
Type II Male	20/31	**65%**	19/34	56%	22/32	69%
Type II Female	30/36	**83%**	28/33	85%	11/12	92%
All Male	34/94	36%	28/84	33%	41/78	53%
All Female	39/74	54%	29/62	47%	22/37	59%
All M + F	73/168	44%	57/146	39%	63/115	55%

Bold indicates significance at $p < .05$

Table 4. Preterit *gave*

	Area D		Area E		Area F	
Type I	3/90	**3%**	4/79	**5%**	9/75	**12%**
Type II	45/57	**79%**	41/65	**63%**	23/44	**55%**
Type I Male	1/55	2%	3/51	6%	3/52	3%
Type I Female	2/35	6%	1/28	4%	7/23	30%
Type II Male	16/24	67%	15/33	45%	14/28	50%
Type II Female	29/33	88%	26/32	81%	10/16	62%
All Male	17/79	**22%**	18/84	**21%**	17/80	**21%**
All Female	31/68	**46%**	27/60	**45%**	17/39	**44%**
All M + F	48/147	33%	45/144	31%	34/119	29%

Bold indicates significance at $p < .05$

Preterit *ran*, nonstandard *run*

Of the eight verb forms examined, the standard preterit *ran* was used by the smallest percentage of informants: only one percent of Type I's in all areas; of Type II's, one-fifth in Areas D and E and one-third in Area F used *ran*. The difference between the two types was significant in all areas, but the difference between males and females was slight, except in Area F, and was nowhere significant.

Preterit *threw*, nonstandard *throwed*

More than 40 percent of all informants in all areas used the standard preterit *threw*, as did more than three-fourths of Type II's. Again, the difference between Type I and II informants was significant. More than half the females of both types in all areas used the standard form, and in Areas D and E this difference between males and females was significant.

Table 5. Preterit *ran*

	Area D		Area E		Area F	
Type I	1/106	**1%**	1/79	**1%**	1/71	**1%**
Type II	12/68	**18%**	16/69	**23%**	14/41	**34%**
Type I Male	1/68	1%	1/51	2%	0/52	0%
Type I Female	0/38	0%	0/28	0%	1/19	5%
Type II Male	6/30	20%	9/34	26%	9/30	30%
Type II Female	6/38	16%	7/35	20%	5/11	45%
All Male	7/98	7%	10/85	12%	9/82	11%
All Female	6/76	8%	7/63	11%	6/30	20%
All M + F	13/174	7%	17/148	11%	15/112	13%

Bold indicates significance at $p < .05$

Table 6. Preterit *threw*

	Area D		Area E		Area F	
Type I	18/81	**22%**	4/54	**7%**	15/67	**22%**
Type II	49/62	**79%**	43/57	**75%**	39/51	**76%**
Type I Male	12/49	24%	3/37	8%	9/50	18%
Type I Female	6/32	19%	1/17	6%	6/17	35%
Type II Male	17/28	61%	18/28	64%	27/36	75%
Type II Female	32/34	94%	25/29	86%	12/15	80%
All Male	29/77	**38%**	21/65	**32%**	36/86	42%
All Female	38/66	**58%**	26/46	**57%**	18/32	56%
All M + F	67/143	47%	47/111	42%	54/118	46%

Bold indicates significance at p < .05

Past participle *torn*, nonstandard *tore*

In Areas D and E, only one-fifth of all informants used the standard participle *torn*; in Area F two-fifths did. The difference between Type I and II informants was significant in all areas; that between males and females was significant in none of them. Again Area F had the highest use of the standard form for both informant types and both sexes.

Past participle *worn*, nonstandard *wore*

The standard participle *worn* was used by more than one-third of the informants in Areas D and E and by three-fifths in Area F, where more than three-fourths of Type II informants used the standard form. The difference between Type I and II informants was everywhere significant. That between all male and female informants was significant in Areas D and E (as with *threw*).

Table 7. Participle *torn*

	Area D		Area E		Area F	
Type I	4/96	**4%**	5/81	**6%**	13/64	**25%**
Type II	30/65	**46%**	26/70	**37%**	32/44	**66%**
Type I Male	2/62	3%	4/54	7%	10/52	19%
Type I Female	2/34	6%	1/27	4%	3/12	25%
Type II Male	13/29	45%	15/36	42%	20/31	65%
Type II Female	17/36	47%	11/34	32%	9/13	69%
All Male	15/91	16%	19/90	21%	30/81	37%
All Female	19/70	27%	12/61	20%	12/25	48%
All M + F	34/161	21%	31/151	21%	42/106	39%

Bold indicates significance at p < .05

Table 8. Participle *worn*

	Area D		Area E		Area F	
Type I	25/99	**25%**	13/78	**17%**	19/44	**43%**
Type II	47/68	**69%**	37/66	**56%**	31/41	**76%**
Type I Male	15/63	24%	8/49	16%	13/33	39%
Type I Female	10/36	28%	6/29	17%	6/11	55%
Type II Male	18/30	60%	13/31	42%	21/30	70%
Type II Female	29/38	76%	24/35	69%	10/11	91%
All Male	33/93	**35%**	21/80	**26%**	34/63	54%
All Female	39/74	**53%**	29/64	**45%**	16/22	73%
All M + F	72/167	43%	50/144	35%	50/85	59%

Bold indicates significance at p < .05

Past participle *written*, nonstandard *wrote*

About one-fourth of all informants in Areas D and E used the standard participle *written*, and nearly half of those in Area F did. The difference between the two types of informants was everywhere significant; the difference between Type I and Type II informants in Areas D and E was particularly striking, with more than half of the Type II informants using the standard form. The difference between males and females was significant only in Area D. In Area F fewer females than males used the standard form, but probably this is owing to an unusually small number of female informants there.

Table 9. Participle *written*

	Area D		Area E		Area F	
Type I	5/93	**5%**	3/66	**5%**	10/50	**20%**
Type II	36/67	**54%**	33/65	**52%**	35/42	**83%**
Type I Male	4/61	7%	3/43	7%	8/36	22%
Type I Female	1/32	3%	0/24	0%	2/14	14%
Type II Male	9/29	31%	20/33	61%	31/37	84%
Type II Female	27/38	71%	14/32	44%	4/5	80%
All Male	13/90	**14%**	23/75	31%	39/73	53%
All Female	28/70	**40%**	14/56	25%	6/19	32%
All M + F	41/160	26%	37/131	28%	45/92	49%

Bold indicates significance at $p < .05$

Table 10 compares the percentages of men and women using the standard form. The difference between them is significant five times in Area D (for *drowned*, *gave*, *threw*, *worn*, and *written*); three times in Area E (for *gave*, *threw*, and *worn*), and only once in Area F (for *gave*). The percentages of males and females using the standard form *gave* is almost the same in all three areas. Informants in Area F quite consistently used standard forms more than did those in the other two areas, perhaps because of the presence of larger cities like Charleston, Savannah, and Augusta.

Table 10. Percentages of men and women using standard forms

	Area D		Area E		Area F	
	M	F	M	F	M	F
blew	28	28	2	20	51	51
drowned	36 *	54	33	47	53	59
gave	22 *	46	21 *	45	21 *	44
ran	7	8	12	11	11	20
threw	38 *	58	32 *	57	42	56
torn	16	27	21	20	37	48
worn	35 *	53	26 *	45	54	73
written	14 *	40	31	25	53	32

* = significant at p < .05 level

Table 11 presents the percentages of all informants using each standard form. *Ran* was used by the lowest rate of speakers in all areas. The percentages of those with *gave* and *threw* were close in all three areas. Only in Area F did informants use the standard form more than half the time (with only three verbs: *blew*, *drowned*, and *worn*).

Table 11. Percentages of informants using standard forms

	Area D	Area E	Area F
blew	28	20	51
drowned	44	39	55
gave	33	31	29
ran	7	11	13
threw	47	42	46
torn	21	21	39
worn	43	35	59
written	26	28	49

Table 12 indicates significant differences between informant types and genders in eight columns, with an asterisk marking where the differences were significant at the p < .05 level. For example, the first column includes Type I and II informants of both sexes, and the differences were significant in all three areas for all verbs. The difference between all male and all female informants (second column) was significant only nine times out of a possible 24. Five of these nine were in Area D, three were in Area E, and one, for the preterit of *give*, was in Area F, the southernmost one. The difference between Type I males and females (third column) was significant only once, again for the preterit of *give*, in Area F.

The differences between Type I and II males (fourth column) were everywhere significant; those between Type I males and Type II females (fifth column) were significant everywhere except for the verb *blow* in Area F. The differences between Type I females and Type II males (sixth column) were significant except for the past participles of *drown* and *wear* and the preterits of *give* and *run* in Area F. Differences between Type I and Type II females (seventh column) were everywhere significant, except in Area F for the use of the standard preterits of *blow* and *give* and the standard participles of *tear* and *wear* in Area F. For *wear*, the difference was not significant in Area E either. Finally, the difference between Type II males and females (eighth column) was significant for only five verbs confined to areas D and E: the preterits of *blow* (D), *give* (E), and *throw* (D), and the participles of *drown* (E) and *write* (D).

The data in the tables also allow a cumulative comparison of the gender usage within Type I and Type II. Among Type I informants, males used the standard form more than did females in 12 of the 24 possible cases; for *blew* (Areas D and E); *drowned* (E); *gave* (E); *ran* (D, E); *threw* (D, E); *tore* (E); *wrote* (D, E, F). Females also used the standard form more in12 cases: *blew* (F); *drowned* (D, F); *gave* (D, F); *ran* (F); *threw* (F); *tore* (D, F); *wore* (D, E, F).

Among Type II informants the picture was different. In Area D the two genders tied in using the standard form at a rate of 53 percent, and in the other two areas the percentages were also similar. Leaving the tie aside, females used the standard form more in 17 of the possible 23 areas and males in six.

Table 12. Significant differences between informant type/gender

Type Gender	I II Both	Both M F	I I M F	I II M M	I II M F	I II F M	I II F F	II II M F
blow								
D	*			*	*	*	*	*
E	*			*	*	*	*	
F	*			*		*		
drown								
D	*	*		*	*	*	*	
E	*			*	*	*	*	*
F	*			*	*		*	
give								
D	*	*		*	*	*	*	
E	*	*		*	*	*	*	*
F	*	*	*	*	*			
run								
D	*			*	*	*	*	
E	*			*	*	*	*	
F	*			*	*		*	
throw								
D	*	*		*	*	*	*	*
E	*	*		*	*	*	*	
F	*			*	*	*	*	
tear								
D	*			*	*	*	*	
E	*			*	*	*	*	
F	*			*	*	*		
wear								
D	*	*		*	*	*	*	
E	*	*		*	*	*		
F	*			*	*			
write								
D	*	*		*	*	*	*	*
E	*			*	*	*	*	
F	*			*	*	*	*	

Males used the standard form more with *blew* (F); *ran* (D, E); *torn* (E); and *written* (E, F). Females used the standard form more often with *blew* (E); *drowned* (D, E, F); *gave* (D, E, F); *ran* (F); *threw* (D, E, F); *torn* (D, F); *worn* (D, E, F); and *written* (D). Clearly the difference between genders seems more marked for Type II informants than for Type I's. This is supported also by the greater number of statistically significant differences between the two groups, five instances for Type II M/Fs (column eight, table 12) versus once for Type I M/Fs (column three).

What conclusions can be drawn from studying these eight verbs? First, as Atwood concluded, social differences were important; they separated Type I and Type II informants for all verbs in all areas. Second, as Van Riper hypothesized, females more often used the standard form than the males did, and in nine of the 24 cases, the difference was significant. The difference between the genders was more marked in Type II informants than in Type I's. Van Riper's hypothesis should now be considered established for verb forms in the Atlas data: women do use standard forms more frequently and consistently than men do.

Most of the LAMSAS records examined here were completed in the late 1930s and 1940s and thus reflect the speech of half a century ago, speech that was shaped in the late 19th century. What would later studies reveal? Material gathered some 20 years ago is available in Lee Pederson's *Linguistics Atlas of the Gulf States*. The two surveys include many of the same items, including verb forms, and in eastern Georgia there is geographical overlap. Here is a rich field for the study of real-time social change in the 20th century.

NOTE

1. Another reason for choosing the chi-square test is that the data here are classificatory, and hence used only to identify the groups to which the informants belong. For example, suppose that in Virginia and North Carolina, *have drank* is evidenced by 32 Type I informants, 18 Type II informants, and 5 Type III informants. Each informant is counted only once, and then put into one category or another (in this case, use or non-use of *have drank*). Parametric

tests are generally used on ordinal and interval (i.e. non-nominal) data and are thus inappropriate here.

A third reason for using the chi-square test involves not the nature of the data, but rather the nature of the test itself: it is a test of goodness of fit for a particular set of nominal data. In other words, the chi-square statistic tells us the probability of getting the results obtained for the particular subjects involved. For example, we obtained these results for linguistic atlas informants in Virginia and North Carolina:

	Type I	Type II	Type III
have drank	32	18	5
have drunk	17	24	14

$\chi^2 = 9.712$; $p < .01$; df = 2

The chi-square test, then, tells us that there is less than one chance in 100 that the distribution of these particular data could have occurred by chance. Now we can say that, in the linguistic atlas records for Virginia and North Carolina, there is a relationship between informant type and the use of *have drank* vs. *have drunk* at the $p < .01$ level of probability.

The Naming of Churches in West Alabama

John Stanley Rich

Compelled to name their surroundings, humans christen both *natural features* such as lakes, valleys, prairies, hills, mountains, creeks, branches, rivers, and springs, and *artificial features* such as settlements, townships, churches, schools, and post offices. The names people give to places, both artificial and natural, speak clearly, often eloquently, and sometimes enigmatically about the topography, the history, and, most especially, the people who settled there, reflecting their knowledge and personal attitudes, their language, and their social and cultural interests and mores. Toponomy, the study of the origins of place names, is an interdisciplinary field involving linguistics, history, geography, archaeology, and folklore. Each of these disciplines sheds its own light on the provenance of names, aiding the researcher in presenting a balanced study of a region's naming patterns. This toponomic study, drawing upon these academic fields, focuses on naming of one artificial feature, the church, as practiced in a small area of Alabama.

Since the early days of settlement in America, the church has had a major influence on the social and cultural development of the people. The building itself has served as a central meeting-place for many social activities of the local community, and in very small settlements the church has been the primary focus of communal gatherings. During an 'In Performance at the White House' held at the Shiloh Baptist Church in Washington, D. C., on 1 December 1983, Leontyne Price observed that for the black church the singing of spirituals and gospel songs in the church has molded a community of people into a cohesive force in American society.

The local church, as a focal point in the forming of social relations for many of the people, thus has significant value for cultural historians and for linguists interested in names and name patterning. This study focuses upon the names of churches in two counties in West Alabama, Tuscaloosa and Greene.

Tuscaloosa County was established on 7 February 1818 as one of the original 22 counties in the Territory of Alabama (Alabama 1818:sec. 2, 16–21). Presently 1,346 square miles in area, it is the second largest county in the state. The Black Warrior River flows diagonally across the county from the mountainous coal-mining region of the northeastern section to the level swamp lands of the southwestern section. Greene County, adjacent to Tuscaloosa County on the southwest, was established on 13 December 1819, one day before Alabama became a State (Toulmin 1823:92). Soon after settlement by whites in 1818, Greene became the foremost agricultural county in Alabama, remaining so until the beginning of the Civil War in 1861. Prosperous plantations covered vast areas of the prairies in this 'Black Belt' region of West Alabama. (See map 6 in Fitts, this volume.) The county is almost entirely bordered by rivers: the Sipsey to the north, the Black Warrior to the east, and the Tombigbee to the west and the south.

For Tuscaloosa and Greene Counties, the naming patterns for places follow the settlers' places of origin fairly clearly. Most of the white settlers who entered the area about 1816, following General Andrew Jackson's bloody drive to wipe out the native Choctaw Indians, were immigrants from the Carolinas and Georgia. Largely Protestant, these new settlers brought to the land sets of names from their older settlements: *Society Hill, Union, Clinton, New Lexington, Greene, Eutaw*, and *Camden* (Foscue 1989:2). These names reveal a group of people with a definable cluster of characteristics: a pioneering people, hardy and adventurous, with a religious idealism which fostered hopes as the frontier was being pushed farther west.

The following sections focus upon the various patterns which developed as churches have been named in Tuscaloosa and Greene Counties, Alabama. First we develop a typology of church naming, as suggested by the practices. Then we look at the naming conventions of the four major denominations (Baptist, Methodist, Presbyterian, and Episcopalian). These findings provide a basis for suggesting how church naming patterns will continue to evolve in this area of West Alabama.

CHURCH NAMING PRACTICES

The importance of establishing churches early in the settlement of a locale may be seen in the total statistics for various types of place names in these two counties. Of 2,489 significant place names in the history of the two counties, church names form the largest corpus, for both artificial and natural features: 370 names. In decreasing numbers are 259 settlement names, 230 creek names, 167 post office names, and 136 branch names. With 370 church names in the counties, this feature makes up a significant 15 percent of the total place names. These figures generally exclude the names of churches which have taken the name of the local settlement (e.g. *Peterson Methodist Church, Vance Baptist Church, Eutaw Presbyterian Church*), since such names are not generally considered linguistically significant (Rich 1979:58–63). With few exceptions, the significant church names fall into four major categories: biblical names, inspirational and symbolic names, descriptive (or site) names, and personal names.

Biblical Names
   As John Leighly has noted in his study of biblical place names in the United States, descendants in the colonies often 'saw themselves in resemblance to the ancient Hebrews seeking and subduing a promised land' (1979:57). This metaphor gave rise to many settlements named for sites or persons mentioned in the Hebrew scriptures. Frequently these names had been transferred from a church to the settlement. In Tuscaloosa and Greene Counties the religious nature of the settlers is seen in the 121 names given for biblical places or persons, 33 percent of the total 370 church names (Rich 1979:61). There are seven *Mt. Zion* churches, six named *Ebenezer*, six *St. Paul's*, five *Bethel*, five *Zion Hill*, and four each of the following: *Mt. Olive, Bethlehem, Salem, Sardis, Shiloh, Zion*. A listing of biblical place names would seem a veritable gazetteer of ancient Palestine, her environs, and the nearby Mediterranean world: *Antioch, Bethany, Beulah, Calvary, Canaan, Carmel, Corinth, Damascas, Galilee, Gilgal, Hebron, Jerusalem, Macedonia, Mt. Carmel, Nazareth, Olivet, Philadelphia, Pisgah, Siloam, Sinai*. The names of Christ's apostles and early disciples are given as numerous saints' names: *St. James, St. John, St. Luke, St. Mary, St. Paul*, and *St. Stephen*.

The settlers' hopes for new life in West Alabama may be seen in their renaming, with the descriptor *new*, several older biblical place names now transferred to the new land: *New Asia, New Bethany, New Bethel, New Mt. Hebron,* and *New Zion.*

Inspirational and Symbolic Names

One of the most fascinating groupings of church names in these two counties is the inspirational and symbolic names. These 71 names comprise nearly 20 percent of all the church names, telling, in their far-ranging variety, of the hopes and aspirations of the pioneering inhabitants (Rich 1979:61). Five churches are named *Liberty*, four each named *Hopewell, New Hope,* and *Morning,* all indicating the premium placed by the settlers upon a new locale. Although Zion is a biblical place (so treated in the tables below), its geographical denotation was allegorized into a spiritual significance, as in the old hymn 'We're Marching to Zion'. This symbolic *Zion* keeps reappearing, as in *Zion Friendship, Zion Grove, Zion Hope, Brush Creek Zion,* and *Beautiful Zion.* A composite listing of inspirational and symbolic names reveals the enduring hopes and spiritual aspirations of the people: *Concord, Enterprise, Freehope, Friendship, Good Hope, Goodwill, Hope, Kingdom, Mt. Liberty, Mt. Pilgrim, New Christian, New Hope, New Light, New Prospect, Pilgrim Rest, Providence, Sinner's Friend, The Solid Rock, True Vine, Union, Unity.* The concept of light appears in several names associated with the sun and stars: *Christian Light, Morning Light, Evening Star, Rising Star, Starlight, New Light, Little Star,* and *Sunflower.* The adjective *little* appears in a small cluster of names, perhaps indicating the spiritual humility of the namers: *Little Mission, Little Star, Little Vine, Little Zion.* The members of *Little Hope Church* must have realized the negative connotations of their church name, for they renamed it *Union Grove. Weeping Mary Church* carries its own poignant signification.

A lovely story of one particular church, *Purity Methodist Church*, long since gone, vividly informs us about the process involved in giving an inspirational/symbolic name. Anson West in his *History of Methodism in Alabama* gives the account as follows:

> There was a Methodist Meeting-house in Jasper County, Georgia, called Purity. By 1820 a number of the members of the Society at that place had

emigrated and joined themselves in a community about twelve miles from Tuskaloosa, Alabama, and east of south from that place. A Society was organized in that community, and the place of worship fixed on Bunche's Creek. The associations of the old church whence these new settlers came were still fresh in their memories, and the affections of these persons still entwined about the sacred place where formerly they had sung the songs of Zion and offered the sacrifices of praise, and which place they had so recently left, and so they did what was most natural for them to do—they named the place of the meeting of their new Society on Bunche's Creek Purity. Purity Church was, from its organization to its discontinuance, one of the appointments of the Tuskaloosa Circuit . . . Purity Church as an organization is extinct, and the place as a place of worship has been abandoned, but there at that sacred spot in the old churchyard repose the remains of many men and women who acted well their part in the drama of life, and who await the resurrection morning and the revelation of the last day. (1893:159–60)

Here, in West's florid Victorian prose, exists a fine account of the motivation behind the naming of one particular place now long gone. For African Americans, a more earthly longing may be reflected in the name *Freehope Church*, early established in Greene County for the workers at Thornhill Plantation. This inspirational/symbolic name appears also as *Free Hope Church* (William M. Branch, p.c. 1978).[1] With the names *Purity Church* and *Freehope Church* we might agree with Thomas Campbell, in his *Pleasures of Hope* (Pt. II, l. 5): 'Who hath not own'd, with rapture-smitten frame, / The power of grace, the magic of a name?'

Descriptive Names

Descriptive names, 70 in all, yield another 20 percent of the church names (Rich 1979:61). *Pleasant* seems to be the key descriptive term, for there are four named *Pleasant Grove*, three *Pleasant Hill*, and three *Pleasant Ridge*. Others are *Pleasant Field*, *Pleasant Valley*, and *Pleasant Wood*. The church namers were generous with their subjective descriptions, including *Belleview, Goodwater, Fairview, Mt. Pleasant*, among the other pleasant places. Locational descriptions are abundant: *Cedar Grove, Cedar Tree, Cloverdale, Flatwoods, Flint Ridge, Green Oak, Highland, Midway, Oak Grove, Oak Hill, Sandy Springs, Pine Grove, Piney Woods, Plum Grove, Prairie, Rock Bluff, Shady Grove,* and *White Oak*. Such descriptive names paint a partial picture of the flora of the region while also portraying the varied topography of West Alabama.

In Tuscaloosa and Greene Counties the features from which names have most often spread to others are the settlement, the church, and the creek. The church name, in particular, was given to 80 schools; 11 creek names were given to churches, such as *Carrolls Creek Church*. The feature to which a name has most often spread first in these two counties is the school; next in order are the post office, the settlement, and the church. A basic pattern emerges in the names involved here: the highest percentage of spreading sequences begins with the artificial feature name, rather than with the natural feature name, and the church name is second in frequency of spreading (Rich 1979:51–57).

This pattern manifests itself clearly in churches named for nearby places. Creek names predominate: *Big Creek Church, Five Mile Creek Church, Grant's Creek Church*. A curious combination of names occurs in *Brush Creek Zion Church*—a coalescing of descriptive, locational, and biblical names. Nearby place names go on to make up 20 percent of the church names. Others include spring names: *Arbor Springs Church, Gum Springs Church, Holly Springs Church, Poplar Springs Church*. Topographical features are also transferred to church names: *Johnson Hill Church, Rose Valley Church, Roupes Valley Church*, and the triple-generic name: *Spring Hill Church*. Churches named for a nearby body of water or stream of water have an unusually high frequency in the total number of names, thus indicating the importance of locating near a convenient source of water for the early settlers.

One locational-descriptive name bears noting for its probable reflection of social dialect, particularly the practice of substituting stops for fricatives (e.g. [d] for [ð]). *The Mount Church*, near the settlement of Mt. Hebron in Greene County, is apparently named for that small town. However, this church name appears on the official *Greene County Highway Map* for 1972 as *Demount Church*, probably a surveyor's misinterpretation of the local inhabitants' pronunciation of the church name (Branch, p.c.).

Personal Names

Churches named for local persons take a variety of generics. There are 44 of these comprising 12 percent of the total (Rich 1979:61). The majority of the personally named structures or local congregations are called *chapels*, as in *Andrews Chapel* and *Jennings Chapel*. This category contains names for many local families: *Morrow, Phillips, Robertson, Shelton, Thomas, Watson, White*. Most Methodist churches in rural West Alabama started as a *chapel*, the generic usually denoting its early status as a 'mission' of a larger church in a nearby town (O. D. Thomas, p.c. 1996). The early structure was usually small, not large enough for a sizeable worshiping congregation (Marvin Harper, p.c. 1996). Another *chapel* designates the first black church in Tuscaloosa County, which existed informally 1856–1861. Formally organized in Tuscaloosa on 2 May 1866, it was later named *Hunter's Chapel* for Edward H. Hunter, a pastor of the African Methodist Episcopal denomination in the 1880s (Glynn 1976:3–4, 26, 30).

The most enigmatic name discovered in this study is that of *Grim Chapel* which appears on the official county highway maps and on the United States Geological Survey 1931 topological map of the area, the Eutaw Quadrangle. The puzzle of such a darkly negative name for a church was solved through a lengthy examination of the *Greene County Deed Books* which revealed the local property owner to be Mr. Dempsey A. Graham (Vol. F, 980). Thus *Grim Chapel* appears on official maps probably through the official surveyor's change to *grim* of the local pronunciation of *Graham*. Perhaps to clear up the confusion, the name was later changed to *New Christian Church*.

The generic *church* appears at the next highest frequency: *Cleveland Church, DeGraffenreid's Church, Gordon's Church*, along with other family names such as *Hargrove, Harkness, Hickman*, and *Porter*. Other generics are less frequent but more colorful.

From the early settlement days comes the generic *preaching place*, confined apparently to only Methodist sites. Each of the five was named for a local family or for an itinerant preacher, the name for the feature no longer in use: *DeGraffenreid's Preaching Place, Everett's Preaching Place, Ray's Preaching Place, Sadler's Preaching Place*, and *Thompson's Preaching Place*. All of these preaching places named for a person carry the genitive suffix, spelled with an apostrophe + *s*. *Preaching place* and *meeting house* (see below) were probably both relatively interchangeable terms among Methodists according to local usage (Duncan Hunter, p.c. 1990). Circuit rider preachers, following

John Wesley's earlier example, often preached at outdoor sites, in someone's home, or even in a general store (Harper, p.c.; Kennard C. Smith, p.c. 1996).

The generic *temple* appears in two instances: *Dobbs Temple* and *Washington Temple*, both located in remote rural areas. The similar generic *tabernacle* appears in *Sherman Tabernacle*, located at a former lumber campsite. The term itself has a long and honored history, especially with its Hebraic implication of a tent offering sanctuary. The choice of this generic may be particularly appropriate, for the tabernacle is named for a local black family, who probably sensed a need for sanctuary in an alien and socially inhospitable land.

One of the earliest Methodist churches in Tuscaloosa County carried the generic *shelter*. *Hardwick's Shelter* was founded in 1818 and in all likelihood, as with the generic *tabernacle*, gave the local inhabitants a sense of rest and safety in the frontier territory. A final generic appears in the long-abandoned name *Sand Mountain Meeting House*, established about 1826 and named for the nearby mountain. Other *meeting houses* gave their names to nearby branches, a *Meeting House Branch* appearing in each of the two counties.

Two of the names given for local families present interesting variations on the generic *church*. The Whitson family gave its name to the local settlement *Whitson* and to the place where the church is located, and thus the name *Whitson Place Church*. The Cook family apparently preferred two generics in giving their name, thus the redundant *Cooks Chapel Church*.

Miscellaneous Names

Only one classical name was given for a church in these two counties. *Mesopotamia Church* was named for the settlement of old *Mesopotamia* in Greene County (La Tourette 1839). Founded by Scotch-Irish Presbyterians in 1818, this 'high place between two rivers', the Tombigbee and the Black Warrior, was named for the ancient Tigris-Euphrates Valley (also mentioned in the Bible). In 1838 the town was succeeded by *Eutaw* when the Seat of Justice was moved from old *Erie* to a site approximately one mile east and southeast of old *Mesopotamia*, thus causing this ancient town to die. The church was established in 1824 and in 1851 was moved to Eutaw, with the grand old name changed to the nondistinctive *First Presbyterian Church* (Snedecor 1856:62, 64).

One anecdotic name exists in a church named *Shake Rag Church*. Established circa 1819, with the meeting house built circa 1830, this church grew out of the old *Sand Mountain Church*. Circa 1844 the church was called *Mt. Pleasant Church*, a name alternating with *Shake Rag*. Several legends exist regarding the origin of the name:

1) In camp meeting days the congregation responded to the preaching by dancing and shouting until they were in rags and tatters.
2) A woman in white would walk up and down the church aisle on stormy nights, now and then lifting angel wings as if in preparation to fly into heaven.
3) A Mr. Phil Cribbs was chased from the church on a stormy night by an apparition in white; later, a demented Negro woman in long, flowing, tattered clothing was found to have taken refuge in the church that night.
4) An old woman shouted and cried in church, waving a tear-wet handkerchief or 'rag'. (Seay n.d.)

All that is left at the site today is Shake Rag Cemetery, in the southeastern area of Tuscaloosa. Dating to 1840, this burial place holds many of the pioneer citizens of the county, including veterans of the Civil War. In recent years an annual homecoming and cleaning of the cemetery have helped restore the memory of the old, historic *Shake Rag Church*. As the Roman poet Lucan says in *The Civil War*, 'There stands the shadow of a glorious name'.

A question may arise regarding the apparent lack of Native American Indian names given for churches in these two counties of West Alabama. (A very small percent of Indian names are given for settlements and water-courses.) In all likelihood, the early white settlers, eager to impose Christian names for the churches, avoided what they would have considered 'pagan' or 'heathen' Indian names. For example, *Black Warrior* in *Black Warrior Church* translates the Indian name *Tuscaloosa*, the force of the native name being thus softened.

Church names, as with all place names, are subject to change and variation. The naming practices reflect a variety of motivations. The areal name *Prairie Church* in Greene County was changed to *West*

Greene Church, for the local settlement. Although *Mt. Pleasant Church* was changed to *Shake Rag Church*, the original name *Mt. Pleasant Church* persists, perhaps to counter the ominous sense of the ghost stories associated with the church's history. The name change from *White Hope Church* to *Whites Chapel* apparently attempted to remove a restrictive racial connotation in this family-named church. The unfortunately paronomastic *Little Hope Church*, as mentioned above, was disambiguated to *Union Grove Church*.

NAMING PATTERNS

Another issue of interest in the study of church names arises: Is there a pattern of name-giving for various church denominations which can be traced through the history of the churches? Rogers, after lengthy correspondence with officials from the major Protestant denominations in the United States, concludes:

> . . . only a few denominations have any fixed onomastic principles or policies. Actually, this is not surprising in the light of the reasons for the establishment of Protestantism, one of the distinctions of which it its general reliance upon the local congregation for self-government, a feature of which is the selection of its own name. (1963:45)

Thus, the major Protestant groups in West Alabama (Baptists, Methodists, Presbyterians, and Episcopalians) leave the local congregations to choose their names, with some consultation with the regional and national bodies to prevent any local duplication of names. (The exceptions nationally are the Christian Scientists, Jehovah's Witnesses, and Latter-Day Saints, for which a central headquarters has a system for naming churches, most of the names being nondistinctive, according to the principles used in this study.)

One way to determine a pattern of name-giving is to look at church names in particular locales and to trace the names as they were given in historical time periods. If a pattern emerges, one could form generalizations towards a theory of naming churches in particular denominations. This study is limited to only major church denominations in the 19th and early 20th centuries for Tuscaloosa and Greene Counties in West

Alabama: Baptist, Methodist, Presbyterian, and Episcopal. While other denominations certainly do flourish in the area, these four have been chosen because they appeared with the earliest settlement in this area. Other denominations (such as the Assembly of God, Church of Christ, Church of the Nazarene, Lutheran Church, and Wesleyan Church) appeared decades later. One of three Roman Catholic churches in the two counties, St. John the Baptist R. C. Church, was established in 1844 in Tuscaloosa, the oldest Catholic church in North Alabama. Otherwise, the Protestant denominations have been the dominant church influence in West Alabama. Thus, for historical consistency and for economy, the four earliest Protestant denominations will be considered here.

Because existing records, especially maps, frequently do not distinguish between black and white churches, this study can only give a general overview of church naming patterns in these two counties without regard to race. The one exception is that the historically black African Methodist Episcopal, African Methodist Episcopal Zion, and Christian ('Colored' until 1956) Methodist Episcopal churches are parenthetically listed in the tables as AME, AME Zion, or CME. However, the overall observations make no racial distinctions.

The tables below treat the four denominations identified above in four categories: churches named for the site (often including the 'descriptive names' discussed above); churches named for biblical places or reminiscent of the Bible; church names which are inspirational or symbolic in nature; and churches named for benefactors, a local family or local person, or some other person (frequently a major figure in the denomination's own history). The tables begin by chronologically listing churches for which the date of establishment is known. These are followed by an alphabetical listing of churches with an uncertain or unknown establishment date. (The undated churches were generally founded in the mid to late 19th century, detailed records being almost non-existent. Such churches were often independent, kept few records, and served transient or very small congregations. With few exceptions, these churches no longer exist.)

Baptist Church Naming

The 256 Baptist churches (tables 1a–d, sources: Tuscaloosa County Baptist Association 1989; Dorothy Davis, p.c. 1990; Hezekiah Tauga Carstarphen, p.c. 1990) comprise the largest number of churches in the two counties . Of these, 94 Baptist churches named for the site (37%) make up the largest grouping (table 1a). From 1819 to 1990, churches have been named for a site in each decade of the more than 170 years of the presence of Baptist churches in the area. While the earlier churches were named for such natural features as creeks, valleys, springs, woods, groves, fields, hills, ridges, and mountains, more recent ones tend to be named for housing subdivisions and sections of urban areas. The current pattern of naming for a site is consistent, and it will probably continue.

The second largest grouping of Baptist churches, 84 in number (33%), comprises those named for the Bible or reminiscent of the Bible (table 1b). In 1818 *Ebenezer Baptist Church* became the first church to be established in Tuscaloosa County. Founded a year before Alabama joined the Union, *Ebenezer* was eventually renamed *First Baptist Church of Tuscaloosa*. Biblical names were given regularly in every decade until the early 20th century. Of the known dates of establishment, just one biblical name appears in the 1920s, the 1930s, and the 1940s, while site names have been given regularly in every decade up to the present.

Fifty-five Baptist churches (21%) were given inspirational or symbolic names beginning with *Friendship Church* in 1825. As table 1c shows, establishment dates have been ascertained for only half of this grouping. Churches have been given inspirational or symbolic names during most of the decades since 1825. The most recent name given is *Beacon Light Baptist Church*, established in March 1990 in Tuscaloosa.

Churches named for benefactors, local families or local persons, or other persons (table 1d), make up the smallest grouping of Baptist churches, only 14 in number (5%). Except for *Camp Church*, established circa 1830, benefactor names have been given for Baptist churches more recently, primarily in the 20th century.

One of the patterns of church-naming history in West Alabama is that while Baptist churches were quite frequently named for biblical places in the earlier settlement period, name-givers today seem mainly to prefer site names as they establish new churches. This and other trends will be discussed below.

Table 1a. Baptist churches named for the site,
establishment date given where known

1819 Sandy Creek

1820 Big Creek

1820 Five Mile Creek

1827 Roupes Valley

1828 Grants Creek

1828 Spring Hill

1830 Holly Springs

1834 Dunn's Creek

1834 Bucks Creek

1836 Little Sandy

1836 Cedar Grove

1838 Big Hurricane

1838 Chapel Hill

1842 Carrolls Creek

1842 Piney Woods

1848 Prudes Creek

1855 Mt. Pleasant

1857 Big Sandy

1857 Pleasant Field

1858 Davis Creek

1859 Moores Bridge

1863 Rock Springs

1864 Pleasant Hill

ca. 1865 Center Chapel

1866 Pole Bridge

1874 Holly Springs

1876 Prairie

1881 Arbor Springs

1883 Mountain Springs

1887 Piney Grove

1888 Flatwoods

1890 Hurricane

1896 Windham Springs

1896 Cedar Grove

ca. 1900 Highland

1906 Goodwater

1908 Rosedale

1912 Little Hurricane

1913 Yellow Creek

1914 Evergreen

1921 Southside

1925 Cedar Cove

1929 Warrior's Chapel

1932 Oak Grove

1936 Forest Lake

1936 Rice's Valley

1938 West End

1948 Hillcrest

1949 Five Points

1952 Circlewood

1953 South Highlands

1957 Ridgecrest

1958 Northwood Hills

1961 Greenwood >
    Trinity

1967 Skyland Boule-
    vard

1969 Eastern Hills

1972 Indian Lake

1976 Central

1985 Woodland Park

1986 Lakewood

1987 Hargrove Road

1987 Valley View

1988 Country

1988 Northway

1988 Northridge

1988 Cedar Tree > Mt.
    Paran

Belleview

Black Warrior

Brush Creek

Brush Creek Zion

China Grove

Dry Creek

Flatwoods

Flint Ridge

Green Oak

Gum Springs

Lower Sulphur Springs

Midway

Mt. Pleasant

New Green Oak

Oak Hill Chapel

Pine(y) Grove

Pleasant Grove

Pleasant Ridge

Plum Grove

Poplar Springs

Shady Grove

South Sandy

Spring Hill

Spring Hill

Square Top

Sulphur Springs

Warrior

Warrior Chapel

Table 1b. Baptist churches named for the Bible or reminiscent
of the Bible, establishment date given where known

1818 Ebenezer	**1888** Mt. Paran	Mt. Olive
1818 Bethel	**1895** Ebenezer	Mt. Olive
1819 Sardis	**1906** Zion Hill	Mt. Sinai
1820 Bethlehem	*ca.* **1911** Calvary <	Mt. Zion
1822 Bethel	Monnish Memorial	Mt. Zion
1824 Philadelphia	**1911** Mt. Nebo	Mt. Zion
1824 Salem	**1914** Weeping Mary	Mt. Zion
1828 Gilgal	**1929** Sardis	Mt. Zoar
1832 Bethany	*ca.* **1930** Zion Grove	Nazareth
1832 Mt. Tabor	**1947** Emmanuel	New Asia
1833 Beulah	Antioch	New Bethany
1834 Rehoboth	Antioch	New Bethel
1834 Ruhama	Bethany	New Bethlehem
1834 Bethel	Bethel	New Zion
1840 Mt. Pisgah	Bethel	St. James
1843 Bethabara	Bethesda	St. John's
1844 Siloam	Bethlehem	St. Luke
1844 Mt. Lebanon	Bethlehem	St. Matthew
1847 Hepzibah	Beulah	St. Matthew
1850 Bethlehem	Canaan	St. Paul's
1850 Mt. Zion	Damascas	Salem
1853 Shiloh	Ezekiel	Sarepta (Greek form
1858 Mt. Olive	Galilee	of Zarephath)
1860 Corinth	Gilgal	Shiloh
ca. **1866** Mt. Zion	Jerusalem	Zion
1876 Bethel	Macedonia	Zion Hill
1880 Mt. Hebron	Mt. Carmel	Zion Hill
1881 (Old) Salem	Mt. Carmel	Zion Hill
1882 Mt. Olive	Mt. Galilee	

Table 1c. Baptist churches given an inspirational or symbolic
name, establishment date given where known

1825 Friendship	**1830** Liberty	**1837** Concord
1830 Hopewell	**1835** Liberty	**1839** Concord

1839 New Hope	**1974** Eastern Gate	Little Vine
1873 Hopewell	**1977** Fellowship	Little Zion
1875 Tabernacle	*ca.* **1980** Trinity <	Morning Star
1876 Providence	Greenwood	Morning Star
1880 New Zion	**1990** Beacon Light	Mt. Pilgrim
1882 Enterprise	Bible	New Christian <
1894 Kingdom	Christian Valley	Graham Chapel
1899 New Prospect	Double Portion	New Home
1908 The Solid Rock	Evergreen	New Hope
ca. **1910** Morning Star	Freehope	New Light
1921 Little Hope	Friendship	Open Door
1923 White Hope	Friendship	Pilgrim's Rest
1924 Union Grove	Friendship	Rising Star
1933 Unity	Goodwill	Starlight
1945 Hope	Liberty	True Vine
1958 Temple	Liberty	Zion Friendship
1972 Faith	Little Mission	Zion Hope

Table 1d. Baptist churches named for benefactor, local family or local person, or other person, establishment date given where known

ca. **1830** Camp	**1941** Stone Memorial
1882 Cornelius Chapel	**1946** Robertson's Chapel
ca. **1888** Elizabeth	**1947** Wilcutt Memorial
1893 Phillips Chapel	Benville/Bienville
1910 Monnish Memorial > Calvary	Graham Chapel
1915 Lloyds Chapel	Harkness Wood
1925 White's Chapel	Rigsby

Methodist Church Naming

Methodist churches (tables 2a–d, sources: Ola Grace Baker, p.c. 1990; Hunter, p.c.; Gary Yarbrough, p.c. 1996) named for the site comprise 23 in number (28%, table 2a). Most of these names were given in the early 19th century, with only three given since 1950. Biblical names, 22 in number (27%, table 2b), have a history almost parallel to the site names. By 1900 Bible names were no longer in vogue, *St. Luke* (1962) and *St. Mark* (1965) being exceptions. Only nine inspirational/symbolic names (11%, table 2c) have been given, the smallest category of the 83 Methodist churches discovered.

In sharp contrast to Baptist churches, Methodist churches named for a benefactor are the largest number with 29 instances or 35% (table 2d). Beginning with *Hardwick's Shelter* in 1818, benefactor names have been steadily given through the decades, especially in the 1830s and the 1870s. The presence of the circuit-riding Methodist preachers may account for many church names in this large category. The pattern for Methodist churches is that benefactor names dominate, appearing fairly consistently until the 1950s. The names vary in use of the possessive form for saints or personal names: *Watson Chapel*, *St. Mark's*, *St. Luke*, *St. Mark*. With no national church onomastic policy, each local congregation decides on the possessive form of the name (Hunter, p.c.).

Table 2a. Methodist churches named for the site,
establishment date given where known

1818 Pleasant Hill (Hargroves)
ca. **1820** Lye Branch
ca. **1820** (Old) Center (Center
   Meeting House)
1826 Sand Mountain Meeting
   House
1830 Pleasant Grove
ca. **1830** Rock Springs (Kindred's
   Chapel)
1834 Pleasant Grove
1836 Clinton Preaching Place
ca. **1840** Big Sandy
1844 Mt. Pleasant (Shake Rag)
1849 Goodwater

1852 Bone Camp
1858 Rose Valley > Union Chapel
1881 Sand(y) Spring
1901 Mt. Pleasant
1950 Forest Lake < Wesley
   Memorial
1958 Druid Hills
1984 Lakeview
Cripple Creek > Good Hope >
   North River
Little Center > Old Center
Pleasant Ridge
Poplar Springs (CME)
Springhill (AME Zion)

Table 2b. Methodist churches named for the Bible or reminiscent
of the Bible, establishment date given where known

1826 Shiloh
1830 (Bethel) Campground
1830 Salem < Sadler's Preaching

Place
1831 Ebenezer > Lambuth
   Memorial

1850 Sardis (Preaching Place)
1873 Sardis
1876 (Porter) St. Paul
1889 St. Mark's (AME)
1892 Weeping Mary
1902 Macedonia
ca. **1930** Shiloh
1949 Trinity < Brandon
Memorial (1910)
1962 St. Luke

1965 St. Mark
Beautiful Zion (AME)
El Bethel
Jerusalem (AME Zion)
Little Zion
Mt. Carmel
Mt. Hermon
Mt. Sinai
St. Peter (AME Zion)

Table 2c. Methodist churches given an inspirational or symbolic
name, establishment date given where known

ca. **1820** Purity
ca. **1821** Hopewell (Hurricane)
1836 Trinity Preaching Place
ca. **1840** New Hope
1850 Backbone (Mt. Bethel)

ca. **1897** Sinner's Friend (AME)
Mt. Liberty
Tabernacle (AME Zion)
Zion Hill

Table 2d. Methodist churches named for benefactor, local family or local
person, or other person, establishment date given where known

1818 Hardwick's Shelter
1818 Hargrove's Church > Pleasant
Hill
1830 Sadler's Preaching Place >
Salem
ca. **1830** Kindred's Chapel > Rock
Springs
1831 Everett's Preaching Place
ca. **1831** Ray's Preaching Place
ca. **1831** Thompson's Preaching
Place
ca. **1836** DeGraffenreid's Preaching
Place
ca. **1836** Watson Chapel
ca. **1837** Gordon's Church
1847 Jennings Chapel

ca. **1856** Hunter's Chapel (AME
Zion)
ca. **1860** Shelton Chapel
ca. **1870** Bailey Tabernacle (CME)
ca. **1870** Cleveland
ca. **1870** Porter (St. Paul)
1872 Andrews Chapel
1879 Haygood Chapel
1910 Brandon Memorial > Trinity
(1949)
ca. **1918** Slaughter Chapel >
Peterson
1923 Sherman Tabernacle
1943 Wesley Memorial > Forest
Lake (1950)
1947 Hargrove Memorial

1954 Lambuth Memorial <	Emerson Chapel
Ebenezer (1831)	Patterson Chapel
Beards Chapel (AME)	Wesley Chapel
Buncome > El Bethel	

Presbyterian Church Naming

Of the 25 Presbyterian churches (tables 3a–d, source: Marshall 1977), 24 spread fairly evenly among names for site (eight, 32%), Bible (nine, 36%), and benefactor (seven, 28%). Most of these were established in the earlier decades of settlement history, with only a few that have distinctive names established more recently. Only one benefactor name (4%) had been given to a Presbyterian church.

Table 3a. Presbyterian churches named for the site, establishment date given where known

1824 Mesopotamia > Eutaw	Beaverdam > Mt. Olivet
1832 Pleasant Hill	Pleasant Valley
1872 Cloverdale	Rock Bluff
1966 University	White Oak

Table 3b. Presbyterian churches named for the Bible or reminiscent of the Bible, establishment date given where known

1818 Bethel (originally Baptist;	**1830** El Bethel
Presbyterian by 1835)	**1835** Mt. Hermon
1820 Bethel	**1836** Bethsalem
1824 Hebron	Mt. Olivet < Beaverdam
1828 Ebenezer	St. Pauls

Table 3c. Presbyterian churches given an inspirational or symbolic name, establishment date given where known

1819 New Hope	Christian Light <	Sunflower
1838 Hopewell	Morrows Chapel	Union
ca. **1860** Liberty	Covenant	

Table 3d. Presbyterian church named for benefactor

Morrows Chapel > Christian Light

Episcopal Church Naming

Episcopal church names (table 4, sources: Emmet Gribben, p.c. 1996; Frederick Hyde, p.c. 1990) are the most consistent category of the four denominations studied. As the table illustrates, six of the seven names are given for persons in the New Testament. One name, *Canterbury Chapel*, is a transfer name reminiscent of Canterbury Cathedral in England. While not biblical per se, it carries a similar authority.

Table 4. Episcopal churches named for the Bible or similar authority

1828 Christ Church (the second EC organized in the State of Alabama)
1834 St. John's (in the Wilderness)
1845 St. Stephens
1850 St. Phillips Chapel (an early church for blacks)
1852 St. Mark's (in the Fork of Greene)
1950 Canterbury Chapel
1961 St. Matthias

TRENDS

Table 5 summarizes the combined figures for the four denominations. Churches named for the site comprise the largest number, 134 in all. Baptists and Methodists have most consistently given site names. Biblical names are second with a total of 122. Methodists and Episcopalians have continued in more recent decades to give biblical names. With inspirational and symbolic names the numbers drop in half, Baptists giving most of these names. Benefactor names form the smallest category, with Methodists giving nearly three times those of the Baptists.

With all this information in mind, is it possible to discern any intentional plan or pattern to naming churches in West Alabama? Do church denominations as institutions have set plans for naming churches? One Baptist church official in Birmingham, Alabama, has stated that there is no church policy or formula for naming churches (Hudson Baggett, p.c. to Matilee Dorough, 1990). Each individual Baptist church decides on its own name. The same principle seems to hold true for both Methodists and Presbyterians also. The Episcopal Church, in West Alabama, appears to name churches primarily for biblical personages, a tradition honored rather consistently throughout the United States.

Table 5. Summary of church name categories

Site names	134	36%
Biblical names	122	33%
Inspirational/symbolic names	70	19%
Benefactor or local family names	44	12%
Total church names	370	100%

The naming patterns for the two largest church denominations in West Alabama, the Baptist and the Methodist, have generally moved away from naming a church for the site or for the Bible; in recent decades, these churches are more frequently given a voguish residential subdivision name such as *Woodland Park, Northwoods,* or *Northridge.* This trend will most likely continue into the near future. Since inspirational and symbolic names have been given consistently to Baptist churches from 1825 to the present, a reasonable prediction would be that this pattern will also continue.

These findings seem to correlate with those of Miller, whose study 'How to Name a Church in the Northern Neck of Virginia' (1990) concludes with a 'doctrine of appropriateness'. The pragmatics of the church-naming phenomenon sets certain social and cultural restrictions on name-giving. For each age we may thus have a certain sense of what is appropriate in naming churches. By analogy, while personal names such as Vida, Lula, Eunice, and Cora Mae were stylish for naming females in earlier times, and male names such as Kevin, Justin, Scott, and Todd are voguish in contemporary American society, so church names may also vary with the social and cultural styles of the times, however unconscious the name-givers may be regarding any definite patterning in their choices.

In *The Apocrypha*, the writer of Ecclesiasticus ('The Church Book') gives a eulogy for the ancestors of Israel's past, exclaiming: 'Let us now sing the praises of illustrious men, the heroes of our nation's history'. In a consideration of the names of churches in Tuscaloosa and Greene Counties in West Alabama, we may not typically have many illustrious men and women who founded and gave names to the more than 370 various churches included in this study, but those ancestors, most of them hardy pioneers settling the frontier of West Alabama in the first half of the 19th century, gave us a rich legacy of names which live on through the generations. Thus, the words of the author of Ecclesiasticus 44:7–8, 14 may yet be applicable for those early name-givers in Tuscaloosa and Greene Counties, Alabama:

> All these won fame in their own generation
> and were the pride of their times.
> Some there are who have left a name behind them
> to be commemorated in story . . .
> Their bodies are buried in peace,
> but their name lives on for all generations.

NOTE

1. I wish to thank the historians of local churches and areas whose personal communications, marked p.c. in this essay, informed much of this study.

Bubba Is within You
John Algeo

Tolstoy's *Anna Karenina* begins with one of the most memorable opening lines in literature: 'All happy families are alike; every unhappy family is unhappy in its own way'. The same is true of election campaigns, except that they, being universally unhappy, are always unique. For example, in the midst of the 1996 campaign one could look back at the events of 1992, which in retrospect seem to have been more innocent and naive, an era when bubba came out of the closet.

Bubba is a quintessential Southernism, both in itself and in its apprehension by the rest of the nation. With alternative spellings *bubbuh*, *bubber*, it is part of a complex that also includes *bub*, *bubs*, *bubby*, and more distantly *bud*, *buddy*, or *buddie*.

The geographical and social distribution of these forms is noteworthy. According to Cassidy's *Dictionary of American Regional English* (*DARE*) it is as follows:

NORTHERN: *Bub* as a term of address for a boy is chiefly Northern and old-fashioned. *Bubby* as a term of address for a boy is especially Northern. *Buddy* as a nickname or term of address for any man is chiefly Northern, North Midland, and Atlantic Coast, used chiefly by men.

MIDLAND: *Bubby* as a term of address for a brother is especially Midland. *Buddy* as a nickname or term of address for a brother or eldest son is widespread but chiefly Midland and Southern and is somewhat old-fashioned.

SOUTHERN: *Bud* as a nickname or term of address for a brother or eldest son is widespread, but especially common in the South and South Midland, though somewhat old-fashioned. *Bubba* as a term of address for a brother is chiefly Southern or South Midland and is especially common among blacks.

OTHER REGIONAL PATTERNS: *Bub* 'brother' is widespread, but rare in New England. *Bud* as a nickname or term of address for any man is found especially on the Atlantic Coast.

The specifically Southern form *bubba* did not find its way into Craigie's *Dictionary of American English* (*DAE*) or Mathews's *Dictionary of Americanisms* (*DA*). There are five instances of it in the *LAGS Concordance* (Pederson, McDaniel, and Bassett 1986): four as instances of a pet name (protocol page 64, line 4, in books 5, 387, 538, and 760) and one as part of a response for the item *Mrs.* (protocol page 67, line 7, book 538) reporting that a woman called herself 'Mrs. Bubba Snead'.

The history of *bubba* can be written only in general terms. *DARE* with commendable caution says in its etymology of the word that it is of uncertain origin but probably a hypocoristic form of *brother*. The evidence for that probability, however, is so great as to amount to virtual certainty.

Barrère-Leland's 1897 *Slang* (as cited by Mathews 1951) says that *bub* or *bubby* 'came from Pennsylvania, where it was derived from the German bube, which is commonly abbreviated to bub'. The *Oxford English Dictionary* also favors a German etymology for *bubby*, commenting that 'Bartlett and Webster say a corruption of *brother*; but the word looks more like Ger[man] *bube*, *bub*, boy'. It is possible that in Pennsylvania the complex was reinforced by German, but that can hardly be the origin of the widespread American use. Variant forms of the word are too widely distributed in the United States at too early a date for a Pennsylvania Dutch origin to be likely, and there are better explanations available for it than the hypothetic German origin.

Similarly, the Pennsylvania miner's use of *butty* or *buttie* for 'partner, helper' may have reinforced *buddy* in that region (aided by the homophony of the two words in typical American pronunciation), but *butty* is not likely to be the source of *buddy*. *Butty* has English dialect origins as 'a fellow-workman . . . an intimate friend', as the *English Dialect Dictionary* (*EDD*, Wright 1898–1905) puts it, and has had a Romany origin suggested for it (Chapman 1986). Thomas P. Beyer's association of *butty* with *butt* or *buttocks* (*American Speech* 1929:389) may be folk etymology, although it is part of a metaphor that, in more vulgar form, appears also in *asshole buddy* (Chapman 1986).

The *brother* etymology of *bub* is strongly indicated by an early pun. The 1837 *Knickerbocker* (10.521) joked, 'Have you at present any of the *chastised idiot-brother* . . . What I want is what *you* call *whipped syllabub*'. The implied pronunciation of *syllabub* as 'silly bub' suggests that *bub* was already easily recognizable in the sense 'brother'. Mathews's *DA* suggests a British etymon for *bub* in the dialectal *bubby* (*EDD* s.v. *booby*), but that only pushes the history back a stage. It is very likely that all the *bub*- and *bud*- forms began as childish pronunciations of *brother* taken up by other members of a family as hypocoristic forms. If so, the forms were probably invented more than once, indeed, perhaps repeatedly.

The specifically Southern form *bubba* is attested first in 1864 by Lighter 1994: 'Poor papa, so faraway from his little girl and mama and bubbers'. *DARE*'s oldest citation is from Ambrose Gonzales's 1922 *Black Border* as a Gullah form. Its semantics is complex and embraces the following senses recorded by Cassidy 1985, Chapman 1986, and Lighter 1994 as a term of address for a brother or a boy, as a nickname, and as a title.

In its earlier development, *bubba* may have been a Black English version of *brother* extended to general Southern use, perhaps by way of child language as part of the whole complex of *hub*- and *bud*- terms. Or perhaps it was just Southern, both black and white. Used for some time as a nickname and a term of address, it acquired distinct regional and social implications. Recently, the term has expanded in new directions, and the election campaign of 1992 brought it into national prominence in a generic sense.

The use of *bubba* as a generic for a politically and socially conservative white Southern male of low-brow and lower socioeconomic status is at least as old as the early 1980s ('Among the New Words', *American Speech* 68.1, Spring 1993). In 1982 the expression *bubba system* was being used of Key West politics in roughly the sense 'old boy network' (or perhaps, considering the region, 'good ol' boy network').

Within the South, in old-fashioned use, *bubba* is still a nickname with connotations of plain-folksness and is not limited to either white or lower-class males. Black use of the nickname is sufficiently inconsistent with current use of the expression for 'good old boy' whites to have been commented upon:

> According to 'The Encyclopedia of Southern Culture', the nickname 'Bubba' has been, along with 'Sonny', 'Buddy', and one or two others,

fairly common for decades among Southern boys and men. It's hardly restricted to whites. A number of celebrated black athletes, including the great Michigan State and NFL lineman Charles 'Bubba' Smith (of Beaumont, Texas), have had the nickname. (Sam Hodges, *Orlando Sentinel*, in *Atlanta Constitution*, 27 April 1992, A6/2)

When used outside the South, *bubba* is usually pejorative. When Southerners use it generically, recognizing the Northern bias connected with such use, it sometimes has an ironic, in-your-face tone. The new word files of the American Dialect Society show that expressions collocating with the generic sense of *bubba* include *beer, blue collar, dogs, drinking, filling station, guns, hunting, liquor, pickup trucks, pork rinds, racism, sexist, tobacco,* and *working class*.

The following examples document the generic use:[1]

McDonald's Bubbacide / In throwing his hat into next year's gubernatorial ring, state Rep. Lauren W. 'Bubba' McDonald (D-Commerce) has become just plain old Lauren McDonald . . . [¶] Could it be that some slick Atlanta political consultant advised Rep. McDonald that his time-honored nickname might smack too much of the General Assembly and the hardware store, thereby detracting from his statewide appeal? (*Atlanta Constitution*, 14 May 1989, D6/1, editorial)

Whether you're a Bubba or a Yuppie or just a Good Old Country (or city) Boy or Girl, Dennis Rogers has a story for you. In his four books, The *News and Observer* columnist has collected the best of almost 12 years of reporting on the people and places he finds along the highways and byways of North Carolina. (Raleigh, N.C., *News and Observer*, 5 Dec. 1989, A12, ad)

Despite his wealth, the Midland oilman and rancher [Clayton Williams, Republican candidate for governor of Texas] has run a populist campaign that rails against liberals in Austin and promises to put youthful drug offenders in boot camps where they can 'discover the joys of bustin' rocks'. Says Austin political consultant Mark McKinnon: 'The Republicans have never had a "Bubba" before. Now they've got one'. (*Business Week*, 22 Oct. 1990, 54/3)

'Bubba', [pollster Claibourne Darden Jr.] says, 'is a high-school graduate, blue-collar or lower white collar. He rides around in a pickup truck with a gun in the back window. He's in construction, farming, factory, forestry, or he's an electrician, plumber, mechanic. And right now Bubba loves George Bush'. (*National Review*, 4 Nov. 1991, 8/3)

So how will news of this letter [from Pat Buchanan to Gerald Ford, asking to be made ambassador to South Africa] be greeted in the roadhouses, diners, and around the gas pumps [of the South]? [¶] Will Bubba say to Junior: 'Doggone, I see where it came out that ol' Pat wanted to be ambassador to South Africa 'cuz he thought he'd get on just fine with that racist, oppressive, mean government that's been shootin' all them native Africans just for stickin' their heads out of their shacks and wantin' to vote and have a say in how they live'. [¶] 'Yeah, I saw that, Bubba, and am just shocked out of my boots that Pat would even imply that he condoned such cruelty to men, women and children just because of the color of their skin. I am deeply disappointed in Pat'. [¶] 'I, too, am gravely disillusioned'. [¶] Sure, and they'll ask the waitress for a slice of quiche. (Mike Royko, Jacksonville, IL, *Journal-Courier*, 29 Feb. 1992, 6)

In the American mindscape, [the South] summons up stubbornly unshakable images: racism; pickup trucks piloted by chaw-cheeked lowbrows; elegant gents courting blushing belles; the problem of Bubba; the passion of Rhett, Scarlett and Ashley. (*Chicago Tribune*, 26 July 1992, sec. 5, p. 7/1)

[Reference to three keynote speakers at the Democratic convention: Bill Bradley, Barbara Jordan, and Georgia governor Zell Miller, who speaks with a strong Appalachian accent:] But the piercing mountain twang in the middle of this three-part harmony was aimed at all of America's straying Bubbas and Jim Bobs and Rosa Maes, from Bakersfield to Flowery Branch. Miller's job was to call them home to the party to which they once belonged. (*Atlanta Constitution*, 14 July 1992, A6/1)

The 'King' [Guy Hunt, governor of Alabama] is a man who says that he is above the laws that govern the rest of the citizens ('Bubbas' as our elected representatives so fondly call us voters). [¶] . . . He [the director of the state Highway Department], like King Hunt, has the welfare of us Bubbas at heart. [¶] It has been reported that the highway director charged personal telephone calls, sometimes $500 a month, to us poor, dumb Bubbas. He stayed at his home in Gulf Shores and charged the state (again us 'Bubbas') per diem. . . . [¶] With a replacement in sight I sleep

like a baby knowing that we 'bathless Bubbas' will get the kind of
governor we deserve. (It's the 'great unwashed' that elect the governor
of 'the Great State of Alabama'.) (*Birmingham Post-Herald* 24 Dec.
1992, A4/4, letter to the editor)

The presidential campaign of 1992 brought the term *bubba* to
national attention. Because both the presidential and vice-presidential
candidates on the Democratic ticket were Southerners and because the
vote in Southern states was seen to be crucial to the outcome of the
election, *bubba* spawned a large number of progeny. Thus, that part of
the Southern vote which it was essential for either party to carry became
the *bubba vote*:

GOP has lock on 11 states of the old Confederacy . . . And it will stay that
way, adds Southern pollster Claibourne Darden Jr. until the Democrats
win back the 'Bubba' vote. (*National Review*, 4 Nov. 1991, 8/2-3)

What's happening here is that Mr. Buchanan is making inroads into the
'Bubba' vote—conservative whites, many of them Democrats, who
because Georgia doesn't register voters by party are free to vote in the
GOP primary. (*Wall Street Journal*, 28 Feb. 1992, A16/1)

But there may not be a Bubba vote [in the March 3 Georgia primary
election]. (NPR, 1 Mar. 1992)

But might not a funky accent hurt him [Paul Tsongas] in Dixie? [¶]
'Maybe with the Bubba vote, but I don't think the Bubba vote is going for
him anyway'. (*Birmingham Post-Herald*, 7 Mar. 1992, A5/2)

The fun part—goofy guys playing in New Hampshire snow, a buncha
white boys fighting across the South for the Bubba vote and the black
bloc vote, feisty finger-pointing debates on television—is over. (*Birmingham Post-Herald* 23 Mar. 1992, A5/1)

Why do political commentators freely talk about 'the Bubba vote' and not
the 'Mick', 'Hymie', 'Julio', 'Ahmad', or 'Linda' votes? . . . Conventional political wisdom says the 'Bubba vote' consists of those white
Southern males who, regardless of socio-economic standing, favor the
death penalty, a strong national defense, constitutional protection of the

U.S. flag and prayer in public schools. (Sam Hodges, *Orlando Sentinel*, in *Atlanta Constitution*, 27 Apr. 1992, A6/2-4)

The combination of two Southerners at the head of the ticket was dubbed the *Bubba ticket* or *double-Bubba ticket*. The fact that neither Bill Clinton nor Al Gore fits the stereotype of a *bubba* was ignored in the coining of that term. Both candidates were yuppy rather than bubba in education, career, taste, and style. The realization of that incongruity led to the coining of the terms *faux bubba* and *weenie-bubba*:

[Preacher Will B. Dunn:] Clinton's a faux Bubba—a phony good ol' boy! A counterfeit cracker! Real Bubbas own dogs—spelled d-a-w-g! Faux Bubbas own cats! Real Bubbas hunt—faux Bubbas jog! . . . [Mechanic Uncle Dub:] Real Bubbas don't use words like faux! ('Kudzu' comic strip, 14 Dec. 1992)

Mr. Clinton is, at best, a weenie-Bubba, having assimilated at Yale and Oxford (on a Rhodes scholarship). (Sam Hodges, *Orlando Sentinel*, in *Atlanta Constitution*, 27 Apr. 1992, A6/2)

Other terms resulting from the presidential campaign are *Bubba and the Brotha* or *Bubba and brother* 'the political coalition of Southern whites and blacks'; *Bubba border* 'Mason-Dixon Line'; *Bubbacracy* 'predominance of Southerners in the 1992 Democratic campaign'; *Bubbadom* 'bubbas collectively'; *Bubba factor* 'conservative Southern votes as an influence in the election'; *Bubbaism* 'the values and lifestyle of bubbas'; *Bubbaland* 'the South'; and *Bubbette* 'a woman of the bubba class'. Terms not directly related to the political campaign, but using *bubba* in the generic sense, are *Bubbacide* 'the replacement of Bubbaism by the malling of America, that is, the extension of yuppy values and lifestyle' and *Bubbaville* 'nickname of a U.S. military camp in Arabia during the Gulf War'.

A human-interest story in the *Atlanta Constitution* of 13 January 1991 (M-2/2) dealt with the conversion of *bubba* from a regional and neutral nickname for persons to a social and derogatory label for a class and with an effort to salvage it:

Look your last on all things Bubba. This most Southern of appellations could be headed for the sanitary landfill—or at least a trip to the re-education camp.

What was once a ubiquitous nickname seems to have dwindled into an ethnic slur, a tag for an embarrassing ancestor of the New South, three branches down the evolutionary tree.

Bubba was never supposed to represent the South in its Sunday best. Beau was the nickname of choice for the image-conscious, a handle with Gallic origins suggesting aristocracy and Eurostyling. Bubba, on the other hand, stood for calluses and shad-bellies, rednecks, white socks and blue tick hounds.

While Beau disappears into the egalitarian Bo, Bubba is vanishing in a different direction. It's being appropriated to describe the Snopesian constituency that Atticus Finch fended off in 'To Kill a Mockingbird'. Some saw that type in Clayton Williams, the two-fisted Texas gubernatorial candidate who, when cautioned to tone down his redneck posturing, declared, 'I am Bubba'.

That's bad news for bubba. But the handwriting was on the wall back in 1988, when Southern Magazine blurbed a cover story: 'Bubba! You Don't Have to BE Dumb, Mean, Fat, Slow, White or Male to Be One'.

Of course, the article went on to explode all these stereotypes about the nickname (and, implicitly, about the South). But which evidence was more persuasive: the multicultural Bubbas featured in the text or the editorial comment on the cover? As the story made clear, there is no shortage of accomplished Bubbas, from ex-jock Bubba Smith to state Rep. Lauren 'Bubba' McDonald. Near the top of the list is Julius B. 'Bubba' Ness, retired chief justice of the South Carolina Supreme Court and a jurisprudence legend. He has made the Palmetto State Bubba-friendly. Fellow jurist Alec Sanders describes Judge Ness's impact this way: 'If William Buckley were named Bubba, then people in Ipswich, Mass., would not think of Bubba the same way'.

Judge Ness, who chews tobacco only when he plays baseball, disregards Bubba's bad rap. 'Nobody ever said anything derogatory to me about the name Bubba', he says. 'When somebody doesn't call me Bubba, I know they either don't know me or they don't like me'.

Southern chronicler John Egerton also makes the case that Bubba is less unenlightened than unpretentious. Jeb Stuart and Daniel Boone would fit in this lineage, he says. 'It's more laid back. Like that country song "I Belong to the Country Club." That's a Bubba song'.

A dualist in the best Southern tradition, cartoonist Doug Marlette avers that Bubba stands for both boneheaded and laudable aspects of this latitude. In Mr. Marlette's 'Kudzu' strip, redneck guru Uncle Dub is declared to be the last of this breed, due to the introduction of Perrier in filling station drink boxes and the encroachment of condos and malls. 'I call it Bubbacide', Mr. Marlette says. 'It's the wiping out of a species'.

Perhaps the only hope for Bubba is radical redefinition. That's the strategy of Pat Jobe and Kim Taylor, Forest City, N.C., residents who publish the Bubba Newsletter. Tracing the nickname to its roots, as a mispronunciation of 'brother', they champion the spirit of Bubba as a Thoreauvian impulse toward kinship with the world.

'We consider ourselves to be at the vanguard of a revival of Bubba-ism at its best', says Mr. Jobe, who counts Jesus, Gandhi and Tennessee preacher Will Campbell as exponents of Bubba. 'When Jesus said the Kingdom is within you, he was trying to say Bubba is within you, it's just that the term wouldn't be created for 1,500 years'.

Bubba is typical of Southern life for a number of reasons:

1) It may have begun as black use, but now is associated distinctively with white Southern culture. Black culture has been strongly influential in the South and continually moves into the dominant regional white culture, the black roots often being forgotten in the process. Much of Southern culture is black in origin.

2) It was probably derived from a complex of native English forms. Like much of black culture, it is not ultimately African but nonstandard or regional British, transformed in the black community.

3) It is typical of a plain-folks style that marks much of Southern life. No other region has provided the nation with presidents known as 'Jimmy' and 'Bill' rather than 'James' and 'William'. In Southern political life, the latter would be perceived as uppity and insincere.

4) It is prominent in political discourse. Despite the 'late unpleasantness' of 1861–65, the South has always been notably influential in American government and politics. That is the case especially in recent years.

5) It is a focus for prejudice and stereotyping. The rest of the nation typically regards the South with condescending bias. When a Milwaukeean named Jeffrey Dahmer lured young men into his apartment as objects of torture and cannibalism, the nation regarded it as a psychopathic aberration. If it had happened in Charleston, it would have been regarded as expected Southern Gothic.

6) It has been prominent in the news because of non-Southern attention paid to it. Despite a widespread bias against the South, many people from other parts of the country seem to find an irresistible fascination in things Southern, whether they are a romanticized Rhett Butler or a caricatured Gomer Pyle.

Perhaps, however, the real reason for the success of bubba is that the stereotype is also an archetype. And like all archetypes, it has both a bright and a dark side that we recognize as not foreign to us. Bubba is as American as apple pie and Texas politics, attractive and repellant according to how you resonate to him. Bubba is within you.

NOTE

1. These citations are from the new-word files of the American Dialect Society, not previously used in 'Among the New Words'; their contributors include Catherine M. Algeo, George S. Cole, the late James B. McMillan, Allan Metcalf, and Patricia Stewart.

APPENDIX

The Publications of Lee Pederson

1959

Thoreau's source of the motto in 'Civil Disobedience'. Thoreau Society Bulletin 67.3.

An unrecorded use of *clout*. American Speech 34.369–71.

1960

La fuenta del lema de Thoreau en 'Disobedienca Civil'. Voluntad 4. Spanish translation by V. Munoz of 1959 item.

1962

An introductory field procedure in a current urban survey. Orbis 11.465–69.

1963

A social dialect survey of Chicago: An overview. Chicago: Science Research Associates. (with Raven I. McDavid, Jr.)

Thoreau's rhetoric and Carew's lines. Thoreau Society Bulletin 82.1.

1964

McDavid's 'Mencken revisited'. Harvard Educational Review 34.459–60.

Non-standard Negro speech in Chicago. Non-standard speech and the teaching of English, ed. by William A. Stewart, 16–23. Washington, DC: Center for Applied Linguistics. Preprint of 1965 item.

The pronunciation of English in metropolitan Chicago: Vowels and consonants. Chicago: University of Chicago dissertation.

Terms of abuse for some Chicago social groups. Publication of the American Dialect Society 42.26–48.

1965

Americanisms in Thoreau's journal. American Literature 37.167–84.

McDavid's 'Mencken revisited'. Language and language learning, ed. by Janet Emig, 459–61. Cambridge: Harvard University Press.

The Mencken legacy. Orbis 14.63–74.

Non-standard Negro speech in Chicago. NAFSA studies and papers: English language series 10, ed. by R. P. Fox, 36–42. New York: National Association for Foreign Student Affairs.

The pronunciation of English in metropolitan Chicago. Publication of the American Dialect Society 44.

Social dialects and the disadvantaged. Language programs for the disadvantaged, ed. by Richard K. Corbin and Muriel E. Crosby, 236–49. Champaign, Ill.: National Council of Teachers of English.

Some structural differences in the speech of Chicago Negroes. Social dialects and language learning, ed. by Roger W. Shuy, 28–51. Champaign, Ill.: National Council of Teachers of English. Preprint of 1966 item.

1966

Negro speech in *The Adventures of Huckleberry Finn*. Mark Twain Journal 13.1 4.

Phonological indices of social dialects in Chicago. Communication barriers to the culturally deprived, ed. by Raven I. McDavid, Jr., and William M. Austin. Cooperative Research Project 2107. Chicago: US Department of Health, Education, and Welfare.

1967

Editor's foreword. Emory Quarterly 23.

Mark Twain's Missouri dialects: Marion county phonemics. American Speech 42.261–78.

Middle-class Negro speech in Minneapolis. Orbis 16.347–53.

1968

Americanisms in Thoreau's journal. English Language Bulletin 1. Oita Kogyo Daigaku. Japanese translation by T. Shigamatsu of 1965 item.

An annotated bibliography of Southern speech. SEL Monograph 1. Atlanta: Southeast Education Laboratory.

Regional and social dialect study. Georgia English Counselor 17.9–10.

1969

The linguistic atlas of the gulf states: An interim report. American Speech 44.279–86.

1970

Review of The categories and types of present-day English word formation by Hans Marchand. 2nd ed. General Linguistics 10.132–38.

1971

An approach to urban word geography. American Speech 46.73–86.

Chicago words: The regional vocabulary. American Speech 46.163–92.

The pronunciation of English in metropolitan Chicago. A various language: Perspectives on American dialects, ed. by Juanita V. Williamson and Virginia M. Burke, 525–48. New York: Holt, Rinehart, and Winston. Reprint of selections from 1965 item.

Some structural differences in the speech of Chicago Negroes. Readings in American dialectology, ed. by Harold B. Allen and Gary N. Underwood, 401–20. New York: Appleton-Century-Crofts. Reprint of Non-standard Negro speech, 1965, and Phonological indices, 1966.

Southern speech and the LAGS project. Dialectology: Problems and perspectives, ed. by Lorraine Hall Burghart, 130–42. Knoxville: University of Tennessee Press.

Southern speech and the LAGS project, Orbis 20.79–89. Revised and corrected version of item above.

Terms of abuse for some Chicago social groups. Readings in American dialectology, ed. by Harold B. Allen and Gary N. Underwood, 382–400. New York: Appleton-Century-Crofts. Reprint of 1964 item.

1972

Black speech, white speech, and the Al Smith syndrome. Studies in linguistics in honor of Raven I. McDavid, Jr., ed. by Lawrence M. Davis, 123–34. University: University of Alabama Press.

An introduction to the LAGS project. In A manual for dialect research, 1972, 1–31.

A manual for dialect research in the southern states. Atlanta: Georgia State University College of Education. (edited with Raven I. McDavid, Jr., Charles W. Foster, and Charles E. Billiard)

1973

Dialect patterns in rural northern Georgia. Lexicography and dialect geography: Festgabe for Hans Kurath, ed. by Harald Scholler and John Reidy, 195–207. Wiesbaden: Franz Steiner Verlag.

Practical phonology in a general dictionary: A discussion paper. Lexicography in English, ed. by Raven I. McDavid, Jr., and Audrey R. Duckert. Annals of the New York Academy of Sciences 211.129–33.

Review of Vocabulary change: A study of variation in regional words in eight southern states, by Gordon R. Wood. Language 49.184–87.

1974

An introduction to the LAGS project. In A manual for dialect research, 2nd ed., 1974, 1–31. Revision of 1972 item.

The linguistic atlas of the gulf states: Interim report two. American Speech 49.216–23.

A manual for dialect research in the southern states, 2nd ed. University: University of Alabama Press. Revision of 1972 item.

On closet terms. American Speech 49.133.

Review of Linguistic atlas of the upper midwest, volume 1, by Harold B. Allen. Journal of English Linguistics 8.71–77.

Tape/text and analogue. American Speech 49.5–23.

1975

Basic methods of dialect research. Trends in southern sociolinguistics, ed. by William G. Pickens, 8–16. Atlanta: Morehouse College.

Biracial dialectology: Six years into the Georgia survey. Journal of English Linguistics 9.18–25. (with Grace S. Rueter and Joan H. Hall)

Fifty years of American speech. American Speech 50.163.

Insular dimensions of southern speech. Trends in southern sociolinguistics, ed. by William G. Pickens, 26–34. Atlanta: Morehouse College.

The plan for a dialect survey of rural Georgia. Orbis 24.38–44.

Questionnaire for a dialect survey of rural Georgia. Orbis 24.45–71. (with Howard G. Dunlap and Grace S. Rueter)

Review of Studies in area linguistics by Hans Kurath. Foundations of Language 12.609–13.

Review of the Urban language series, nos. 1–9, ed. by Roger W. Shuy. American Speech 50.98–110.

Sourmilk. American Speech 50.49.

1976

Aims and methods in a Chicago dialect survey. Sprachlisches Handlen/Soziales Verhalten, ed. by Wolfgang Viereck, 193–204, 364. München: Wilhelm Fink.

American *rap*: Three more times. American Speech 51.279–81.

A datum for *podunk*. American Speech 51.108.

The linguistic atlas of the gulf states: Interim report three. American Speech 51.201–7.

Review of Placenames in Georgia by John H. Goff, ed. by F. L. Utley and M. R. Hemperley. Verbatim 3.2.10–1.

1977

A compositional guide to the LAGS project. Atlanta: Emory University, Administrative Services.

The dugout dairy. Tennessee Folklore Society Bulletin 43.88–89.

Grassroots grammar in the gulf states. James B. McMillan: Essays in linguistics
    by his friends and colleagues, ed. by James C. Raymond and I. Willis
    Russell, 91–112. University: University of Alabama Press.
The randy sons of Nancy Whisky. American Speech 52.111–21.
Review of A glossary of Faulkner's south by Calvin S. Brown. Verbatim
    4.3.6–8.
Structural description in linguistic geography. Papers in language variation:
    SAMLA/ADS collection, ed. by David L. Shores and Carole P. Hines,
    19–24. University: University of Alabama Press.
Studies in American pronunciation since 1945. American Speech 52.262–327.
Toward a description of speech. Papers in language variation: SAMLA/ADS
    collection, ed. by David L. Shores and Carole P. Hines, 25–31. University:
    University of Alabama Press.

1978

Flying jenny. American Speech 53.198.
Right on. American Speech 53.80.
Sociolinguistic aspects of American mobility. Amerikastudien/American
    Studies 23.299–319.

1979

Composition of the LAGS urban complement: Atlanta words. Orbis 28.223–41.
    (with Charles E. Billiard)
Editors' preface to Dialects in culture: Essays in general dialectology, by Raven
    I. McDavid, Jr., xxiii–xxv. University: University of Alabama Press. (with
    William A. Kretzschmar, Jr., James B. McMillan, Roger W. Shuy, and
    Gerald R. Udell)
Review of Kentucky moonshine by David W. Maurer. American Speech
    54.52–55.
Review of Lexicalische und grammatische Ergebnisse des Loman-Survey von
    Mittel- und Südengland, 2 vols., by Wolfgang Viereck. Zeitschrift für
    Dialektologie und Linguistik 46.231–46.
The urban work sheets for the LAGS project. Orbis 28.45–62. (with Charles E.
    Billiard)

1980

Calvary camels and the knockaway tree. American Speech 55.158–59.
Lexical data from the gulf states. American Speech 55.195–203.

1981

A compositional guide to the LAGS project. 2nd ed. LAGS working paper, 1st series, no. 5. In Linguistic atlas . . . basic materials, 1981, fiche 1183–84. (edited with Susan E. Leas)

A conference to plan a linguistic atlas of the southeastern states, May 16–17, 1968. LAGS working paper, 1st series, no. 1. In Linguistic atlas . . . basic materials, 1981, fiche 1178.

E-80, Negro: Argot from the game of life. American Speech 56.78.

Hey, Lucy. American Speech 56.63.

Introduction to the basic materials. In Linguistic atlas . . . basic materials, 1981, fiche 1.

Introduction to the LAGS working papers, 1st series. In Linguistic atlas . . . basic materials, 1981, fiche 1176.

LAGS demographics: Communities and localities. LAGS working paper, 1st series, no. 11. In Linguistic atlas . . . basic materials, 1981, fiche 1192.

LAGS fieldworkers: Styles and contributions. LAGS working paper, 1st series, no. 13. In Linguistic atlas . . . basic materials, 1981, fiche 1194.

LAGS scribes: Idiolects and habits of composition. LAGS working paper, 1st series, no. 14. In Linguistic atlas . . . basic materials, 1981, fiche 1195.

Linguistic atlas of the gulf states; The basic materials. In two formats; 1199 fiche/55 reels. Ann Arbor, Mich.: University Microfilms International. (edited with Guy H. Bailey, Marvin W. Bassett, Charles E. Billiard, and Susan E. Leas)

The linguistic atlas of the gulf states: Interim report four. American Speech 56.243–59.

A manual for dialect research in the southern states, 3rd ed. In Linguistic atlas . . . basic materials, 1981, fiche 2–4. (edited with Charles E. Billiard, Susan E. Leas, and Marvin W. Bassett)

A plan for the LAGS concordance. LAGS working paper, 1st series, no. 9. In Linguistic atlas . . . basic materials, 1981, fiche 1190. (with Susan E. Leas)

Raven I. McDavid, Jr.: A tribute. English World-Wide 2.225–26.

The regional and social dialects of East Tennessee: A preliminary overview. Final report to NCTE Research Foundation. LAGS working paper, 1st series, no. 8. In Linguistic atlas . . . basic materials, 1981, fiche 1187–89.

Review of A bibliography of Scandinavian languages and linguistics, 1900–1970 by Einar Haugen. American Speech 56.125–28.

Review of Ein Profil Soziolinguistischer Variation in einer Amerikanischen Kleinstadt by G. Redden. English World-Wide 2.264–65.

Review of The ecology of language by Einar Haugen. American Speech 56.118–25.

Toward the publication of the Linguistic atlas of the gulf states. LAGS working paper, 1st series, no. 4. In Linguistic atlas . . . materials, 1981, fiche 1182.

1982

The bootlegger's legacy. American Speech 57.239.

Bush, busher, bushest. American Speech 57.154–56.

Language, culture, and the American heritage. American Heritage Dictionary, 2nd college ed., 17–29. Boston: Houghton Mifflin.

1983

East Tennessee folk speech: A synopsis. Bamberger Beiträge zur Englischen Sprachwissenschaft 12. Frankfurt am Main: Peter Lang. Revision of 1981 item,The regional and social dialects of East Tennessee.

'Press the collar'. American Speech 58.95. (with Marvin W. Bassett)

Review of Language of the underworld by David W. Maurer. Modern Philology 81.105–7.

1984

The LAGS concordance. American Speech 59.332–39. (with Susan L. McDaniel and Marvin W. Bassett)

Review of The mirth of a nation: America's great dialect humor by Walter Blair and Raven I. McDavid, Jr. Journal of English Linguistics 17.97–102.

1985

Language in the Uncle Remus tales. Modern Philology 82.292–98.

Systematic phonetics. Journal of English Linguistics 18.14–24.

1986

An electronic atlas in microform. LAGS working paper, 3rd series, no. 4. In Linguistic atlas . . . a concordance, 1986, fiche 10.

An English technical alphabet. LAGS working paper, 3rd series, no. 1. In Linguistic atlas . . . a concordance, 1986, fiche 7.

A graphic plotter grid. LAGS working paper. 3rd series, no. 3. In Linguistic atlas . . . a concordance, 1986, fiche 9.

A graphic plotter grid. Journal of English Linguistics 19.25–41.

Grassroots grammar in the gulf states. Dialect and language variation, ed. by Harold B. Allen and Michael D. Linn, 162–79. Orlando: Academic Press.

Introduction. In Linguistic atlas . . . a concordance, 1986, fiche 1. (with Susan L. McDaniel)

Introduction to LAGS working papers, 2nd series. In Linguistic atlas . . . a concordance, 1986, fiche 2.

Introduction to LAGS working papers, 3rd series. In Linguistic atlas . . . a concordance, 1986, fiche 3.

The LAGS grid. LAGS working paper, 2nd series, no. 2. In Linguistic atlas . . . a concordance, 1986, fiche 5.

Linguistic atlas of the gulf states. Volume 1: Handbook. Athens: University of Georgia Press. (edited with Susan L. McDaniel, Guy H. Bailey, and Marvin W. Bassett)

Linguistic atlas of the gulf states: A concordance of basic materials. Ann Arbor, Mich.: University Microfilms International. (edited with Susan L. McDaniel and Marvin W. Bassett)

Mapping phonetics in the gulf states. LAGS working paper, 3rd series, no. 5. In Linguistic atlas . . . a concordance, 1986, fiche 11. (with Susan L. McDaniel)

Microcomputing in linguistic geography: Files and maps. LAGS working paper, 3rd series, no. 7. In Linguistic atlas . . . a concordance, 1986, fiche 13. (with Susan L. McDaniel)

A reference tool for southern folklore study. LAGS working paper, 3rd series, no. 6. In Linguistic atlas . . . a concordance, 1986, fiche 8. (with Susan L. McDaniel)

A survey in deductive phonetics. LAGS working paper, 3rd series, no. 2. In Linguistic atlas . . . a concordance, 1986.

1987

An automatic book code (ABC). Journal of English Linguistics 20.48–71.

Rewriting dialect literature: 'The wonderful tar-baby story'. Atlanta Historical Journal 30.3–4.57–70.

A survey in deductive phonetics. Zeitschrift für Dialektologie und Linguistik 53.289–309.

1988

Electronic matrix maps. Journal of English Linguistics 21.149–74.

Linguistic atlas of the gulf states. Volume 2: General index. Athens: University of Georgia Press. (edited with Susan L. McDaniel and Carol M. Adams)

Zum Einsatz von Schnelldruckerkarten in der Dialektkartographie, trans. by S. Sieglinde and C. Moss. Zeitschrift für Dialektologie und Linguistik 55.306–31.

1989

AAM phonology. Computer methods in dialectology: Special issue. Journal of English Linguistics 22.54–62.

Linguistic atlas of the gulf states. Volume 3: Technical index. Athens: University of Georgia Press. (edited with Susan L. McDaniel, Carol M. Adams, and Caisheng Liao)

Linguistic geography in Wyoming. Computer methods in dialectology: Special issue. Journal of English Linguistics 22.18–24. (with Michael W. Madsen)

1990

Linguistic atlas of the gulf states. Volume 4: Regional matrix. Athens: University of Georgia Press. (edited with Susan L. McDaniel, Carol M. Adams, and Michael B. Montgomery)

1991

Linguistic atlas of the gulf states. Volume 5: Regional pattern. Athens: University of Georgia Press. (edited with Susan L. McDaniel and Carol M. Adams)

Linguistic atlas of the gulf states. Volume 6: Social matrix. Athens: University of Georgia Press. (edited with Susan L. McDaniel, Carol M. Adams, and Michael B. Montgomery)

1992

A Georgia word geography. Old English and new: Studies in language and linguistics in honor of Frederic G. Cassidy, ed. by Joan H. Hall, Nick Doane, and Dick Ringler, 384–99. New York: Garland.

Linguistic atlas of the gulf states. Volume 7: Social pattern. Athens: University of Georgia Press. (with Susan L. McDaniel)

A natural history of English: Language, culture, and the American heritage. American heritage dictionary, 3rd ed., xv–xxiii. Boston: Houghton Mifflin.

1993

An approach to linguistic geography. American dialect research, ed. by Dennis R. Preston, 31–92. Amsterdam and Philadelphia: Benjamins.

A southern phonology. SECOL Review 17.36–54.

1995

Elements of word geography. Journal of English Linguistics 23.33–46.

1996

LAMR/LAWS and the main chance. Journal of English Linguistics 24.234–49.

LAWCU project worksheets. Journal of English Linguistics 24.52–60.

Piney woods southern. Focus on the USA, ed. by Edgar W. Schneider, 13–23. Amsterdam and Philadelphia: Benjamins.

References

Alabama. 1818. Acts of the general assembly of the Alabama territory. St. Stephens, Ala.: Thomas Eastin.

Allen, Harold B. 1973–76. Linguistic atlas of the upper midwest. 3 vols. Minneapolis: University of Minnesota Press.

Allen, Harold B. 1986. Sex-linked variation in the responses of dialect informants. Journal of English Linguistics 19.149–76.

Atwood, E. Bagby. 1953. A survey of verb forms in the eastern United States. Ann Arbor: University of Michigan Press.

Babitch, Rose Mary, and Eric Lebrun. 1989. Dialectometry as computerized agglomerative hierarchical classification analysis. Journal of English Linguistics 22.83–90.

Bailey, Guy. 1986. A social history of the gulf states. LAGS working paper 1, 2nd series. Addendum to Pederson, McDaniel, and Bassett 1986.

Bailey, Guy, and Marvin Bassett. 1986. Invariant 'be' in the Lower South. Language variety in the South: Perspectives in black and white, ed. by Michael B. Montgomery and Guy Bailey, 158–79. University: University of Alabama Press.

Bailey, Guy, and Cynthia Schnebly. 1988. Auxiliary deletion in the Black English Vernacular. Language change and contact, ed. by Kathleen Ferrara, et al., 34–41. Austin: University of Texas Linguistics Department.

Bailey, Guy, Tom Wikle, Jan Tillery, and Lori Sand. 1991. The apparent time construct. Language Variation and Change 3.241–64.

Battistella, Edwin. 1990. Government and binding analysis of double modals. Paper read at forty-second meeting of the Southeastern Conference on Linguistics, Greenwood, South Carolina.

Battistella, Edwin. 1991. The treatment of negation in double modal constructions. Linguistic Analysis 21.49–65.

Battistella, Edwin. 1995. The syntax of the double modal construction. Linguistica Atlantica 17.19–44.

Bernstein, Cynthia. 1988. A variant of the 'invariant' be. American Speech 63.119–24.

Beyer, Thomas P. 1929. Anent 'Buddy'. American Speech 4.389.

Bloomfield, Leonard. 1933. Language. New York: Holt.

Boertien, Harmon. 1986. Constituent structure of double modals. Language variety in the South: Perspectives in black and white, ed. by Michael B.

Montgomery and Guy Bailey, 294–318. University: University of Alabama Press.

Brown, Penelope, and Stephen Levinson. 1978. Politeness: Some universals of language usage. Cambridge: Cambridge University Press.

Brown, Vivian R. 1991. Evolution of the merger of /ɪ/ and /ɛ/ before nasals in Tennessee. American Speech 66.303–15.

Butters, Ronald. 1973. Acceptability judgments for double modals in southern dialects. New ways of analyzing variation in linguistics, ed. by Charles-James N. Bailey and Roger Shuy, 276–86. Washington, D.C.: Georgetown University Press.

Butters, Ronald R. 1989. The death of black English: Divergence and convergence in black and white vernaculars. New York: Peter Lang.

Carr, Joseph W. 1905. A word list from northwest Arkansas. Dialect Notes 3.68–103.

Carver, Craig. 1987. American regional dialects: A word geography. Ann Arbor: University of Michigan Press.

Cassidy, Frederic G., et al., eds. 1985–. Dictionary of American regional English. Cambridge, Mass.: Belknap Press.

Chambers, J. K., and Peter Trudgill. 1980. Dialectology: An introduction. Cambridge: Cambridge University Press.

Chapman, Robert L., ed. 1986. New dictionary of American slang. New York: Harper & Row.

Clauß, Günter, and Heinz Ebner. 1978. Grundlagen der Statistik für Psychologen, Pädagogen und Soziologen. Berlin: Volk und Wissen, 6th ed.

Cleland, Herdman. F. 1920. The black belt of Alabama. Geographical Review 10.375–87.

Coleman, William. 1975. Multiple modals in southern states English. Bloomington: Indiana University dissertation.

Craigie, William A., and James R. Hulbert, eds. 1940. A dictionary of American English on historical principles. 4 vols. Chicago: University of Chicago Press.

DARE, see Cassidy et al. 1985–.

Davis, Alva L. 1949. A word atlas of the great lakes region. Ann Arbor: University of Michigan dissertation.

Davis, Alva L., Raven I. McDavid, Jr., and Virginia G. McDavid, eds. 1969. A compilation of the work sheets of the linguistic atlas of the United States and Canada and associated projects. Chicago: University of Chicago Press.

Davis, Lawrence M. 1983. English dialectology: An introduction. University: University of Alabama Press.

Davis, Lawrence M., and Charles L. Houck. 1992. Is there a midland dialect area?—again. American Speech 67.61–70.

Davis, Lawrence M., and Charles L Houck. 1996. The comparability of linguistic atlas records: The case of LANCS and LAGS. Focus on the USA, ed. by Edgar W. Schneider, 51–62. Amsterdam and Philadelphia: Benjamins.

Dearden, E. J. 1943. Dialect areas of the south Atlantic states as determined by variations in vocabulary. Providence, R.I.: Brown University dissertation.

Dickson, R. J. 1988. Ulster emigration to colonial America, 1718–1775. 2nd edition, with an introduction by Graeme Kirkham. Belfast: Ulster Historical Foundation.

Dieth, Eugen. 1948. Linguistic geography in New England. English Studies 29.65–79.

Di Paolo, Marianna. 1986. A study of double modals in Texas English. Austin: University of Texas dissertation.

Dumas, Bethany K. 1987. Double modals in Ozark folk speech. Paper read at New Ways of Analyzing Variation meeting, Austin, Texas.

Ecclesiasticus. Trans. The New English Bible and the Jerusalem Bible.

Eckert, Penelope. 1989. Jocks and burnouts: Social categories and identity in high school. New York: Teacher's College, Columbia University Press.

Faneuf, Mildred A. 1939. Dialect study of Auburn, Lee county, Alabama, made as a preliminary investigation for the preparation of work sheets for the linguistic atlas. Auburn: Alabama Polytechnic Institute thesis.

Fasold, Ralph. 1990. Sociolinguistics of language. Oxford: Blackwell.

Feagin, Crawford. 1979. Southern white in the English language community. Variation and change in Alabama English, 243–68. Washington, D.C.: Georgetown University Press.

Fennell, Barbara. 1993. Evidence for British sources of double modal constructions in Southern American English. American Speech 68.430–6.

Fitts, Anne Malone. 1989. Words of the black belt and beyond: A study of Alabama lexical patterns in the linguistic atlas of the gulf states. Tuscaloosa: University of Alabama dissertation.

Foley, Lawrence M. 1969. A phonological and lexical study of the speech of Tuscaloosa county, Alabama. Tuscaloosa: University of Alabama dissertation. Condensed and published in 1972 as Publication of the American Dialect Society 58.

Foscue, Virginia O. 1966. Background and preliminary survey of the linguistic geography of Alabama. Madison: University of Wisconsin dissertation.

Foscue, Virginia O. 1971. A preliminary survey of the vocabulary of white Alabamians. Publication of the American Dialect Society 56.

Foscue, Virginia O. 1989. Place names in Alabama. Tuscaloosa: University of Alabama Press.

Francis, W. Nelson. 1983. Dialectology: An introduction. London: Longman.

Gilliéron, Jules, ed. 1902–10. Atlas linguistique de la France. 13 vols. Paris: Champion.

Girard, Dennis, and Donald Larmouth. 1993. Some applications of mathematical and statistical models in dialect geography. American dialect research, ed. by Dennis R. Preston, 107–32. Amsterdam and Philadelphia: Benjamins.

Glynn, Robert L. 1976. How firm a foundation: A history of the first black church in Tuscaloosa county, Alabama. Tuscaloosa: Friends of the Hunter's Chapel A. M. E. Zion Church; City of Tuscaloosa, Alabama Bicentennial Committee.

Greene county [Alabama] deed books. 1990. Eutaw, AL.

Grizzard, Lewis. 1987. The compleat southerner: A refresher course in the essentials. Southern Magazine 2.1 (October), 49–55.

Jaberg, Karl, and Jakob Jud. 1928–40. Sprach- und Sachatlas Italiens und der Südschweiz. 8 vols. Zofingen.

Johnson, Ellen. 1996. Lexical change and variation in the southeastern United States 1930–1990. Tuscaloosa: University of Alabama Press.

Kerr, Grace. 1989. The onset of variation: The treatment of the /hj/ cluster in Texas. College Station, Tex.: Texas A & M University thesis.

Keyser, Samuel J. 1963. Review of Kurath and McDavid 1961. Language 39.303–16.

Kretzschmar, William A., Jr. 1992. Isoglosses and predictive modeling. American Speech 67.227–49.

Kretzschmar, William A., Jr. 1996a. Foundations of American English. Focus on the USA, ed. by Edgar W. Schneider, 25–50. Amsterdam and Philadelphia: Benjamins.

Kretzschmar, William A., Jr. 1996b. Quantitative areal analysis of dialect features. Language Variation and Change 8.13–39.

Kretzschmar, William A., Virginia G. McDavid, Theodore Lerud, and Ellen Johnson, eds. 1994. Handbook of the linguistic atlas of the middle and south Atlantic states. Chicago: University of Chicago Press.

Kretzschmar, William A., Jr., and Edgar W. Schneider. 1996. Introduction to quantitative analysis of linguistic survey data: An atlas by the numbers. Thousand Oaks, Calif: Sage.

Kroll, Harry Harrison. 1925. A comparative study of upper and lower southern folk speech. Nashville: George Peabody College thesis.

Kurath, Hans. 1928. The origin of the dialectal differences in spoken American English. Modern Philology 25.385–95.

Kurath, Hans. 1949. A word geography of the eastern United States. Ann Arbor: University of Michigan Press.

Kurath, Hans. 1972. Studies in area linguistics. Bloomington: Indiana University Press.

Kurath, Hans, et al., eds. 1939. Handbook for the linguistic atlas of New England. Providence, R.I.: Brown University.

Kurath, Hans, and Raven I. McDavid, Jr. 1961. The pronunciation of English in the Atlantic states. Ann Arbor: University of Michigan Press. Reprinted, University of Alabama Press, 1982.

Labov, William. 1963. The social motivation of a sound change. Word 19.273–309.

Labov, William. 1981. Resolving the neogrammarian controversy. Language 57.267–308.

Labov, William A. 1991. The three dialects of English. New ways of analyzing sound change, ed. by Penelope Eckert, 1–44. New York: Academic Press.

Labov, William A., Paul Cohen, Clarence Robins, and John Lewis. 1968. A study of the non-standard English of Negro and Puerto Rican speakers in New York City. 2 vols. Philadelphia: US Regional Survey.

Labov, William A., Malcah Yaeger, and Richard Steiner. 1972. A quantitative study of sound change in progress. Philadelphia: US Regional Survey.

LAGS, see Linguistic atlas of the gulf states.

LAMSAS (Linguistic atlas of the south and middle Atlantic states), see Kretzschmar et al. 1994 (handbook).

La Tourette, John. 1839. Mississippi, Louisiana, and Alabama [map]. Mobile, Alabama.

LAUM (Linguistic atlas of the upper midwest), see Allen 1973 76.

Leighly, John. 1979. Biblical place-names in the United States. Names 27.46–59.

Leyburn, James G. 1962. The Scotch-Irish: A social history. Chapel Hill: University of North Carolina Press.

Lighter, J. E., ed. 1994. Random House historical dictionary of American slang. Vol. 1, A–G. New York: Random House.

Linguistic atlas of the gulf states.
    Basic materials, see Pederson, Billiard, Leas, Bailey, and Bassett, eds. 1981.
    Concordance, see Pederson, McDaniel, and Bassett. 1986.
    Handbook, vol. 1, see Pederson, McDaniel, Bailey, and Bassett, eds. 1986.
    General index, vol. 2, see Pederson, McDaniel, and Adams, eds. 1988.
    Technical index, vol. 3, see Pederson, McDaniel, Adams, and Liao, eds. 1989.
    Regional matrix, vol. 4, see Pederson, McDaniel, Adams, and Montgomery, eds. 1990.
    Regional pattern, vol. 5, see Pederson, McDaniel, and Adams, eds. 1991.
    Social matrix, vol. 6, see Pederson, McDaniel, Adams, and Montgomery, eds. 1991.

Social pattern, vol. 7, see Pederson and McDaniel, eds. 1992.

McDaniel, Susan L. 1989. Databases of the LAGS automatic atlas. Journal of English Linguistics 22.63–8.

McDavid, Raven I., Jr. 1949. Application of the linguistic atlas method to dialect study in the south-central area. Southern Speech Journal 15.1–9.

McDavid, Raven I., Jr. 1958. The dialects of American English. The structure of American English, by W. Nelson Francis, 480–539. New York: Ronald.

McDavid, Raven I., Jr. 1967. Needed research in southern dialects. Perspectives on the South. Agenda for research, ed. by Edgar T. Thompson, 113–24. Durham: Duke University Press.

McDavid, Raven I., Jr. 1994. Dialect areas of the LAMSAS region. Handbook of the linguistic atlas of the middle and south Atlantic states, ed. by William A. Kretzschmar, Jr., et al., 147–54. Chicago: University of Chicago Press.

McDavid, Raven I., Jr., William A. Kretzschmar, Jr., and Gail J. Hankins, eds. 1982–86. Linguistic atlas of the middle and south Atlantic states and affiliated projects: Basic materials: Pennsylvania. Microfilm MSS on cultural anthropology 68.363. Chicago: Joseph Regenstein Library, University of Chicago.

McDavid, Raven I., Jr., and Richard C. Payne, eds. 1976–78. Linguistic atlas of the north central states: The basic materials. Manuscripts on cultural anthropology XXXVIII, no. 200–208. Chicago: University of Chicago.

McDavid, Virginia G. 1956. Verb forms in the north-central states and upper midwest. Minneapolis: University of Minnesota dissertation.

McDavid, Virginia G. 1987. Twelve verbs: Gender and educational differences. Paper read at American Dialect Society, San Francisco.

McDavid, Virginia G. 1988a. Sex-linked differences among atlas informants: Irregular verbs. Methods in dialectology, ed. by Alan R. Thomas, 333–39. Clevedon and Philadelphia: Multilingual Matters.

McDavid, Virginia G. 1988b. Sex-related variation in verb forms in the north-central states and upper midwest. Paper read at American Dialect Society, New Orleans.

McDavid, Virginia G. 1988c. Verb forms in the middle west: Evidence from LANCS and LAUM. Paper read at Midwest American Dialect Society, St. Louis.

McDavid, Virginia G. 1989. Grammatical items in the linguistic atlases of the north-central states and upper midwest: Educational and gender differences. Paper read at American Dialect Society, Washington, D.C.

McDavid, Virginia G. 1990. Irregular verb forms in Michigan, Wisconsin, and Minnesota: Educational attainment and gender differences. Kansas Quarterly 22.4.31–43.

MacDonald, Christine. 1981. Variation in the use of modal verbs with special reference to Tyneside English. Newcastle: University of Newcastle-on-Tyne Ph.D. thesis.

McMillan, James B., and Michael B. Montgomery, eds. 1989. Annotated bibliography of Southern American English. Tuscaloosa: University of Alabama Press.

Marshall, James William. 1977. The Presbyterian church in Alabama. Ed. Robert Strong. Montgomery: Presbyterian Historical Society of Alabama.

Mathews, Mitford M., ed. 1951. A dictionary of Americanisms on historical principles. 2 vols. Chicago: University of Chicago Press.

Maynor, Natalie. 1981. Males, females, and language propriety. Journal of English Linguistics 15.17–20.

Miller, J., and K. Brown. 1982. Aspects of Scottish English syntax. English World-Wide 3.3–17.

Miller, Mary R. 1990. How to name a church in the northern neck of Virginia. Unpublished essay.

Miller, Michael I. 1988a. Quantification of sociolinguistic data. Studies in English Literature and Language (Taipei) 14.137–48.

Miller, Michael I. 1988b. Ransacking linguistic survey data with a number cruncher. Methods in dialectology, ed. by Alan R. Thomas, 464–79. Multilingual Matters 48.

Miller, Michael I. 1990–95. Dialect, dialect area, and social dialect: The linguistic atlas of the gulf states. Journal of English Linguistics 23.78–88.

Milroy, Lesley. 1987. Language and social networks. 2nd ed. Oxford: Blackwell.

Mishoe, Margaret, and Michael Montgomery. 1994. The pragmatics of multiple modals in North and South Carolina. American Speech 69.3–29.

Montgomery, Michael. 1979. A discourse analysis of expository Appalachian English. Gainesville: University of Florida dissertation.

Montgomery, Michael. 1991. The roots of Appalachian English: Scotch-Irish or southern British? Journal of the Appalachian Studies Association, ed. by John Inscoe, 177–91. Johnson City, Tenn.: East Tennessee State University Center for Appalachian Studies and Services.

Montgomery, Michael. 1993. Review of The linguistic atlas of the gulf states. American Speech 68.263–318.

Montgomery, Michael. 1995. Does Tennessee have three 'grand' dialects?: Evidence from the linguistic atlas of the gulf states. Tennessee Folklore Society Bulletin 57.69–84.

Montgomery, Michael, and Stephen J. Nagle. 1993. Multiple modals in Scotland and the Southern United States: Trans-Atlantic inheritance or independent development? Folia Linguistica Historica 14.91–107.

Norusis, Marija J. 1983. SPSSX introductory statistics guide. Chicago: SPSS.

O'Cain, Raymond K. 1979. The linguistic atlas of New England. American Speech 54.243–78.

Pampell, John R. 1975. More on double modals. Texas Linguistic Forum 2, ed. by Susan F. Schmerling and Robert D. King, 110–21. Austin: University of Texas.

Payne, Leonidas. 1908/09. A word-list from east Alabama. Dialect Notes 3.279–328, 343–91.

Payne, Richard C. 1976. The linguistic atlas of the north-central states: Publication of the basic materials. Typescript.

Pederson, Lee. 1964a. Non-standard Negro speech in Chicago. Non-standard speech and the teaching of English, ed. by William A. Stewart, 16–23. Washington, D.C.: Center for Applied Linguistics.

Pederson, Lee. 1964b. Some structural differences in the speech of Chicago Negroes. Social dialects and language learning, ed. by Roger W. Shuy, 28–51. Champaign, Ill.: National Council of Teachers of English.

Pederson, Lee. 1965. The pronunciation of English in metropolitan Chicago. Publication of the American Dialect Society 44.

Pederson, Lee. 1966. Phonological indices of social dialects in Chicago. Communication barriers to the culturally deprived, ed. by Raven I. McDavid, Jr., and William M. Austin. Chicago: US Department of Health, Education, and Welfare.

Pederson, Lee. 1969. The linguistic atlas of the gulf states: An interim report. American Speech 44.279–86.

Pederson, Lee. 1971. An approach to urban word geography. American Speech 46.73–86.

Pederson, Lee. 1974a. The linguistic atlas of the gulf states: Interim report two. American Speech 49.216–23.

Pederson, Lee. 1974b. Tape/text and analogue. American Speech 49.5–23.

Pederson, Lee. 1976. The linguistic atlas of the gulf states: Interim report three. American Speech 51.201–7.

Pederson, Lee. 1977a. A compositional guide to the LAGS project. Atlanta: Emory University, Administrative Services.

Pederson, Lee. 1977b. The dugout dairy. Tennessee Folklore Society Bulletin 43.88–9.

Pederson, Lee. 1980a. Calvary camels and the knockaway tree. American Speech 55.158–9.

Pederson, Lee. 1980b. Lexical data from the gulf states. American Speech 55.195–203.

Pederson, Lee. 1981a. Hey, Lucy. American Speech 56.63.

Pederson, Lee. 1981b. The linguistic atlas of the gulf states: Interim report four. American Speech 56.243–59.

Pederson, Lee. 1983. East Tennessee folk speech: A synopsis. Bamberger beiträge zur Englischen sprachwissenschaft 12. Frankfurt/ Main: Peter Lang.

Pederson, Lee. 1985. Systematic phonetics. Journal of English Linguistics 18.14–24.

Pederson, Lee. 1986a. An electronic atlas in microform. LAGS working paper 4, 3rd series. Addendum to Pederson, McDaniel, and Bassett 1986.

Pederson, Lee. 1986b. A graphic plotter grid. Journal of English Linguistics 19.25–41.

Pederson, Lee. 1986c. The LAGS grid. LAGS working paper 2, 2nd series. Addendum to Pederson, McDaniel, and Bassett 1986.

Pederson, Lee. 1987. An automatic book code (ABC). Journal of English Linguistics 20.48–71.

Pederson, Lee. 1988. Electronic matrix maps. Journal of English Linguistics 21.149–74.

Pederson, Lee. 1990–95. Elements of word geography. Journal of English Linguistics 23.33–46.

Pederson, Lee. 1993. An approach to linguistic geography. American dialect research, ed. by Dennis Preston, 31–92. Amsterdam and Philadelphia: Benjamins.

Pederson, Lee. 1996. Piney woods southern. Focus on the USA, ed. by Edgar W. Schneider, 13–23. Philadelphia: Benjamins.

Pederson, Lee, and Charles E. Billiard. 1979. The urban work sheets for the LAGS project. Orbis 28.45–62.

Pederson, Lee, Charles E. Billiard, Susan E. Leas, Guy Bailey, and Marvin Bassett, eds. 1981. Linguistic atlas of the gulf states: The basic materials. Microform collection. Ann Arbor: University Microfilms.

Pederson, Lee, and Susan Leas McDaniel, eds. 1992. The linguistic atlas of the gulf states, vol. 7: Social pattern. Athens: University of Georgia Press.

Pederson, Lee, Susan Leas McDaniel, and Carol Adams, eds. 1988. The linguistic atlas of the gulf states, vol. 2: General index. Athens: University of Georgia Press.

Pederson, Lee, Susan Leas McDaniel, and Carol Adams, eds. 1991. The linguistic atlas of the gulf states, vol. 5: Regional pattern. Athens: University of Georgia Press.

Pederson, Lee, Susan Leas McDaniel, Carol Adams, and Caisheng Liao, eds. 1989. The linguistic atlas of the gulf states, vol. 3: Technical index. Athens: University of Georgia Press.

Pederson, Lee, Susan Leas McDaniel, Carol Adams, and Michael Montgomery, eds. 1990. The linguistic atlas of the gulf states, vol. 4: Regional matrix. Athens: University of Georgia Press.

Pederson, Lee, Susan Leas McDaniel, Carol Adams, and Michael Montgomery, eds. 1991. The linguistic atlas of the gulf states, vol. 6: Social matrix. Athens: University of Georgia Press.

Pederson, Lee, Susan Leas McDaniel, Guy H. Bailey, and Marvin H. Bassett, eds. 1986. The linguistic atlas of the gulf states, vol. 1: Handbook. Athens: University of Georgia Press.

Pederson, Lee, Susan Leas McDaniel, and Marvin Bassett. 1984. The LAGS concordance. American Speech 59.332–39.

Pederson, Lee, Susan Leas McDaniel, and Marvin Bassett. 1986. The linguistic atlas of the gulf states: A concordance of basic materials. Ann Arbor, Mich.: University Microfilms.

Pederson, Lee A., Raven I. McDavid, Jr., Charles W. Foster, and Charles E. Billiard, eds. 1972. A manual for dialect research in the Southern states. Atlanta: Georgia State University. Revised ed. 1974, University of Alabama Press.

Petyt, K. M. 1980. The study of dialect: An introduction to dialectology. London: Deutsch.

Reed, Carroll E. 1953. English archaisms in Pennsylvania German. Dialect Notes 19.3–7.

Report of the conference on a linguistic atlas of the United States and Canada. 1929. Linguistic Society of America Bulletin 4.20–47.

Rich, John Stanley. 1979. The place names of Greene and Tuscaloosa Counties, Alabama. Tuscaloosa: University of Alabama dissertation.

Rogers, P. Burwell. 1963. Naming Protestant churches in America. Names 11.44–51.

Romaine, Suzanne. 1982. What is a speech community? Sociolinguistic variation in speech communities, ed. by Suzanne Romaine, 1–24. London: Arnold.

Saussure, Ferdinand de. 1959[1915]. Course in general linguistics. Ed. by Charles Bally and Albert Sechehaye. Trans. by Wade Baskin. New York: McGraw-Hill.

Schneider, Edgar W. 1988. Qualitative vs. quantitative methods of area delimitation in dialectology: A comparison based on lexical data from Georgia and Alabama. Journal of English Linguistics 21.175–212.

Schneider, Edgar W., and William A. Kretzschmar, Jr. 1989. LAMSAS goes SASsy: Statistical methods and linguistic atlas data. Journal of English Linguistics 22.129–41.

Seay, John L. n.d. 3:15A–16A, 26A. In the Thomas P. Clinton Collection, Scrapbooks. University of Alabama Library. Special Collections.

Snedecor, Victoria Gayle. 1856. A directory of Greene County for 1855–6. Mobile: Strickland. Ed. and rpt. Franklin Schackelford Moseley. Eutaw, Ala.: Office of the Greene County Democrat, 1957.

Stockwell, Robert. 1959. Structural dialectology: A proposal. American Speech 34.258–68.

Thomas, Alan. R. 1967. Generative phonology in dialectology. Transactions of the Philological Society 179–203.

Tillery, Jan. 1989. The merger of /ɔ/ and /a/ in Texas: A study of sociological and linguistic constraints. College Station, Tex: Texas A & M University thesis.

Tillery, Jan, and Guy Bailey. 1990. The status of two southernisms. Paper read at NWAVE meeting, Philadelphia.

Toulmin, Harry. 1823. Digest of the laws of the state of Alabama. Cahawba, Ala.: Ginn and Curtis.

Turtledove, Harry. 1992. The guns of the south: A novel of the civil war. New York: Ballantine.

Tuscaloosa County Baptist Association. 1989. Annual. 1929 to 1989. Birmingham, Ala.: Birmingham Publishing.

United States Geological Survey. 1931. Topographic map: Eutaw Quadrangle.

Van Riper, William R. 1977. Usage preferences of men and women: 'Did', 'came', and 'saw'. Paper read at the Chicago Conference on Language and Cultural Pluralism. Revised in 1979 for American Speech.

Van Riper, William R. 1979. Usage preferences of men and women: 'Did', 'came', and 'saw'. American Speech 54.279–84.

Viereck, Wolfgang. 1973. The growth of dialectology. Journal of English Linguistics 7.69–86.

Wardhaugh, Ronald. 1992. An introduction to sociolinguistics. 2nd ed. Oxford: Blackwell.

Weinreich, Uriel. 1954. Is a structural dialectology possible? Word 10:388–400. Reprinted in Dialect and language variation, ed. by Harold Allen and Michael Linn, 20–34. Orlando: Academic Press, 1986.

West, Anson. 1893. A history of Methodism in Alabama. Nashville, Tenn.: Publishing House, Methodist Episcopal Church, South, 1893.

Whitley, M. Stanley. 1975. Dialectal syntax: Plurals and modals in Southern American. Linguistics 161.89–108.

Wilson, William Julius. 1978. The declining significance of race. Chicago: University of Chicago Press.

Wilson, William Julius. 1988. The truly disadvantaged. Chicago: University of Chicago Press.

Wolfram, Walt, and Donna Christian. 1976. Appalachian speech. Arlington, Va.: Center for Applied Linguistics.

Wood, Gordon R. 1961. Word distribution in the interior south. Publication of the American Dialect Society 35.1–16.

Wood, Gordon R. 1963. Dialect contours in the southern states. American Speech 38.243–56.

Wood, Gordon R. 1971. Vocabulary change. A study of variation in regional words in eight of the southern states. Carbondale: Southern Illinois University Press.

Wright, Joseph, ed. 1898–1905. The English dialect dictionary. 6 vols. Oxford: Frowde.

Contributors

John Algeo, Alumni Foundation Distinguished Professor Emeritus of English at the University of Georgia, has served as President of the American Dialect Society, the American Name Society, and the Dictionary Society of North America. He served as editor of *American Speech*, and with his wife, Adele, he co-edited "Among the New Words," a regular feature of *AS,* for ten years. He is currently working on *English in North America*, vol. 6 of the *Cambridge History of the English Language*, and a dictionary of Briticisms.

Anne Malone Fitts was a LAGS fieldworker for Alabama and wrote her University of Alabama dissertation on Alabama speech. She teaches English at Concordia College-Selma.

Joan Houston Hall is Associate Editor of the *Dictionary of American Regional English* at the University of Wisconsin-Madison. She has written numerous articles about *DARE*, and co-edited *Old English and New: Essays in Language and Literature in Honor of Frederic G. Cassidy* (Garland, 1992).

William A. Kretzschmar, Jr., is Professor of English and Linguistics at the University of Georgia and serves as Director of its Linguistics Program. He publishes widely in the field of language variation, serves as editor of the *Journal of English Linguistics*, and works on American English pronunciations for the Oxford English Dictionary and other Oxford dictionaries. He is editor-in-chief of LAMSAS and of LANCS, is on the advisory board for the Linguistic Atlas of Oklahoma and the Linguistic Atlas of the Rocky Mountain Region, and served on the LAGS advisory board.

Susan Leas McDaniel completed her doctorate at Emory University and worked for LAGS from 1976 until the completion of the project, variously as scribe, field worker, assistant editor, and associate editor. She is a member of the Richard III Society and a certificated teacher of Scottish Country Dancing.

Virginia G. McDavid, Professor Emerita of English at Chicago State University, has served as president of the American Dialect Society and the Dictionary Society of North America. She has been actively involved in many of the Linguistic Atlas projects and is Associate Editor of LAMSAS.

†**Michael I. Miller** taught at Augusta College, Virginia Commonwealth University, and Chicago State University, and served at Chicago State as Associate Vice President for Academic Affairs before his premature death in 1994. He completed his dissertation on the speech of Augusta, Georgia, on the basis of which he wrote important essays on lexical and grammatical variation in Southern American speech. His work on statistical exploration and testing of linguistic atlas data has been very influential.

Michael B. Montgomery, Professor of English and Linguistics at the University of South Carolina, has published widely on the English of the American South, Ulster, and Scotland. He was Assistant Editor for the *Linguistic Atlas of the Gulf States* from 1987 to 1988 and Consulting Editor for Language for the *Encyclopedia of Southern Culture*. At present he is Associate Editor of *American Speech* and is editing a dictionary of southern mountain English.

Thomas E. Nunnally is Associate Professor of English at Auburn University, numbering among his courses Old English, the history of English, and lexicography. He co-organized the second LAVIS conference and co-edited *Language Variety in the South Revisited* (Alabama, 1997).

John Stanley Rich teaches in the Department of English at the University of South Carolina-Aiken where he enjoys courses in English linguistics, classical mythology, British literature, and peace studies. His special areas of scholarly research are American English regional dialects and place names.

Edgar W. Schneider is Full Professor of English Linguistics at the University of Regensburg, Germany, after having held appointments at universities in Bamberg, Georgia, and Berlin. He has published several books and many articles in the fields of English dialectology, sociolinguistics, language history, and lexical semantics, with his books including *American Earlier Black English* (Alabama, 1989), *Focus on the USA* (ed., Benjamins, 1996), and *Englishes Around the World* (2 vols., ed., Benjamins, 1997). He is also the editor of the journal *English World-Wide* and the book series *Varieties of English Around the World*.

Index